Theodore & Eliza

VIEW OF THE SOUTH QUARTER OF MOCHA.

Theodore & Eliza

The True Story

by

Susan Harvard.

Susan Harvard

In fond memory of Kitty's great-grandson, the late
Theodore 'Ted' Crombie.

THEODORE & ELIZA

The True Story

By

Susan Harvard

Copyright © Susan Harvard 2018

This book is published by HARVARD WORKS OF ART

in conjunction with WRITERSWORLD

ISBN: 978-1-9995952-1-0

WRITERSWORLD

☎ +44 1993 812500

www.writersworld.co.uk

This book is produced entirely in the UK by HARVARD WORKS OF ART in conjunction with WRITERSWORLD. It is available to order from most bookshops in the United Kingdom and globally via UK based Internet book retailers.

*The paper on which this book is printed is produced from sustainable and/or recycled sources

Contents

PART IV: SACRED AND PROFANE

TAIL PIECES

List of Colour Illustrations

Preface

When the engagement of HRH Prince Charles to Lady Diana Spencer was announced from Buckingham Palace, it ended months of speculation, but instantly the eyes of the world were upon Diana. There was a seemingly insatiable hunger for any information, however slight, about the future bride of the Prince of Wales. All aspects of her life, past and present, came under scrutiny. But it soon became apparent that royal genealogists trying to trace her maternal lineage were baffled. They had to admit that they could go no farther back than four generations. Their researches had brought them to July 1818, to the baptismal record of five-year-old Katherine 'Kitty' Scott Forbes, in the register for the Bombay Presidency of the Honourable East India Company.

The child's father, Theodore Forbes, came from the ranks of the Scottish landed gentry but it seemed that no one knew anything about her mother, Eliza Kewark. She had metaphorically 'stuck her foot out' from the folds of Princess Diana's illustrious pedigree and brought researchers to a stumbling halt. Her precise ethnicity and whether she was legally married to Theodore was a mystery. There was no record of their marriage or the birth, in December 1812, of their daughter Katherine. A media hunt set out to find a skeleton in the royal scullery.

Genuine ignorance in 1981, of Eliza's origins, was represented by Lady Colin Campbell in her book *The Real Diana* (2005) as deliberate subterfuge – a conspiracy on the part of the Spencers and the Royal Family to conceal an unpalatable truth. Eliza is described as a 'dark-skinned native of Bombay, who lived without benefit of matrimony with... Theodore Forbes.' To this day no one can claim to know the exact tone of Eliza's skin, but she lived in Surat, and it is certain that she and Theodore were married in the Armenian Church there.

Recent DNA analysis by Professor Jim Wilson of Edinburgh University has found that Eliza Kewark's maternal grandmother was Indian, making Diana's grandmother Ruth Fermoy one 64th Indian: hardly enough to necessitate a conspiracy of deceit. But Lady Colin Campbell insisted that Eliza's 'true race' had been 'expunged from the family tree' and that she had 're-emerged as an Armenian'. Given that spelling had not been standardised at this period, Kewark is easily recognisable as a variant of Kevork; one of the commonest of all Armenian names. Her charge that it was a "fiction… maintained, even after Diana married the Prince of Wales" is manifestly untrue. Princess Diana's worldwide popularity and tragic death coincided with the dawn of the Internet. Speculation continued about Theodore and Eliza and the legitimacy of their children, and many inaccurate stories circulated. Their daughter, Katherine Scott Forbes, known as Kitty in the family, knew that her mother was Armenian but she did not know the exact circumstances of her own birth. The proof of that can be found in the nineteenth century Aberdeen census returns.

Kitty had been a young woman of twenty-four, married for less than three months, when King William IV died and was succeeded by his niece, the teenage Princess Victoria. During the Queen's reign her presence in Aberdeenshire was recorded in five successive censuses. Her given place of birth was different in every single one. Only in her last census return, in 1891, two years before she died, was she able to give even the approximate location of where she was born.

Following the announcement of the royal engagement, press interest in Kitty prompted her great-grandson, the late Theodore 'Ted' Crombie, to begin research into Eliza's origins. The late Merlynn and Morrice Henderson were his cousins who told me what they knew about Theodore and Eliza. Their son, Arnold 'Jamie' Henderson, produced the only known photograph of Kitty.

The scant sum of family knowledge was that Theodore Forbes had fathered an illegitimate son, Frederick, before he left for India, by Anne Macdonnell, a 'Scottish country lass'; that Eliza Kewark was a 'Native of India'; that they 'were married after the manner of the country where they lived'; that 'they had three children, one of whom died young'; that 'he was not allowed to keep Eliza with him in Bombay'; that the remaining 'two children were sent to Scotland to live with their grandparents at Boyndlie, near Fraserburgh'; that Theodore 'died at sea on his way home'; that 'Eliza remained in India and died a wealthy woman'. All have turned out to be true with the exception of the very last point, which has yet to be proved.

At the time of the 1891 census, Kitty's prosperous surroundings in Bon Accord Square, Aberdeen, confirm that her parents' hopes for her had been amply fulfilled. She was one of the lucky ones; of the thousands of children of mixed marriages, uprooted and sent to Britain from throughout the Empire, many never felt they truly belonged anywhere. Her younger brother, Alexander 'Aleck' Scott Forbes, was dark complexioned and did not arrive in Scotland until he was ten-years old. His early education had been poor and he found it difficult to settle; subsequently he became unfairly known in the wider family as the 'ne'er-do-well' and it is said that he returned to India.

Theodore 'Ted' Crombie died in 1982 without having discovered anything further about Eliza apart from confirming from her signature that she was indeed Armenian. Some years later I decided to try and complete the task he had set himself. The Hendersons sent me photocopies of some of Eliza's letters. An extensive jumble of correspondence and other papers had been deposited in the library of Aberdeen University by the Ogilvie-Forbes family, largely unsorted, unread and in need of transcription. It was there, in Ms 2740 of the special collections in King's College Library that, against the odds, the details of Eliza's poignant story had survived. Unlike most mixed-race marriages of that time, the story of Kitty's parents, though hidden and almost forgotten, was not lost. It exists still on the worn pages of Theodore's letter book, kept only for his own reference and almost illegible; it exists in letters from his brother-in-law and confidant, Agah Aratoon Baldassier of Surat, neatly folded in Solander boxes; it exists in bundles of letters from other correspondents, still tied with pink linen tape; but, above all, it exists in Eliza's letters to Theodore, dictated to a Parsi scribe in her broken English, written in his immaculate copperplate hand and always signed in Armenian script 'Sahiba [Lady/Mrs] Forbes' and in English 'your affectionate Mrs Forbes'.

Eliza's voice speaks from the page. It tells of the separation imposed on her by the man she loves; of how her initial disbelief turns to a determination not to accept his cruel injunction; of how she discovers that he intends to make the break permanent; how she uses his love for his children to spearhead her campaign to win him back even though it might mean giving them up for ever.

Acknowledgements

Firstly, my thanks are due to Kitty's great grandson, the late Theodore 'Ted' Crombie, art historian, who began researching her story. He suggested that, given the dearth of knowledge in1981, I might write a novel based on the story of Theodore & Eliza. My late husband Michael Harvard and our children: Ted's godson James, and our daughter, Elizabeth, they and Elizabeth's fiancé, Huw J Davies, military historian, all deserve my gratitude for their patience over the years and for their continuing encouragement to bring this project to a conclusion. Thanks also to my partner Otto for his continuing support and his unwavering faith in the project.

A special thank you must go to Jamie Henderson for providing and letting me use the only known photograph of Kitty, and kind remembrances of his parents who sent me the photocopies of letters in Aberdeen *Ms. 2740* that started my journey of research after Ted's death. Mary Roche, another of Kitty's great grand-children encouraged me to continue my research and always took an interest in my progress.

In Scotland the following deserve my unreserved thanks: John Brose, who was kind enough to allow me to photograph family portraits at Boyndlie and gave his permission for the publication of extracts from the Ogilvie-Forbes archive; Alexander Morison, who gave me access to the Frendraught muniments; the staff of the special collections of King's College who have been unfailingly helpful; Professor Roy Bridges who kindly offered to tie up loose ends in Ms.2740 and whose enthusiasm and encouragement inspired me to persevere; Professor Jim Wilson of Edinburgh University who was generous with information from his recent DNA analysis to pin-point Eliza's ethnicity more precisely.

Thanks are overdue to my friend Diana Brown for saying 'yes' at a moment's notice and coming with me to that beautiful and tragic country, Yemen, in 1994, where we were fortunate to be able to pay a brief visit to Mocha and to meet Caroline Stone and the late Dr Paul Lunde, who translated several letters from the Arabic, and who were both unfailingly enthusiastic. Elizabeth von Petersdorf read an early draft and I am grateful for her time and comments and, above all, her encouragement to make the book accessible to a general reader with no previous knowledge of the area and period.

Unfortunately, only belated thanks are possible to the late Peter de Jong and John Hewitt of BACSA for taking an interest in my project and giving me contacts in Bombay. I am also grateful to Dr Andrew S Cook, of the India Office Records, at the British Library for allowing me to pore over the very large map of Surat, before it was removed for conservation; Dr Rosie Llewellyn of BACSA, Gillian Tindall, and Nancy Um have all kindly answered queries and aided my research.

Liz Chater has published photographs and translations of inscriptions on gravestones in the old Armenian cemetery of Surat, which have been of great help in establishing Eliza's partial genealogy. She continues to do a valuable job in documenting many aspects of the Armenian diaspora and deserves the thanks of all who have an interest in its history.

I am especially grateful to Graham Cook of Writersworld for seeing me through the chicanes of publishing; to Ian Large my proof reader and copy editor for his patience over my numerous changes, his unerring eye for wayward punctuation and his application of Capital Punishment to my habitually over-capitalised nouns; and to Jag Lall for his considerable skill in ordering, editing and realising my vague ideas for the cover.

PART I

SEA & SAIL

Chapter 1

Burial at Sea, 1820

1

Indian Ocean, September 24th 1820

Theodore Forbes was buried at sea in a sailcloth shroud, with a stitch through his nose and a 'sinker' at his feet. He was thirty-two-years old. Some might call it karma – his just deserts for the cruel betrayal of the woman who loved him – his 'Dear Betsey' – the mother of his children and, in his own words, his 'most faithful and affectionate partner', Eliza Kewark. He was a rich Scottish merchant from Bombay, a partner in Forbes & Co. and former Honourable East India Company Servant. The ship, on which he had been fated to take his final passage from this world to the next, was the *Blenden Hall*, Captain Greig, bound for London from Bombay. He had died off the East Coast of Africa, halfway between Madagascar and the Cape of Good Hope.

The *Blenden Hall* was an elegant three-masted barque. The Red Ensign of Britain and the red and white striped flags of the Honourable East India Company flew at her stern and at her mastheads. At her prow a 'handsome representation of a highland chieftain' breasted the waves, and the dark faces of her cannon ports stared boldly out from her sleek sides. They punctuated the entire length of her graceful white mid-line, as if to reinforce the message that she was strong as well as beautiful. She was fully armed against attack by pirates or privateers, equipped with a powder magazine, an armoury of smaller guns and a superabundance of manpower.

In the emptiness of the Indian Ocean, in those far-off days when Africa was still 'The Dark Continent', there was no one to witness the moment when Captain Greig brought the ship about to face into what wind there was; to see the sails being hauled down and her flags being lowered at his command, or to hear the scrape and rattle of the chain as a drift anchor was dropped.

Within a few minutes he had sent for Robert Perry, ship's

carpenter, and James McCulloch, sailmaker, and given them orders to make ready for a burial. While the carpenter looked for a length of iron chain or some heavy cannon-shot for the sinker, McCulloch busily stitched the corpse into its shroud. He worked quickly. There was no time to lose; to have a dead body on board in this heat would be unpleasant; to keep it for burial on dry land could bring bad luck on the ship and all who sailed in her.

When Perry returned carrying the sinker, the two men weighted the bag. McCulloch sewed deftly to close it, punching and driving the needle into the stout canvas and pushing it through with the thick leather pad on the heel of his hand. Hesitating for a moment, he brushed the sweat from his brow with his forearm, then with a sweeping stroke, he plunged the needle inside the bag. Carefully, he drew it back out, pulling the twine through and muttering some private imprecation under his breath. The last stitch had closed the corpse's nostrils and held the nose pressed against the rough canvas. Reaching for a small marlinspike, he tugged the cord tight. Perry looked on without emotion; he had served under Captain Greig for nigh on seventeen years. He had seen the end of countless shipmates: the death of a passenger did not worry him.

For burial at sea the last offices were never finished without closing a corpse's nostrils, it had been so when McCulloch was a lad – and long before that. Some said that it was done to check that the man was really dead. But in the tropics there was never any doubt – the sailmaker's own nose would soon tell him the man was dead. Mariners through the ages and across the globe shared a long-held superstition that the last stitch prevented the spirit of the dead man from coming back to haunt them. They needed to be certain that his unquiet ghost could not rise up again from the depths and follow their ship forever.

When the tropical sky above the *Blenden Hall* changed from azure and gold to green and purple, the sea began to darken and the shadows on board to lose their definition. As the last rays of the sun were fading from the masthead the ship's bell began to toll. The sombre knell summoned Theodore's fellow passengers to the spar deck. Leaving the helmsman at the wheel, Captain Greig, book in hand, stationed himself by the leeward rail. According to his son he was 'a handsome man, a confident sailor in vigorous middle age'. He turned to the page he had marked in his well-thumbed *Book of Common Prayer* and glanced up to wait for his audience to be silent and still:

'Forasmuch as it hath pleased Almighty God,' he began, 'in his wise providence, to take out of this world the soul of our deceased brother, Theodore...' He looked up again to check the progress of the burial party, as the passengers and crew, who had gathered in two groups, stepped back respectfully. The form of a body was still evident despite the stiffness of the enveloping sailcloth. Theodore's servant Walloo, standing apart from the others, bowed his head and lightly touched his forehead as six stout sailors carried the canvas-shrouded corpse to the gunwale and placed it reverently on the gangplank – a hefty piece of timber, slightly bowed, and polished with the wear of embarking and disembarking feet. Perry had made sure there was no scuffing or roughness to interfere with the passage of the deceased into the waves below.

The darkening sky had turned to bloody red and, as the sun sank below the violet smudge of the African coastline, all felt the chill of night descend. The captain resumed:

'We therefore commit his body to the deep,' he intoned. At which, the sailors tilted the plank until the heavy burden slid off the end and into the sea. Gently he began to close his prayer book. 'Looking for the general resurrection in the last day,' he continued gravely. There was a pause while the pall bearers watched anxiously. The canvas ballooned up, the bundle floated for an instant, then slipped silently below the surface. A patch of turbulence and a trail of silver bubbles marked its descent into the depths of the Indian Ocean. With a final movement of his hands, Captain Greig snapped the book shut and looked up – 'and the life of the world to come.'

'Amen,' responded the passengers and crew with finality and more than a hint of relief.

In his final hours, Forbes may not have known what date it was. It was September 24th, a date which should have held a melancholy significance for him: it was the third anniversary of his infant son's death. The child was born in the old Mughal stronghold of Surat, in western India, on Monday, 27th January 1817 in 'the house of Saleh

Chellabee' in the Deriah Mahal. On that day his proud father had made the following note in his private letter book:

'This night at a quarter to eleven P.M. my dear Betsey was safely delivered of a boy.' He was the third child born to the couple in little more than four years. Fraser Forbes, known for most of his short life by his baby name, Chotabhoy – 'Little Boy' in Hindi – was only two months old when Theodore deserted his 'dear Betsey'. Six months later, on September 24th 1817 Chotabhoy died of a fever brought on by teething. After more than a year had gone by, Theodore had still not visited Eliza and his other children, or settled the bill for his baby son's funeral. Her letters begging to see him again were mostly put aside marked 'Answer unnecessary'.

Theodore's illness had affected everyone on board the *Blenden Hall*. They had sailed from Bombay on the inauspicious 13th day of August 1820. He was in good health when he embarked and was delighted to find that among his fellow passengers were old friends: Captain John Cameron 'of the Hon. Company's Madras Establishment', and Mrs Dickinson, the 'Lady' of Captain Thomas Dickinson of the Bombay Engineers, who was escorting her three young children back to England for their education. 'After being at sea for about three weeks, he was attacked with a bilious and bowel complaint,' according to the account given to his brother James, 'which increased until they reached the Isle de France [Mauritius] – where he lived for a week in the house of the principal surgeon, to see if his condition might improve with a spell on dry land.' Theodore's status as a former British Resident in The Arabian Gulph, as the Red Sea was then known, had assured him of preferential attention in this recently acquired outpost of the Bombay Presidency.

He seemed to show definite signs of recovery, and on the 16th of September the *Blenden Hall* had resumed her voyage home. The captain set a southerly course past the jungly island of Madagascar. But hopes of improvement in the patient's condition soon proved to be ill-founded. The sickness known as 'bilious fever' was also known as 'remittent fever', which turned out to be an apt description. The ship had barely crossed the Tropic of Capricorn and lay off the southern tip of Madagascar, Cape St Mary, when the remission of his fever ended and his symptoms returned with such violence that the sick man became convinced that he could not survive until they reached Cape Town. Throughout his debilitating illness he was attended by Dr Shanks, waited on by his personal servant Walloo and was the focus of Mrs Dickinson's 'extremely kind attention'.

She had been a 'kind and sympathetic companion' from the moment Theodore fell ill, and had taken on the unpleasant duties of nursing her dying friend through his 'bilious fever'. Just three days before he died, he called her to his side and asked her to fetch pen and paper. Though, like all who attend the bedside of the sick, she tried to tell him that he would recover, he insisted that even in that unlikely event, the time had come to set down his final wishes. His illness had given him opportunity and time to reflect on the years he had spent in India; time to think back to the Scottish home he had left a mere twelve years earlier; and time also to consider the children he had fathered since then. He began to dictate:

'I, Theodore Forbes, being of disposing mind but infirm in body, do hereby make my last will and testament, revoking all former ones whatsoever...' It is a long document, and his 'bilious and bowel complaint' must have meant many interruptions, but one thing is clear – it had been well thought out in advance. Bequests of personal items, legacies and annuities, and directions for their payment in Bombay Rupees or Pounds Sterling are all clearly stated. He even left Mrs Dickinson's three children a very generous sum of money:

'To Master Sebastian Dickinson, Misses Fanny and Eliza Dickinson, son and daughters of Captain Thomas Dickinson of the Bombay Engineers, the sum of five hundred pounds/ £500, each, as a small memorial of their mother's extremely kind attention to me during my last illness.' Five hundred pounds each does seem excessive as a 'small memorial', especially in the light of his other bequests. Five hundred pounds was the same sum he had left to his eldest brother Alexander and to his younger sister Jane. In view of the eventual shortfall in his estate, was it possible that he meant 500 rupees each, roughly equivalent to sixty pounds? Could this be the reason he overestimated the funds at his disposal? To the officers and crew of the *Blenden Hall* he left 'fifty/ £50 – to be divided as Captain Greig may think proper.'

The document closes with the words:

'Given, published and declared as my last will and testament on board the ship *Blenden Hall*, at sea in Lat.26 S. and Long.48.4 E. this twenty first day of September, in the year of our Lord, one thousand Eight Hundred and Twenty, where no stamps are used or procurable.' It was duly witnessed by his friend John Cameron, 'of the Honourable Company's Madras Establishment' to whom he left his 'hookah and smoking apparatus', and Dr Shanks, the ship's surgeon, to whom he left twenty five pounds.

After drawing up his will he suffered for another two daysand three nights in the gloom below decks; stifling in the stagnant air of the cabin, sweating in the humidity of a sub-tropical spring and enduring the discomfort of the unremitting movement of the ship: it was a harrowing end. His body was 'committed to the deep' somewhere between Madagascar and the Cape of Good Hope. The *Blenden Hall* sailed on.

At the very moment that he lay dying off the east coast of Africa, Eliza was on the other side of the Indian Ocean, in the port city of Surat, praying for the soul of her dead baby. It was time for the child's anniversary requiem and it had fallen on a Sunday. She had been to morning service at the Armenian Church before gathering with close friends and family at the baby's graveside for the requiem. The couple's oldest child, Katherine, had been sent to Scotland almost exactly a year before Theodore's departure. The baby's five-year-old brother, Aleck, clung close to his mother as they gathered solemnly around the little tomb. Eliza would pray to God, as she always had, for Theodore's good health and later, on this September evening, still in happy ignorance, she would kiss Aleck goodnight and say a prayer with him for his big sister Kitty, in Scotland, and their 'Papa' on his way to join her there. She would continue the daily ritual until the time, still some weeks away, when news of his death would reach her and she would realise how vain her supplication had been and how futile all her prayers.

When the ship arrived off Cape Town, Captain Greig made ready to take provisions on board and exchange mail packets with other ships. But on Friday October 13th the wind dropped and the *Blenden Hall* had the bad luck to be becalmed. It was exactly two months since they had sailed from Bombay; Mrs Dickinson and the other passengers were able to take advantage of the delay to receive visitors from other British ships in port and try to escape the depressing effect of their fellow passenger's demise. Captain Greig went ashore for fresh supplies and was able to find a ship by which to send news of Theodore's death to his partners in Forbes & Co., Bombay.

Two days later there was a sudden change in the weather. A heavy swell began to build and the crew prepared to sail. The *Blenden Hall* left Cape Town in gale force winds and rough seas on Sunday October 15th. She made good speed for the rest of the voyage and anchored off Deal on December 11th. Two days later she reached Gravesend. Again it was the 13th day of the month but at least it was not a Friday this time. Captain Greig immediately sent word of Theodore's death to Forbes & Co.'s London Office.

His death had left three children fatherless: his eldest boy, Frederick, aged twelve, born after Theodore sailed for India in 1808; Kitty, almost eight; and Aleck, just short of his sixth birthday. Theodore's will makes provision for them all; evidently they are his priority. All are described as his 'reputed natural' children and are the first beneficiaries to be mentioned. But the 'first of the first' is not his son Frederick, as might have been expected, or even his younger son Alexander. The principal legatee is his daughter Kitty: 'In Primis, Katherine Scott Forbes, my reputed natural daughter by Eliza Kewark and now in Great Britain'; next comes Kitty's younger brother Alexander 'Aleck' Scott Forbes and finally, 'My reputed son Frederick Forbes by Anne MacDonnell of Aberdeenshire N.B. and now residing there.'

Katherine, more usually known as 'Kitty', was to receive the largest legacy under her father's will: fifty thousand Bombay rupees – more than six thousand pounds. By contrast, Alexander was only to receive half that sum and he was, his father added, 'now in India where it is my wish that he should remain.' Frederick was to receive the least amount – twenty thousand rupees. It is not surprising that Kitty was his favourite: she was the first of his children to be born in wedlock – and the first that he had been able to hold in his arms. He was enchanted. From that moment she had gradually become the most important person in his life. When he left Eliza and the children in Surat at the start of 1817, Alexander had been a toddler incapable of coherent speech or of walking unaided, and baby Fraser was barely six-weeks old. He did not see them again for nearly two years. Kitty was the only one of his children with whom he had enjoyed any prolonged contact. Everyone knew that his vivacious little girl was the undisputed 'apple of her father's eye'.

On August 8th 1819, almost exactly a year before he boarded the *Blenden Hall*, Theodore had put the six-year-old Kitty aboard the ship *Katherine Stewart Forbes* with her trusted nurse Fazagool for the long sea voyage to England. His plan had been to be reunited with his beloved little girl at his family home in Scotland, and recover his health in his native land. But as he lay and sweltered below decks in the grip of his bilious fever, he realised that he could not survive until the end of the voyage. Despite the efforts of Dr Shanks, he would never see Kitty again. As he drew up his will he had the consolation of knowing that she was already safe with his parents in Aberdeenshire and that Fazagool was still with her. In the grip of his feverish imaginings he must have thirsted for a cool Scottish autumn, for the smell of the loam, and the caress of a temperate breeze. Most of all though, he longed to see his little girl again.

In a hundred and seventy years' time it was this little girl, Kitty Scott Forbes, who was to become the focus of press interest in her parentage when her descendant, Lady Diana Spencer, married the Prince of Wales. Theodore might otherwise be forgotten as just one of the many thousands of young Scots who went out to India as Servants of the Honourable East India Company and never saw their native land again. Kitty, too, was one of the many mixed-race children who were sent on the long voyage from India to Britain to improve their future prospects. As she grew up, the lack of information about her breeding, and the consequent suspicion of coloured blood, greatly diminished the likelihood of Miss Katherine Scott Forbes making a satisfactory match among the local gentry. Although her father came from a laird's family, well-respected in Aberdeenshire, too many questions remained unanswered. Her mother was known as Eliza Kewark, or was it

Kuwark or Kework, or even Kewurk perhaps, as written in different copies of Theodore's will? The correct spelling did not matter – all they knew was that Eliza was a 'native of India'; a foreigner of some sort, married to Theodore, so it was said, 'after the custom of the country where they lived'. Their fears were reinforced by the dark complexion of her younger brother Alexander.

A further disincentive, to any well-bred suitor at this time, was the implication that she might be illegitimate. Her older half-brother Frederick was cited as supporting evidence for this assumption. He had been born to a local lass, Anne MacDonnell, six months after Theodore left for India. If Forbes had fathered a bastard in Scotland before he was twenty one, how likely was it that the girl with an Indian mother was legitimate?

In an apparent last act of betrayal, Theodore refers to Eliza in his will as 'my housekeeper in Surat'. It may be that he baulked at the prospect of showing his true affection for her in front of Mrs Dickinson, or of admitting their marriage. More likely though, is that he knew that the legitimacy of their marriage could not be proved in a British court. There was no doubt that Kitty was his daughter, but he referred to her as 'my reputed natural daughter' because, had he described Kitty simply as his daughter and Eliza as his wife, their legacies might have been successfully challenged by his residual legatee, his father, John Forbes of Boyndlie. At that time there was no such thing as a civil ceremony, and only marriages solemnised in the Church of England or Scotland were officially recognised. But there is no doubt that Eliza and Theodore were married.

Confirmation of their marriage in the Armenian Apostolic Church in Surat is found in Eliza's references to a traditional Eastern Orthodox wedding ceremony in her letters to Theodore:

'The whole world knows that only you are of my crown of head and adorn till my life,' she writes. This sentence, puzzling as it may at first seem, is an unambiguous reference to the Armenian wedding ceremony. The couple would have made their vows before the assembled congregation – 'The whole world'. As they stood before the altar, the priest would have blessed a pair of wedding crowns for each to place on the other's head – 'before God'. This mutual coronation, along with the exchange of rings, crystallised for Eliza the concept of an equal partnership in the holy estate of matrimony. The couple were entering into a contract which could only be broken by the death of one of the parties or, as she puts it, 'till my life'. For her this ceremony was the foundation stone of the life they would build together and later, when they are separated, she frequently reminds Theodore of it.

In 1812 the young couple started their married life with a great adventure. Almost immediately after their wedding they embarked for Yemen, where Theodore was to take up his appointment as 'British Resident in the Arabian Gulph'. Little more than ten months passed after the church ceremony in Surat before Eliza gave birth to their firstborn child, Kitty, in Mocha in the official residence known as the 'British Factory'. But while the couple were enjoying the novelty of parenthood in Arabia, forces as yet unknown to them were gathering strength in British India; forces that were to test their marriage to breaking point. The depth of Eliza's commitment to their sacred wedding vows was not to be matched by Theodore's. His behaviour later would prove that, under pressure, he, along with the majority of the British community, did not place the same weight on an Armenian marriage as he might have on one solemnised in an English or Scottish church.

Theodore's appointment to the Residency in Mocha had precipitated their marriage. Eliza was from a respectable Armenian family. Her brother-in-law, Aratoon Baldassier, merited the title Agah. She was not just a *bibi*, and would not have agreed to go with him without the status and security marriage conferred. Passionately in love, Theodore could not contemplate going without her. At that moment being together was the only thing that mattered. Only death should, or would, part them. Soon after they married they left family and friends behind and committed themselves to an uncertain future in an unknown land.

Only four years had passed since Theodore left Scotland. Now, Eliza too was abandoning all she had ever known. But they were in love and they were young. Theodore was twenty-three and Eliza was even younger than her husband – in her teens – barely more than a girl. The busy Red Sea port of Mocha was to be their home for the next three and a half happy years and there they would enjoy an untrammelled intimacy and lay the foundations of a family and a fortune. Having arrived as newlyweds they would leave as a loving couple with two young children, and every prospect of enjoying a long and happy life together.

That sweet prospect ebbed away and all hope was extinguished in the fetid belly of the *Blenden Hall*. How the dying man must have wished for the dry heat of Mocha; for the light and airy upper floors of the British Factory; how he must have longed to be young and virile again and hold his 'Dear Betsey' in his arms once more.

Chapter 2

The Red Sea, 1812

View of Mocha from the South.

Plate from *Valentia's Travels* – drawn by Henry Salt, 1805.

2

The Red Sea, 1812

When Theodore arrived from India with his young bride, Mocha was in its heyday and the city was the undisputed queen of the Red Sea. The busy port drew ships of all kinds from India and beyond, plying the ancient trade routes that were already well-established long before any of the European Companies had gained access to the markets of the east. The larger vessels dropped anchor in the Mocha Roads – deeper waters farther offshore – to stay bare-masted, straining at their moorings and riding the swell. Flotillas of smaller boats of shallow draught danced attendance on them, busily carrying passengers and cargo to and fro across the wide-mouthed bay. It was from one of these that the new Resident tenderly handed his bride ashore onto the busy quayside. They may already have known that she was pregnant.

Today the greater part of ancient Mocha lies deserted and crumbling on Yemen's Red Sea coast, just a short distance away from Africa, across the Strait of Bab-el-Mandeb. Only a few decaying ruins bear witness to the former greatness of the city and hint at the beauty of its classical Ottoman architecture. The brilliant white buildings of old have greyed to dust, as the combined force of wind and sand has whipped the lime-wash off their unbaked bricks and cast them down forever. Timbers have weathered to pearly skeletons. Mosques and minarets, prophets' tombs and merchants' elegant houses are now mostly reduced to mounds of rubble, spread over a wide expanse of empty desert.

Yet, when the sea breeze freshens and sucks the sands up into whirling dust devils, then the dangling shutters creak and bang, parched wooden lintels start to shift, and the wind whistles through the hollow bones of those silent and forsaken houses. It seems as if a million forgotten souls, steeped in dreams of wealth and empire, are bringing an eerie resonance to a *danse macabre* among the cadaverous remains of their once vibrant city. Homes that attested, not so very long ago, to every human passion, and stood so proudly up along the margin of the antique shore, now sink slowly down, into the sandy waste.

Disintegrating merchant house, Mocha 1994.

©Susan Harvard

Interior of merchant house illustrated on previous page;
chunam plasterwork, now presumed lost. Mocha 1994.

©Susan Harvard

Published with my sincere thanks to the Yemeni boy, about ten years old, who guided me to the ruined house, in 1994, without whose appreciation of the craftsmanship within, and friendly beckoning to a foreigner with a camera, this beautiful building might have sunk into the sand unrecorded.

May he live and thrive throughout his country's troubled times.

While scarcely a heartbeat remains of the Mocha of old, the sea breathes rhythmically in sensual contrast; sucking in and spitting out sparkling millennia of sand and grit, spangling her emerald shallows and lighting up the limpid swell. The gentle swish of her lace-edged breakers dragging the shingle back echoes the refrain of centuries past and whispers a constant reminder of her immortality. Her voice pervades the oceans of the Earth; her sepulchral depths nurse the spectral hulks of countless wrecks and their encrusted secrets; her waters are suffused with the atoms of a myriad of lost seafarers, whose hopes and prayers are still borne in futile suspension beneath the living waves. Here, from the briny depths of a distant African coast, some inert speck of Theodore's being has perhaps at last been drawn back to the happy shore of *Arabia Felix*.

In 1812, when the young Resident and his bride climbed down into the ship's jolly boat and were carried closer in to the old city, they would have seen that a light band above the tide line, apparent when they first dropped anchor, was a long sea wall with Arabian-style serrated battlements and fortified bastions. The fortifications were reminiscent of Eliza's home city of Surat – another great port with stout defensive walls. But while Surat was founded on the banks of a river, winding like a silver ribbon damascened upon the verdigris margin of Gujarat, Mocha basked in the brilliance of the Arabian Coast, like a pearl in a setting of gold.

From their low viewpoint, seated in a small boat and looking across the foreshortened cityscape, the young couple could just see, over the battlemented wall and crenellated rooftops, the portly domes of the city's mosques, and their tapering minarets, banded with stucco ornament and ringed with balustrades, rising, shimmeringly elegant, above them. The brilliance of the white city walls, and all the buildings within, was due to the lime render known as *chunam*, speckled, some of it, with glittering crystal fragments and tiny shells. This luminous cityscape was punctuated by the tops of innumerable nodding palm trees, striking dark accents to counterpoint the lustre of the buildings and the brightness of the clouds against a fathomless blue Arabian sky.

Straggling along within its gently curving shallow bay, Mocha's irregular roofscape dominated the level shoreline. With her fortified gates providing the only ways in and out to the landward sides, the ancient city faced boldly out from behind her defensive sea wall and projecting sea gate, towards the setting sun. This confident front was sustained to north and south by two arching spits of land, which extended out at either end of the bay, like the horns of a buffalo. At each tip a fort was strategically positioned, armed with cannon to repel any attack from the sea. They looked impressive, but Lord Valentia had earlier commented that the Arabs had enlarged the touch-holes to such an extent that 'the guns are useless, except to return a salute'. These, then, were the guns that boomed out across the city to signal the hour and salute the arriving and departing ships. The young Resident was newly 'benedict' or blessed, as the slang of the day described a married man, and before long he would be a father. He and his young bride would have been greeted by just such a volley and, before the year was out, their infant daughter in her cot would have had to become accustomed to these distant but regular explosions.

Everything was new and exciting to the young couple. Their first sight of the flags fluttering above the various foreign factories and consulates, where the different nations conducted their commercial and political business, allowed the pair to spot the position of their new home long before their boat drew alongside the quay. The British Factory was a prominent building standing only a short distance back from the sea front with the Union Flag of Great Britain fluttering from the mast on its roof top. It was said to be one of the best houses in Mocha.

The *Furda* or customs house stood close by in the centre of the quay, marked out by its great green flag. Emblazoned in white on the emerald field was the powerful image of the double-bladed sword of Ali. This was the standard of the Zaydi Imam of Sana'a, who ruled the city through his appointed governor, the Dola. Clustered around the customs house and the Dola's stately residence were the houses of the foremost merchants, descending into the distance in order of height, opulence and prestige according to their status. Beyond the walls, at the periphery of the city that was to be their home for the next few years, the newlyweds might just have been able to make out the low dark humps and mounds of a number of scattered shanty villages. This was where, beneath the palm-leaf thatch of their domed mud huts, like human termites, the poorest members of Mocha's multicultural society scraped a living on the barren desert sands beyond its walls.

Unfortunately for Theodore and Eliza, their first footfall through the sea gate, as many earlier travellers had found, soon dispelled any fancies of the attractiveness of the ancient city, which they might have enjoyed while viewing it from afar. In his *Travels*, less than ten years earlier, Lord Valentia's first impression from the sea was of a 'tolerably handsome' city: an impression rapidly dispelled by 'the filth that abounds in every street and more particularly in the open spaces, which are left within the walls by the gradual decay of the deserted habitations which once filled them.'

The large number of open spaces, filled with the debris of fallen buildings, is one feature of the old quarter of Mocha that has remained unchanged since Valentia's day; but now the buildings that remain upright are even fewer and the spaces much greater. The shallow bay has largely silted up and, above the small harbour that remains, loud flocks of gulls wheel and squabble. The foreshore has been abandoned to a mixed pack of feral dogs, quarrelling and scavenging along the tide line or sleeping below it on the cool damp sand left behind by the receding tide. A multitude of gaily-coloured plastic bags litters the shore, each signalling its presence by waving and fluttering in the intermittent breeze. Wooden-hulled fishing boats bask idly at the top of the beach, beside their modern fibreglass counterparts. As the old city bakes in the relentless heat, very few of the resident Mochans are to be seen – and even fewer visitors. Her days of glory are long gone, but the breadth and scale of the rubble-strewn sand gives a sad intimation of just how grand the city was when it was well-populated and prosperous and Eliza and Theodore made their first home together there.

There is no description of the exact protocol surrounding Theodore's arrival from Surat, but he was carrying letters of introduction from Jonathan Duncan, Governor of Bombay, to the Dola of Mocha and the Imam of Sana'a and must have merited a decent salute. His predecessor in the post, Captain Henry Rudland, would certainly have turned out to greet him on the quayside and escort him through the sea gate, where they would be met, as was customary for all important visitors, by the Dola's musicians. His best Arab horses, richly caparisoned in scarlet leather and quilted velvets were usually led in front of important visitors. It must have been a fantastic spectacle as the high-spirited steeds cavorted to the beat of the drums, their burnished coats glowing with vitality, their harnesses decorated with silver and gold, jingling and jangling as their turbaned grooms walked close beside them and curbed them tightly to hold their eagerness in check.

It would be good to think that while the men paid their respects to the Dola, Mrs Rudland was welcoming Eliza warmly, and taking her to the Factory for refreshment, and perhaps showing her round the building that was to be her home for the next few years. Captain and Mrs Rudland were to take their passage to Bombay a week or two later and Eliza would suddenly find herself accorded the respect due to the Lady of a British Resident. To be treated with deference was a novelty for her. As the unmarried younger sister of a married woman she had little status in the Armenian community of Surat. Her marriage and her husband's new rank had meant that within the space of a few months she had become a woman of some importance.

As soon as he was able to take up his duties, the new Resident turned his attention to the vexed question of piracy – more precisely, to the arrest of one particular pirate, Sayyid Mohammed Akil, presumed chief of the Joassimée pirates of Ras al-Khaimah. Theodore had brought orders with him from Bombay to capture the Sayyid and 'find witnesses willing to testify against him' allegedly 'for piracy' almost six years earlier, against the American ship *Essex*, from Salem, Massachusetts. The captain and some of the crew had been murdered and a young cabin boy kidnapped and enslaved. But the case was not as clear-cut as it was at first said to be. The eagerness of the government in Bombay to catch the 'pirate' may have had more to do with his open support of the French, with whom Great Britain was still at war, than with a desire to bring him to justice for crimes against citizens of America. They had been after him for years. What a coup for the young Resident if he could catch the wily rascal!

George Viscount Valentia, who had been acting-Resident for a time in 1803, recalls in his *Voyages and Travels* that he had met the so-called pirate in Mocha and greatly enjoyed his company. The Sayyid was, according to Valentia, 'a man of very considerable property' and the Viscount had been entertained by him, he said, in 'the best house in Mocha', seated in European style, in chairs, as opposed to reclining on cushions. They had a light-hearted chat over a glass of coffee scented with cloves. 'He was a *Wahabee*, and much hated by the Dola,' says Valentia, adding ironically, 'we abused the Dola most cordially.' The two men had parted as equals and friends. But the friendship between the pair soured when the Sayyid was caught exporting undeclared cash to India and Lord Valentia brought him to court.

Then, in 1806, after Valentia had returned home to England, the incident of the *Essex* occurred. It was alleged that Mohammed Akil sent his men on board the *Essex*, on the pretext of providing an escort up the Red Sea. During the night the ship's American captain, Captain Orme, with his English supercargo, and the crew were all murdered and the ship was plundered. It was said that the perpetrators were acting on the Sayyid's orders and that he was personally responsible for kidnapping a young American boy, Johannes Poll, converting him to Islam and keeping him as a slave. In fact the lad later declined the offer of a free passage home to Salem.

In his book *The White Shaik*, H.H. Sheikh Sultan Mohammed al Qassimi writes that Henry Rudland had an opportunity to retrieve the 'captive' Johannes Poll from the Sayyid's ship in Mocha in 1810 but was outfaced by the strength and numbers of the Sayyid's men. Theodore too failed in this task soon after his arrival. Johannes Poll became like a son to Mohammed Akil and married into his household. The Sayyid adopted him and he was appointed to the command of one of his adoptive father's ships under the name Abdullah bin Mohammed bin Akil. The American 'captive' was eventually to become the Sayyid's most trusted captain.

Despite having failed to arrest the wily sea wolf or 'find witnesses willing to testify against him', Theodore could pride himself that the Sayyid did not leave his lair again during his Residency and the pirates had largely steered clear of the Red Sea. Lord Valentia's earlier assessment of the hunt for the pirate was that: 'As a retreat is ever open to him in Arabia, there are but little hopes of his meeting with the fate he merits.' It seems that this remark held true during Theodore's residency. Amongst his earliest reports from Mocha in his first year there were several on the subject of Mohammed Akil, and in August he wrote to inform his bosses in Bombay that though the pirate chief had visited the ports of Loheia, Hodeida and Mocha, he had been unable to catch him 'either on land or at sea'. Like Valentia before him Theodore too 'abused the Dola', but not at all 'cordially', unequivocally blaming the governor's lack of cooperation for this early failure.

At the close of the expedition, described in Valentia's *Voyages and Travels to India, Ceylon, the Red Sea, Abyssinia and Egypt*, Lord Valentia, Rudland and Henry Salt had gone back to London. Shortly afterwards Rudland returned to India, bringing his wife with him. He was immediately appointed to the Mocha Residency – mainly because he already knew the area well from his travels with Valentia. The powers in Bombay may also have hoped that the presence of his wife might help to prevent him from following the example of his predecessor Pringle who, Valentia wrote, had 'an unfortunate attachment to spiritous liquors'.

Rudland seems to have stayed sober but was comprehensively outwitted by the local coffee merchants, dismissed from the post and summoned to Bombay to explain his poor trading account. His coffee purchases were later to be described in Company records as comparing to 'great disadvantage with those made by Mr Theodore Forbes'. The Rudlands left for Bombay after handing over the Factory to Theodore and Eliza. The Resident needed to be a loyal British subject, a diplomat, politician, spy and counter-spy and yet he must still be able to trade profitably in coffee on behalf of the Hon. Company. Perhaps it had been unfair to expect a military man like Rudland suddenly to develop a talent for business. But Theodore had the advantage of a wife with a mercantile background and a flair for languages.

Theodore's masters back in Bombay also wanted their new Resident to develop good relations with local chiefs along the Red Sea coast of Africa, with a view to exploiting any opportunities for trade with the, as yet, unexplored interior of the 'Dark Continent'. They also needed intelligence on political movements within the declining Ottoman Empire. Theodore was intelligent and personable and had experience of general trade back in England. In short, he fulfilled all the requirements for the job.

The raw coffee berries brought from the mountain villages in the highlands of Yemen to the markets of Beit al-Faqih and Mocha were the principal commodity shipped from Yemen. It was the seemingly insatiable demand for coffee from the growing number of coffee houses in both Europe and America that had brought the agents of so many nations to set up their factories in the port, vying with each other to source the finest berries and close the best deals. At the age of twenty three, Theodore was to be responsible for buying and shipping the East India Company's entire annual consignment of coffee. Their monopoly on British trade from India ensured a handsome profit for the Company, a steady tax revenue for the Dola and opportunities for lucrative private trade for the Resident. His domestic arrangements in the British Factory with the multi-lingual Eliza and, later, their two young children, assured him of a far easier acceptance among the local merchants than either Pringle or Rudland.

Apart from coffee, all sorts of other goods passed through Mocha: dates, grapes and honey; herbs, spices and incense; Arabian horses and African slaves; rhinoceros horn; coral, ivory, pearls and gold for the markets of the Persian Gulf, India and the Far East. These were precious cargoes well worth protecting. A certain degree of protection for this long-established two-way traffic between the ports of Western India and the Red Sea could be gained from sailing in convoy. Some captains and supercargoes, keen not to lose the advantage of being first into port, chose to take the risk of sailing early – more heavily armed and manned – but alone. Merchant vessels, bound for Surat and Bombay, laden with goods of such tempting value, provided rich pickings, but if they escaped the notice of the pirates off the Gulf of Aden and across the Arabian Sea, the 'windfall' of being first to bring their goods into an empty market could net them and the owners a tidy profit.

Theodore had already served a useful apprenticeship with Charles Grant of Cushion Court, Broad Street in London, whose original hand-written reference is preserved in the India Office Library:

'I herewith certify that Mr Theodore Forbes was in my employment about two years,' writes Grant, 'during which time he acquired a thorough knowledge of mercantile accounts.' The paper is signed and dated 11th April 1808, and the 20-year-old Theodore had reported for duty at East India House the very next day. It seems though, that the master may not have been as competent as his pupil – only two and a half years after Theodore embarked for India the bankruptcy was announced in the *London Gazette* of Charles Grant of Cushion Court, 'merchant, dealer and chapman'. A chapman was a general dealer in low-value articles; 'chap' being, in this case, a corruption of 'cheap'.

Clearly Theodore must have demonstrated great potential in the three years' service he had so far completed with the Hon. East India Company to have been given so much responsibility at such an early age. But the appointment of 'Mr Theodore Forbes of the Bombay Civil Service' was not all it seemed to the wider public. In addition to buying coffee for the Honourable Company, he was a political agent directly responsible to Richard Goodwin, chief of the Secret and Political Department of the Bombay Government. In other words, he was a British spy. This was an important role at this point in time. The Napoleonic wars with France were not over and within a few weeks of his arrival in Mocha, America declared war on Britain. Although the battles of the war of 1812 were fought on a different front in the Americas and in Canada, the British Resident was now required to watch ships of both nations in the strategic area of the Red Sea. He was also asked to report pirate attacks on merchant shipping and assist some of the earliest British travellers in Africa and Arabia.

It would have been a novelty for many of the merchants and travellers, who came to the door of the Mocha Factory, to see the human face of a Briton abroad with a beautiful young wife and a growing family. The fact that the wife was Armenian might also have been looked on with some surprise. But many would remember that there had been a precedent for a British diplomat bringing an Armenian wife to his post: some years earlier, Lieutenant Robert Taylor was accompanied by his Armenian wife Rosa Hovanessian to take up his post as Assistant to Samuel Manesty the British Resident in the Persian Gulf at Bushire.

In 1808, Mrs Taylor was quite a celebrity. The pirate fleet had intercepted a convoy which included Manesty's ship *La Minerva*, bound for Bombay. Taylor's wife and baby son were on board when the ship was attacked by around fifty pirate dhows. After attempting to outrun them and putting up a spirited resistance lasting two days, they were overwhelmed. Most of the crew and passengers were said to have been put to the sword and thrown overboard. But Mrs Taylor and her baby son were spared. The pirates took them back to Ras al-Khaimah, where she was put up for sale by the Jowassim chief and bought as a prize for ransom. Samuel Manesty is said to have paid her Arab purchaser 1,000 Maria Theresa Thalers to release her. Her infant son survived to grow up and she and her husband had several more children in the course of his long and distinguished diplomatic career.

The story of Rosa Taylor's kidnap, ransom and release was well-publicised, and the grisly details of the deaths of the captain and his crew, though unsubstantiated, were widely circulated. She was evidently a courageous woman and had helped in the attempt to repel the boarders by filling cartridges for the defending crew. She was still the talk of the town when Theodore arrived in Bombay from England later in the year. Attacks by the same pirate fleet had even been carried out off Surat in 1808 and later in the same year, operating out of Ras al-Khaimah, the pirates intercepted ships off the coast of Sind. The economic consequences of hindering the passage of merchant ships between Mocha and Surat were considerable. Lured by the promise of shared booty, captains of dhows from all around began flocking to join the pirate ranks. By early 1809 an estimated sixty large bugalahs and more than eight hundred dhows were at the pirates' disposal. Their combined crews were estimated at more than 19,000 men. At the time, just two ships of the Bombay marine, *Mornington* and *Teignmouth* were deployed to protect the route.

These incursions were still hot topics when Theodore arrived from England and enrolled as an assistant in the Secret, Political and Foreign Department. He was still in Bombay in September 1809 when a British expeditionary force sailed for Ras al-Khaimah. The following month he moved to Surat as Assistant Registrar. Once there, he rented a house and garden from Dhossabhoy Pestonjee for the huge sum of sixty rupees per month. This was the time when talk of pirates was on everybody's lips and when news of the sack of Ras al-Khaimah reached India. This was an exciting time for an ambitious twenty-one-year-old; it was also the time when he first saw Eliza and fell in love.

At the start of 1812, when Theodore married Eliza and they sailed together for Mocha, they must both have been aware of an increased risk of attack from the pirates all along their route. A voyage across the Arabian Sea was a risky undertaking even in the Company cruiser or a ship of the Bombay marine; their decision to leave India could not have been taken lightly. The dangers faced, both in reality and in the imagination, were many. After all, these were the days of great sea battles, of tattered sails and shredded rigging; of noise and smoke; of boarding parties and hand-to-hand fighting. There could be times when their lives would depend on Theodore's skill with the sword he had recently bought from Lewis Collett in Surat. He might have pictured himself helping to defend the ship and protecting his lovely bride against a pirate raiding party; keeping his footing on unsteady decks when the sun-bleached boards were slippery with blood. Perhaps Eliza saw herself upholding her nation's pride in Rosa Taylor's courage; staying by her new husband's side to the end and plying him with powder and shot. The cut throats and grisly beheadings, so frequently reported in the press, were enough to put anyone off embarking on a voyage that would take them so close to the pirates' stronghold. What a sigh of relief they both must have breathed when they reached Mocha without incident.

Chapter 3

Mocha, 1812 – 1815

View from the Roof of the British Factory Mocha, Yemen.
This is the building where Katherine Scott Forbes was born on December 1st 1812.

Original engraving from a drawing by Henry Salt, made c. 1805 and published in 1811 in Valentia's *Voyages and Travels to India, Ceylon, the Red Sea, Abyssinia and Egypt*.

3

Mocha, 1812 – 1815

The British Factory was a large building standing a little way back from the seaward ramparts, only separated from the Dola's mansion by his stables, and close enough for the Resident to consider him as a neighbour. The artist, writer, Egyptologist and diplomat, Henry Salt, stayed there in 1805 and 1809 and drew the *View from the Roof of the British Factory* during his first visit. Salt's *View of Mocha from the South*, drawn during the same visit is a fair representation of the view that met Theodore and Eliza as they transferred from ship to shore and his sketch of the *View from the Roof* is the same vista that the couple would have enjoyed as they explored their new home.

Not long after Theodore and Eliza moved into the Factory, the merchant fleet sailed for Bombay and Mr and Mrs Rudland with it. By August of the same year Theodore had other matters on his mind. Eliza was now six months pregnant. When they arrived, at the tail end of the 1811/12 trading year, she had been available to help him with his important first introductions and business deals with the local Arab traders, Gujarati *banians* and, of course, Armenian merchants. Theodore evidently had some knowledge and experience on his side, but Eliza spoke and wrote Farsi, Hindi and probably Arabic and Gujarati. Her linguistic talents and mercantile background must have contributed greatly to the superiority of Theodore's trading record over Rudland's.

Theodore's new title was 'Commercial and Political Agent in the Arabian Gulph' and the political aspect of his work was as important to British interests as his commercial undertakings. When he and Eliza arrived in Mocha, Napoleon Bonaparte was still the talk and the terror of all Europe, and a cause for concern in British India and all its outposts, especially in the Red Sea area. At a time when the self-declared emperor was simply the autonomous Commander-in-Chief of the French Army, he had taken it upon himself to establish a land base between the

Mediterranean and Red Seas. He assembled a landing force of 40,000 strong, in the French port of Toulon ready to embark for Egypt, where they would be well positioned to sail down the Red Sea to India.

Napoleon's plan had been to mount a diplomatic mission from Suez and persuade as many Indian rulers as possible to help him drive the British out of India. Money was deemed to be 'the sinews of war' and by disrupting their Indian trade he anticipated cutting off a valuable source of British funding for the war in Europe. He needed to back his mission with credible military might. But in 1798 the Royal Navy under Nelson had defeated the French fleet off Aboukir. Less than a year later the French invasion force was destroyed. For the moment Bonaparte's Indian ambitions had been frustrated, but even fourteen years later the British Government and the Hon. Company believed that the French might still harbour designs on their 'possessions' in India.

The young Resident had grown up with tales of 'Boney' as a bogeyman. In his native north-east Scotland, in the closing years of the eighteenth century, a French sea-borne invasion was thought to be a very real threat. He was born in 1788 and between the years 1797 and 1800, when he was an impressionable young boy, this threat was the subject of energetic debate across the whole country. The patriotic feelings of the citizens of 'North Britain', as it was then widely called, even by the Scots themselves, seem to have been heightened along with the raising of volunteer forces and building of coastal defences against the common enemy.

Half a century earlier the French had been the Scottish rebels' friends, and their king had given shelter to the exiled Old Pretender and his family; but the failure of the '45 rebellion at Culloden had ended the hopes of a Jacobite succession for all but the most optimistic of Scots. After that, Scotland had increasingly turned away from Catholicism towards Protestantism and its reformed branches. Though he came from a family which had suffered for the Jacobite cause, Theodore and most of his fellow Lowland Scots were now proudly British. During his time as Resident he was to receive the news of Bonaparte's retreat from Moscow, his defeat, abdication, exile to Elba and subsequent escape. Not until a fortnight before he relinquished his post did Wellington's victory at Waterloo signal the end of any further aggression by 'Boney' and his army.

With Eliza at his side, Theodore would prove to be diligent in carrying out his many duties. The roof of the British Factory had an excellent outlook and from this vantage point, with a telescope to hand, he could keep watch over the whole of the bay, identify the ships as they dropped anchor in the Roads and observe the colourful potpourri of people who stepped ashore from them. As well as the regular reports on politics and piracy that he sent back to the Presidency, he noted in his private letter book his dealings with local merchants and the chain of correspondents he established through Hodeida, Jeddah, Suez, Alexandria, Malta and beyond. Through these he was able to anticipate demand in European markets for Eastern commodities and lay the foundations of a profitable private trading account.

In Theodore's day, Mocha was a truly cosmopolitan port. Commerce was the driving force and religious and racial tolerance was taken for granted. These days, new deep docks have been developed farther to the south with modern cargo handling facilities, and the choppy waters of the bay are sprinkled with only a few native craft, plying their lonely way over an empty tract of sea. The huge modern ships, like fabled Leviathans, are glimpsed only from afar, churning their way past without the need to put in for provisions. Pilgrims fly to Mecca from all over the Indian subcontinent instead of taking a passage from Surat in a sailing ship. Global trade is but a distant dream. The remains of the proud old port of Mocha have been abandoned to the local fishermen, to refugees from Africa, to smugglers and perhaps to the modern-day pirates from the Horn of Africa.

On December 1st 1812, the British Factory was filled with the cries of Theodore's new-born daughter. It was Eliza's first baby and Theodore, anxious for her, made sure that the surgeon to the Mocha establishment, Dr William Aitken, was on hand in case there should be any complications. In the event it seems there were none. She was a pretty pink and white baby with a dusting of brown hair and won her father's heart from the first moment he set eyes on her. Without hesitation he named the infant Katherine Scott Forbes: 'Katherine' after his mother and 'Scott' after his brother-in-law, Alexander Scott, a widely respected doctor and founder of the eponymous charity and hospital that still exist in Huntly, Aberdeenshire. Baby Katherine Scott Forbes soon became known by family and friends as 'Kitty'.

Eliza did have a nurse to help with the baby; her name was Fazagool. She was a much-loved member of the household who would later accompany Kitty on the long sea-voyage to England, be left a small annuity by Theodore and stay with Eliza into old age. Fazagool's origins are a mystery; her name does not tell of belonging to any particular nation. Searches within the Indian subcontinent and the Ottoman Empire throw up no clues as to its origin. A close match is found in the African place name Fazughli. Fazughli is the name of a region in South Sudan close to the Ethiopian border. The town of the same name lies on the banks of the Blue Nile, where its waters flow from the highlands of Ethiopia and mingle with the White Nile to flow as one through the ancient kingdom of the Pharaohs and out into the Mediterranean Sea. Fazughli was a centre of the valuable Nubian gold trade and also of the age-old Arab slave trade, through which thousands of Africans were sent to the fair at Berbera and traded onwards into the markets of Yemen, India, and the Persian Gulf. The frequency of naming slaves from their place of origin suggests strongly that Fazagool was from Christian South Sudan and possibly even brought to Mocha or Surat as a slave. It is easy to imagine how a frightened Sudanese girl, captured in the interior of Africa and traded through the markets of Berbera and Mocha, might blurt out the name of a place, when her own name was demanded by her purchaser.

The chance of finding a Christian nurse in Mocha, with an adopted son who goes by the Armenian name of Markar, is slight. Less than eight years later Theodore describes her as 'the faithful female servant'. Eight years hardly qualifies a servant as 'faithful', so it is more likely that she was a free slave already employed in Eliza's family. She may have been nurse to Eliza as a baby, and to her older sister Guyane's children. Eliza could easily have sent to Surat for her in time for the birth of her first baby. It is impossible to tell whether Markar was truly Fazagool's adopted son or her own illegitimate child fathered by an Armenian. It does seem unlikely that a single female African servant would be allowed to adopt a child from the same community as her employers unless it was her own. A Minas Margarian is mentioned by Mesroub Jacob Seth as the head of one of the households still living in Surat in 1820. Perhaps Fazagool was a slave in his household. She may have been passed on pregnant, as a wet nurse, to avoid his embarrassment.

Opposite – View from the Roof of the British Factory Mocha, the birthplace of Katherine 'Kitty' Scott Forbes on December 1st 1812.

Engraving made from a sketch on the spot by Henry Salt in 1807 and later published in Valentia's *Voyages and Travels*.

The South Fort, the island of Perim and the 'Roads' are clearly visible.

Note: The Flag on the Customs House signifies that it is under the authority of the Zaydi Imam of Sana'a.

Inappropriate later colouring in red has almost completely obscured the outline double-bladed sword of Ali, which should be displayed on a field of green.

The scaffolding can still be seen on the Dola's new Mansion.

The British Factory, where Kitty Scott Forbes was born, was one of the best-situated and best-appointed houses in Mocha. These merchant houses were grand buildings, constructed in traditional Ottoman style and possessing features common to the architecture found in many of the ports along both shores of the Red Sea. As well as being family homes, they were places of work where the prosperous merchants of the city carried on their business. Houses were usually constructed of dried mud bricks. Those of the richer merchants tended to have more than two storeys. These prime properties were first built up on a high foundation of stone block-work with outer walls that were wider at the base and sloped very slightly inwards as they rose higher. Upper storeys of brick, either baked or unbaked, were added as required. The thick walls of the ground floors were deep and strong, with few windows that might attract the unwelcome attentions of burglars and thieves. These lower rooms were consequently darker and much cooler than the rest of the house. Stout metal grilles set deep within the tiny window embrasures made them very secure – perfect for their customary use as storerooms. The top floor was generally where the women's quarters were. This is where, in the British Factory, the infant Kitty's nursery would have been.

Here, in the beautiful and exotic surroundings of one of the grandest houses in Mocha, Kitty Scott Forbes, ancestress of British royalty, was to spend her earliest years – the years that, as an adult, she could not recall, in a city she did not remember, in a country whose name she did not know. This is where, on the upper floors of the Factory, the dark-skinned Fazagool, cool in white muslin, cradled the rosy-cheeked infant in her arms and held her tightly when she lifted her up to point and chuckle at the noisy seagulls and their aerial squabbles, or to look down on the top of her Papa's head, as he crossed the square below, towards the Dola's house. This is where Kitty Scott Forbes took her first steps, formed her first words, and grew from a helpless babe into a pretty and high-spirited child. Theodore probably saw more of his little daughter during her first few years than most European men did at that date, due to the arrangement of the household, the absence of society and the fact that he worked from home.

The birth of a baby to the British Resident's Lady was an unusual, possibly unprecedented, event in Mocha and would have been a great help to Theodore in finding common ground with merchants and Yemeni officials. He was young and ambitious and keen to learn their language and acquaint himself with their customs. This, coupled with his affable nature and Eliza's ethnicity, would have presented the British Resident to the merchants of Mocha as a man with whom they could do business without fear of prejudice. Much of his day-to-day business would have been conducted from home.

Due to the long-established trade route between the two cities, most of the Gujarati merchants in Mocha originated from Surat. Eliza's contacts within the Armenian, Parsee, Hindu and Muslim merchant communities in her home city would have been a great help to her husband in his new undertaking. Her knowledge of languages and her upbringing and culture would also have contributed to her role, not just as a wife but as a helpmeet. The extent to which Eliza assisted her husband in his work can only be guessed at, but Armenian women had always been accorded a degree of freedom that females of other races could only dream of.

In *Western India in 1838*, Marianne Postans reports that 'They have very considerable influence in their families, understand business admirably and are commonly entrusted with the full control of their own property.' It was well-accepted practice amongst the peripatetic merchants and businessmen of the Armenian diaspora to rely on their wives to conduct business on their behalf during their absence. So it seems that during the time the couple spent in Mocha, Eliza would have expected to take an interest in her husband's business affairs and help him wherever possible. Mrs Postans' remarks were probably not made without a hint of envy; another fifty years would pass before British law accorded married women the same rights as the Armenian ladies of Western India in her day.

Mrs Postans also comments that, when she was in Surat, the Armenian ladies there passed their time 'engaged in the care of their families, in receiving or paying visits, drinking coffee or sherbet, embroidering and making delicious confections of Hulwah and various sweetmeats.' If Kitty had not been sent to England at the age of six, but had grown up in Eliza's care with all the advantages of close contact with a loving mother, she would have learned to make the 'delicious confections of Hulwah' and to embroider beautiful traditional motifs in bright silks on luxurious fabric. Importantly, she would have known more about her early years because she would have been able to ask her mother as many questions as she wanted to about their time in Mocha.

Eliza might have told her little girl how Papa had been an important man there, so young and handsome when he arrived to take over from Captain Rudland; how, with her knowledge of languages, she had soon heard about the tricks the coffee merchants had played on poor old Rudland, laughing behind his back when they sold him lowest quality goods for top prices; how she soon put a stop to that, earning for her husband an appreciative report from his superiors in Bombay, as well as the respect of the locals. She might have told her daughter how proud she was to be Sahiba Forbes, 'The British Resident's Lady'; how young they were, how in love and how happy in each other's company! She might have regaled Kitty with amusing stories of how Papa 'set a hen on three goose eggs, and at the same time gave three to the doctor to set also' – Dr Aitken, surgeon to the Mocha Establishment, an educated man, older than Theodore and master of a separate household in the city, who took his orders from her husband.

Her little girl might have giggled at the funny noises of Papa's hubble-bubble – the cool hookah pipe that he loved to smoke after meals. Perhaps she would have learned how the nurse, Fazagool, 'her daydee', whom she loved and who was devoted to her, came into the household. Just maybe, Fazagool would have told her stories – some funny, some frightening and some sad – about her own childhood in Africa, deep in the mountainous centre of Sudan beside the Blue Nile, where no white man like Papa had ever been seen, and had only featured in fable and rumour.

December 1st 1814 in the British Factory was to be an exciting day for Kitty. It was her second birthday; the first in which she could play an active part. Even if she was accustomed by now to being the centre of attention, on this special day everyone would be making an extra effort to make her so. Not only was it her own birthday but, more importantly, her mother was about to give birth to a baby brother or sister. Everyone around her knew what it meant; that her days as an only child were coming to an end. Of course she would not understand that until long after the day, just over a week later, when her brother, Alexander was born. Theodore loved his daughter and he knew that he must send her and any subsequent siblings to England for their education – preferably before they were six years old – if they were ever to be accepted into British society.

Theodore proudly records Alexander's birth in his private letter book under the date Friday 9th December 1814. He refers to Eliza by his pet name for her: 'This day at 11a.m. My Dear Betsey was safely delivered of a boy.' The baby was quite different to Kitty; his skin was darker than hers and his chubby face shone out from under a crest of silky black hair. Theodore would have been incredulous at any suggestion that the dark colouring of this baby boy could ever become a matter for public speculation, or that the Armenian lineage of the lively, pretty and fair-complexioned little girl beside him would be widely discussed and even disputed. But Kitty was the one achievement for which, two hundred years later, he was destined to become a subject of interest. But over the years the question of her mother's precise ethnicity and the child's legitimacy was to be hidden away, barely talked about except in whispered conversations within the family, until gradually they were made into a mystery – tacitly acknowledged but seldom discussed.

If Kitty had been given the opportunity to remember and share happy times with her parents, and to reminisce about the details of her early life, she might have passed them on to her own children, and this section of a royal lineage would not have been lost to posterity. Had she remained for longer in her parents' care, perhaps the false charge of tampering with the pedigree of her descendant, Princess Diana, would never have been made against the houses of Spencer and Windsor. But all too soon, the details of Theodore's successful career and the couple's marriage and life together in Yemen would be lost. He had good reason to suppose that one day history might count his diplomatic achievements in Mocha worthy of note. But as the Raj devolved from Charter to Imperial and finally to Independent, the records of the 'John Company' Secret and Political Department were left behind in Bombay. The diaries of the Bombay Presidency, with details of Theodore's time in office, are still there. Fortunately though, through the generosity of H.H. Sheikh Sultan Mohammad Al-Quasimi, Exeter University has some typescripts.

Exactly one week after Kitty had skipped excitedly into the nursery to see her new brother, Theodore received distressing news from India about his own brother. He sat down to record the following melancholy note in his letter book: 'Friday 16th December 1814 –This morning arrived Moozroo's two Dows from Bombay & by them I received the afflicting intelligence of the death of my dear brother William.'

This event was the catalyst for his resignation from the post of Resident and the family's subsequent return to Bombay. William had named Theodore as his executor, and so he needed to return to India as soon as it was feasible. Though William was his older brother, he had arrived in India almost a year later than Theodore. William's twin, Alexander, had decided not to take up the place allocated to him and William had been allowed to take it instead, without first attending the East India Company's academy and school at Haileybury. William and Theodore were both stationed at Surat for a while, and there was a four-month overlap in their postings when they had shared a house and garden there. At the time of his death, William was still in Surat in the post of Assistant to the Commercial Resident.

When Moozroo's dhows arrived with the sad news of his brother's death, Theodore could not just decamp from the Factory and return to India. First he had to send to Bombay for permission to return on furlough – and then wait two months or more for an answer. Depending on the political situation, he might have to hang on for the appointment and the arrival of a successor. There were other considerations; Eliza needed time to rest, and his baby son was too young to be taken on a dangerous sea voyage; there was business still in train, unpaid debts to call in and his own debts to pay. Some of these bills were not able to be dealt with until nearer to the close of accounts, in July – at the end of the current trading season. He would have to wait for a suitable ship and the favourable winds of the south-west monsoon before he could pack up and return to Bombay.

Two months after Moozroo delivered the fateful letter from Bombay, Theodore wrote: 'Sunday 19th February 1815. This day baptized my little boy by the name of Alexander Scott, Dr Aitken standing Godfather.'

But it would be not until a further four months had passed that he was finally ready to embark for India. During that time his duties kept him very busy. Five days after he baptised his baby son, a large ship from Surat, the 600-ton *Fath-al-Rahman* was taken by pirates after prolonged fighting and much bloodshed. The incident occurred close to the Bab-el-Mandeb, through which the family would shortly have to pass at the start of their voyage to India. Mocha was buzzing with consternation at the savagery of the pirates and their proximity to the port. Theodore seems to have kept a cool head but sent a report to Bombay in which he mentions an atmosphere of near panic among the population. By the end of June, preparations had been made for the evacuation and return of the whole establishment.

Even today, when the great age of sail is long past, pirates are active once again off the Horn of Africa and across the Arabian Sea. The threat to shipping has returned with the pirate fleets operating from fast motorboats instead of sailing dhows. Huge fortunes can be made from the ransom of ships and their crews. By July 1815, when Theodore embarked for India, pirate numbers were once again on the increase, and their dhows had begun harassing shipping all along the route from Mocha to India. The merchant fleet would be getting ready to return to India in convoy with the protection of a cruiser of the Bombay Marine. Theodore and his family were to sail at the end of the trading year, with the summer monsoon at their backs to fill the sails and speed them on their way. But now he had a young family with him. After the *Fath-al-Rahman* incident he, more than anyone, knew the dangers they might face on the voyage.

Chapter 4

Duties of the Resident, 1813 – 1815

James Silk Buckingham and his wife in Turkish costume.

From the portrait by Henry Pickering, Royal Geographical Society, London.

4

Mocha, 1814 — 15

Theodore's duties as Resident, during his time of office, had also included playing host to any British visitors who might arrive on their way to India by way of the Red Sea. Among those who called in was the traveller, author and, much later, Member of Parliament, James Silk Buckingham. In Buckingham's *Autobiography* he describes staying at the Factory for a whole week at the beginning of February 1815 on his way from Jeddah to Bombay. This colourful but somewhat mendacious character devotes a whole chapter to his visit. He describes the results of his conversations with Dr Aitken about the fate of the German traveller Ulrich Jasper Seetzen, and quotes in full the letter he says he sent to the explorer Jean-Louis Burckhardt, travelling in disguise to Mecca. Although Buckingham boasts of his friendship with 'Hajji Ibrahim', as Burckhardt was calling himself, the intrepid Swiss Hajji was later to write an excoriating critique of Buckingham, which has survived in the Erskine Papers now in the British Library.

Having parted from 'Ibrahim' in Jeddah, Buckingham obtained a passage in the Bombay country ship the *Suffeenut ul Russool*, Captain John Boog, bound for Bombay, and he describes his 'kindly' reception by Theodore, who immediately invited him to stay in the Mocha Factory 'as long as the ship should be in port'. The arrival of the *Suffeenut ul Russool* on its way down the Red Sea had coincided with that of the Hon. Company's ship *Mercury*, Captain Blast from Bombay, on its way up the Red Sea to Suez.

An insight into Theodore's genial character and, possibly, Eliza's 'excellent' kitchen management, can be got from Buckingham's description of the dinner party held at the Mocha Factory for the visitors from the two ships:

'At dinner,' Buckingham writes, 'which was served in the Anglo-Indian style, with abundance of excellent dishes, including curries of various kinds, cool claret wine, and hookahs after the meal, a party of seven English gentlemen met together, the greatest number of my countrymen that I had seen at any one time since leaving Smyrna and a very unusual number for so remote a station as Mocha… these were General Wilkinson, late commander in chief of the army in Bombay, a veteran King's officer, who had seen much service, and whose simplicity of dress and manners were remarkable for a man of his rank and position; Captain Blast, of the Indian Navy or Bombay Marine, commanding the Company's ship *Mercury*, bound for Suez to convey General Wilkinson thus far; the surgeon of the ship; Mr. Aikin, the medical officer of the Residency; Mr. Forbes, Captain Boog and myself.'

Buckingham was just one of many British travellers grateful for Theodore's hospitality and in his *Autobiography*, published in 1855, he quotes a fulsome letter of thanks he says he sent to Theodore from Makullah. He was known to be a 'ladies' man', and it is a shame that though he stayed at the Factory for eight days and must have seen and talked to Eliza, he did not leave a description of her. In the *Autobiography* he makes frequent references to his manuscript journal, now missing, and describes it as being very detailed and full of interesting anecdotes. He gives a tantalising account of the size of the missing work, claiming that it occupied 28 volumes of more than 500 closely written large folio pages, and expressing the hope that the 'hitherto unpublished portions of these may yet perhaps see the light, if I am spared to live'. He was not. He died in July of the same year. A striking double portrait of him, seated with his wife, both in Turkish costume, belongs to The Royal Geographical Society – but it seems that the extensive and weighty manuscript journal he describes has completely disappeared.

When Theodore resigned, the whole 'Establishment' had been recalled including the small detachment of the Bombay Marine and the 'surgeon to the station', Dr Aitken who, Buckingham notes in February 1815, had 'been here upwards of five years'. Despite being slightly older, and having already completed several years or more in the post before Theodore arrived, Aitken had soon come to respect him. A few hastily scribbled notes from the doctor in January and February 1814 have survived. They are very untidily penned, and scratches, smudges and ink spots give the impression that the 'Medical Officer of the Residency', like poor Pringle, may have occasionally indulged in rather 'too much spiritous liquor'. According to Aitken's note, the Dola had apparently sent an armed party of sepoys to his house in the centre of the old city:

'My dear Sir,' writes Aitken to Theodore, 'I am sorrow to inform you that the Doolas Servant has just been at me with four Sepoys desiring me never to rid on horse back again in the inside of the town, the bearer will be able to inform you more than I can do at present.'

Clearly a damaging escalation of bad feeling was best avoided by removing the object of the Dola's irritation, Dr Aitken, to the safety of the Factory, until the fuss died down. There he would be under the official protection of the Resident and the Company Marines on guard there. Theodore's response shows how calmly he took his responsibility. He jotted down a copy of his reply on the back of the doctor's letter:

'Dear Dr.,' it reads, 'As we have nothing in our power, it is of no use remonstrating with these rascals and I therefore beg you will come and sleep at the Factory tonight –Yours truly, (Signed) T. Forbes. Sunday 16th January 1814.'

Though he had managed to defuse the situation it was only three weeks or so later that another scrawled note from the doctor was handed to Theodore. The exchange gives a good picture of the tricky relationship between the Resident and the Dola. In the note, Aitken says that the Dola's servant had 'been at' him again, bringing a summons to present himself before the Dola 'instantly'. This time he shifts the responsibility straight onto the younger man's shoulders, telling Theodore: 'My answer was that I could not go unless the Dola got your permission for me to go, as you are my commanding officer in this place, and whoes only order I will obey.' While the doctor's servant waited, Theodore sat down and penned an instant response:

'You have given a very proper answer,' he writes, adding: 'If the beast wants you let him send to me – [signed] Yours truly, T. Forbes. Tuesday 8th Feb 1814.' Later the same evening Theodore sent a boy to the doctor's house with an afterthought: 'If Fakee should send to you again,' he warns, 'do not go to him – on any account whatever.' The boy soon returned with Aitken's reassurance:

'Sir, depend upon it I will never go near such a rascal as Fukee again, without your order in writting, and my answer was that I would not go to see Fukee without your order, your being my commanding officer here.' Fukee was evidently a difficult man to deal with and riding a horse within the town walls, or through the gates, remained a sensitive issue until a new treaty was signed with the Imam of Sana'a, after the bombardment of the city in 1821, assigning this privilege, amongst other concessions, to the British.

Henry Salt, distinguished artist, diplomat and Egyptologist, was another who had expressed a high opinion of Theodore's abilities. From London in 1813, he wrote to Lord Valentia, 'I will send you in a day or two a copy of all my letters from Pearce and the new resident Mr. Forbes at Mocha. The latter I am glad to find a sensible plain dealing man and he appears anxious to promote our views.' His opinion was based largely on the help Theodore had given to Nathaniel Pearce during his long sojourn in Abyssinia in the service of the Ras of Tigré. Again, this compares favourably with Rudland's performance, who was responsible for several fiascos that put the lives of Pearce and his friend Coffin at risk.

As late as 1817, two years after Theodore had left his job in the Secret and Political Department, Pearce would still be writing to him from Abyssinia and, confident of his reputation, simply addressing him as 'Theodore Forbes Esq., Bombay or Elsewhere'. The profound disappointment he expressed that his 'good friend', Mr Forbes, was leaving Mocha is perhaps explained by a letter Salt wrote to Pearce describing an example of Rudland's incompetence, and which is quoted in J.J. Hall's *The Life and Correspondence of Henry Salt. F.R.S. His Britannic Majesty's Late Consul General in Egypt.*

Cairo, April 28th 1816:

'...About a year back I received letters from Major Rudland in India giving me a circumstantial account of your death; you may easily believe how much I was shocked at this intelligence, as were all your other friends in England. This report of course prevented my writing, as I thought my letters were likely to fall into bad hands. I was also induced on the same account to keep back a letter from your brother, whom I often saw in England, strongly expressive of his attachment to you; indeed I assure you that your reported death gave real concern not only to every branch of your family but also to every person who had read the narrative of your proceedings in Abyssinia, which I published in the account of my last mission to that country... Poor Rudland, since he wrote to me, is as you may have heard, himself dead. He died at Surat of a violent fever.'

'Poor' Rudland's own death was announced in *The Gentleman's Magazine* in 1815. It is not clear if his political and diplomatic career was terminated by his superiors when he was summoned from Mocha in 1812, or if he had never given up his commission in the Hon. Company's army when he took up the post of Resident. In either case, it seems that his army career had not been affected by the poor balance sheet of his coffee trading account, or his incompetence in support of his fellow countrymen in Africa. He had been promoted Brevet Major, commanding the 52nd Batt. 8th Regt. Bombay Native Infantry, stationed at Surat and was still in that post when he died. In the announcement, *The Gentleman's Magazine* makes no mention of his time as Resident. He had died on December 3rd 1814, a little over two years after he left Mocha. He was buried the same day in Surat's impressive English Cemetery, and poor Mrs Rudland, who had been with him in Mocha, joined the multitude of widows left to find their own lonely way home from India.

In the year after Theodore left the British Factory, British shipping would once again be attacked within sight of Mocha and it was to counter this continuing threat that the government of Bombay eventually felt compelled to appoint his successor. The unfortunate new Resident, Ramsay, was dead in little more than a year, but in that time had presided over a steady deterioration in relations with the Dola. By contrast, Theodore had proved invaluable in many ways during his tenure, but unlike Rudland and Ramsay, he had an Arabic speaker at his side. With Eliza's help he had made his posting a success.

Theodore had personally overseen the purchase and shipping of the Company's consignment of coffee for the British market and had done so to their 'great advantage'; he had carried out commissions for

Forbes & Co. and others, while making a small fortune for himself in trading bills of exchange for cash in specie, taking advantage of fluctuations and disparities in the different rates of exchange, and using regular European commodity price lists, received from his contacts farther up the Red Sea, to inform his purchases.

When Buckingham left for Bombay aboard the *Suffeenut ul Russool*, Theodore makes only the briefest reference to the event in his letter book. However, because he was already fully occupied in visiting the Mocha *shroffs*, buying gold and silver coinage prior to his own departure he devotes several pages to making detailed lists of the names of native bullion dealers, including the weights and the prices paid for the various types of coins that he has bought from them.

Parallel with the increase in his wealth was the increase in his family, but this happy circumstance would turn out to bring him more problems than joy. Bombay society had altered during the couple's three and a half years' absence; mixed marriages and the resultant children were beginning to be looked at with disapproval, largely due to the growing influence of the British middle classes. His little girl was light-skinned and with the right education she should be well-equipped to integrate into British society; but his little boy was a chubby dark-skinned infant whose origins were evident at a glance. It was this circumstance that was to bring about an unhappy conflict between his ambition and his love for his 'Dear Betsey'.

Besides the *Suffeenut ul Russool*, another ship that called in at Mocha while Theodore was awaiting confirmation of his resignation from office, was the *Durya Beggy*, Captain Preston Wilson, bound from Bombay to Suez, carrying cargo for Forbes & Co. Theodore had entertained Captain Wilson at the Factory and planned to take a passage for himself, his family and household on the ship's return journey. He wrote letters of introduction for the captain, to his contacts at Jeddah and Suez, including the Swiss Hajji, Burckhardt, so recently mentioned to him by Buckingham:

'Wrote to the English traveller (I believe his name is Buckard) who travels disguised as an arab under the name of Hajee Ibrahim, Mocha 17th March 1815, asking him to assist Capt Preston Wilson carrying cargo to Jedda for Forbes & co. Also introduced Capt Wilson to Lieut P--

- of the *Mercury* Cruizer.'

It transpires that Theodore's recommendations did not have the desired effect, moreover, he may have unwittingly hindered the progress of Captain Wilson up the Red Sea. On May 6th he wrote to Forbes & Co. that: 'The *Durya Beggy* has to my great surprize and regret been stopped at Juddah and entirely prohibited from proceeding to Suez. She will therefore be obliged to dispose of all the cargo at the former place.'

However, Forbes and Co. apparently suffered no financial loss by off-loading their goods at Jeddah; the Swiss Hajji seems to have been able to continue his journey successfully in disguise and Captain Wilson arrived safely back in Mocha with *Durya Beggy*.

Importantly for the Secret and Political Department in Bombay, Theodore's period in office had been marked by political as well as commercial success. The years of his time in Yemen had coincided with the ongoing decline of Ottoman authority and the Wahabee insurgency. The rise to power of Mehmet Ali, Pasha of Egypt, required him to keep track of the many fragile alliances up and down the Red Sea. The treacherous murder of the entire Mamluk leadership in the Cairo citadel had been carried out on the orders of the ruthless Pasha just 12 months before Theodore took office. For the whole of his time there the city had been in a state of alarm, beset by rumours of the advance of the Wahabees or the progress of the invading forces of the Ottoman army under Mehmet Ali's sons. Shifting allegiances among local chiefs along the shores of the Red Sea were not always easy to follow, but Theodore seems to have managed to establish a network of correspondents, sufficient to allow him to stay well-informed. In the face of the machinations of the Sherriff of Abu-Arish and other Wahabee chiefs, he managed to deal with the tricky political situations that arose. To that end he had corresponded with rulers and merchants throughout the entire area. Among the native merchants, he left many friends who continued to write to him for some years after his return to India.

Bombay government had considered it important to maintain good relations with Mehmet Ali and the Imam of Sana'a. With Theodore's efforts and the help of his correspondent, Henry Salt, recently appointed to the post of British Consul-General in Egypt, Britain seems to have succeeded in keeping the Viceroy's friendship. Shortly before Theodore returned to India there was a lull in hostilities and Mocha remained part of the Ottoman Empire, still under the delegated power of the Imam of Sana'a.

While Britain had been busy at war with both France and America beyond the confines of the Red Sea, Theodore had kept a constant watch on the activities of both nations in his area of responsibility. Despite the many disturbances across the whole area, his residency was marked by diplomatic stability. To what extent this can be credited to his influence is difficult to say. But he does seem to have managed to keep on good terms with the many ethnic and religious factions active within Yemen. Theodore's happy domestic circumstances and Eliza's origins in multicultural Surat may have helped. But he was evidently a talented linguist himself and there is no doubt that he was, as Buckingham described him, a natural 'diplomatist'. People liked him. His native servants chose to go with him when he sailed for India, and remained loyal for the remainder of his life. Perhaps because he was a middle son in a family of six boys, his personality was ruled, in both his private and his business life, by the imperative of impartiality and trying to accommodate everyone's wishes. Being 'all things to all men' might be seen as desirable in a career diplomat, but it would be prove to be a weakness in his private life and shake the foundations of his marriage.

A brief exchange with the newly-established Bombay Bible Society illustrates Theodore's reluctance to be a cause of disappointment or offence. In March 1814 the committee sent him 'a few copies of the Bible in the Arabic tongue,' in the hope that he would 'assist them in so laudable and praiseworthy an undertaking as... disseminating the knowledge of divine truth amongst the natives of Arabia'. Theodore knew with absolute certainty that this was a vain hope for the evangelists and a pointless exercise for him, but he was unwilling or unable to dismiss it out of hand. He waited six months and then sent back a politely discouraging reply:

'I beg leave to assure you that it would afford me the greatest pleasure to promote, by every means in my power, the laudable objects which have led to the institution of the Bombay Bible Society. In this country, however, the obstacles to the dissemination of Christian knowledge are peculiarly great, and indeed, in my humble opinion, altogether insuperable. The Arabs'… blind veneration for their faith is such, that they regard both the professors of Christianity, and the divine truths contained in the Holy Scriptures, as objects of their greatest contempt and execration. I have as yet only distributed two of the Arabic Bibles, but should there be any probability of a greater number being usefully disposed of I shall not fail to inform you thereof.'

Theodore had come to know the Yemeni Arabs well and it is fairly certain that he had not disposed of any of the Bibles – and would not have even tried. But in case the elders of the society had any doubts about his sincerity, he was confident that the one hundred rupees he had instructed Forbes & Co. to subscribe in his name would soon dispel them. He was right; in the minutes of their subsequent meeting, the committee reported that they had 'endeavoured to diffuse a knowledge… of the gospel amongst the natives of Arabia and the coasts of the Red Sea' but, as Theodore had predicted, they had to admit they had done so 'without success'.

Dr Aitken certainly had a high opinion of Theodore's diplomatic talents. So much so that, two years after their departure from Mocha, he wrote to him from Porbandar, passing on news of an incident that was destined in August 1820 to lead the Governor in Bombay to order a naval blockade of all the Imam of Sana'a's Red Sea ports and resulted in the bombardment of Mocha:

'Several Boats arrived here from Mocha a few days ago,' he writes, 'they say that the commander [Lieut. Bartholomew Dominicetti] of the cruizer [*Mercury*] had a severe flogging from Hadjee Fauts Ascarries, and that they plundered the Factory of almost everything.' He tells Theodore that 'I am well convinced that such conduct would never have happened if you had been there.' His new posting at Porbandar he describes as 'a dull & out of the way place even worse than Mocha, which last I am truly sorry at ever having given up.' This, despite the fact that on his return to India he had met and married Ann Kitson, who accompanied him to Porbandar. They had a son, but poor Dr

Aitken died when the child was only four-years old.

It transpires that the incident referred to by Aitken occurred when Theodore's successor, Ramsey, having made arrangements for the shipping of the Company's coffee purchases for the year 1817, died suddenly of natural causes before the cargo could be loaded. Hearing of Ramsey's death, the owner of the Surat ship commissioned to carry the coffee to Bombay, refused to fulfil his contract. Lieutenant Bartholomew Dominicetti of the Bombay Marine, then in port with HCS [Honourable Company's Ship] *Mercury*, assumed the authority of Acting-Resident and ordered that the cargo immediately be loaded as agreed. When the crew refused, Dominicetti ordered his marines to board the ship. It was later admitted that he had exceeded his authority by this high-handed act. The quarrel escalated until eventually the Dola's militia, along with a large mob, marched on the Factory. The lieutenant, who had been taken sick, was in bed when the mob burst in. He was dragged from his sickbed and, reports *The Asiatic Journal and Monthly Miscellany*:

'He was attacked and beaten with large sticks, and the butt-ends of their matchlocks, until he became senseless, and in that state, and nearly naked, was kicked along the passage leading to the stairs of the factory, was forced to the Dola's house, where he was scoffed at with the opprobrious epithets of dog and coffer by the Dola's headmen; was dragged up and down stairs three times successively, was ordered to prison and confined in irons: was again taken up to the Dola's house, and again buffeted, and spit upon, and obliged to stand in their presence without his shoes, and reviled in language the most opprobrious. After having been thus degraded, he was sent back to the factory, and there detained a close prisoner; most of the sepoys being confined in jail with irons on both of their legs. The British factory was ransacked and plundered.'

During this upheaval, the graves of the unfortunate Resident Ramsay and the doctor were opened, their corpses desecrated and dragged through the streets. It later transpired that the contract mentioned as the cause of the trouble 'was with the ship owning brother of the pirate Mohammed Akil. He is the owner of the *Deriah Beggi*, the involved ship.'

This revelation gives an ironic twist to Theodore's departure from Mocha two years earlier. Though spelled differently in his letter book, the *Deriah Beggi* mentioned in the *Bombay Courier* was the very same *Durya Beggy* in which he was to sail to India with his family. As the departing British Resident went aboard in July 1815, the hunter was effectively in the jaws of the hunted. How the Sayyid must have laughed when he heard of it!

Chapter 5

Departure, 1815

The *rawshan* or *mashrabiya* of a prosperous merchant's house in Mocha.

5

Mocha, Yemen, July 1815

On the afternoon of Saturday 1st July 1815, the British Resident and the whole establishment of the British Factory were about to leave Mocha for ever. While Fazagool carried baby 'Aleck' in her arms, Kitty, like any excited two-and-a-half-year old, would doubtless have skipped excitedly from parent to parent. Theodore's two personal servants were with the party. The Christian Yemeni 'Old Antoon' and the Ethiopian Coptic Christian Walloo had both chosen to chance a voyage into the unknown with their master and mistress. A teenage boy, Markar, Fazagool's 'adopted' son made up the party; only two years away from his own wedding, he was strong enough to assist with bags and baggage. Theodore's much-loved dog Tipoo was also going to India with the family, under the care of 'Old Antoon'.

Back in February Theodore had sent his Arab horse ahead, aboard the *Sufeenut ul Russool* with Captain Boog and James Silk Buckingham. He was confident that his mount would be well cared-for during the voyage because every day during Buckingham's week-long stay they had ridden out together and Theodore noticed how his guest had appreciated the quality of their mounts. Theodore's faith in his new friend was rewarded; when he reached Makullah, Buckingham had taken the opportunity to send a note by a passing ship to reassure him that his horse was 'in excellent health'.

It was not far to the waterfront from the Factory; a walk of just a few minutes. But, as Lord Valentia found, 'its proximity to the Dola's stables, where… the horses were, in the daytime… fastened by their hind legs with chains to the ground, and by the head to the wall' meant 'that it requires some precaution to pass between them, and still more to enter the gates of the factory, from the crowd of children belonging to the stable-keepers, who demand rather than petition for, charity.'

On this fine afternoon, as he closed the Factory door for the last time,

Theodore was able to be rather more liberal than usual with his time and his *baksheesh*. To be free of the little ragamuffins, all that was required of him was to dip his hand into his breeches pocket and fling wide a handful of small change. While the urchins scrambled for the broadcast coins, the Resident and his party made good their escape, picking their way across the square between the piles of dung and armies of flies.

'The form is gone through every morning of sweeping a path across the square from the Dola's house to his stables,' says Valentia. 'Yet at the same time a dunghill is formed under his windows by the filth thrown out from his Zenana, so extremely offensive as often to induce the Europeans to take a circuit to avoid it.' Having skirted the offending heaps, Theodore's party headed for the Dola's house. As might be expected, the Dola had the most magnificent and best situated of all the grand Ottoman-style merchants' houses in Mocha. It might more properly be termed a mansion. The building was three storeys high and occupied a large area right on the seafront. Looking out to sea across the ramparts and *Furda*, or customs house, it dominated the centre of the port. When Theodore and Eliza arrived, their neighbour's residence had only recently been completed at huge expense. In Salt's view from the roof of the Factory, scaffolding is still visible on the rooftop of the Dola's new mansion; it was no longer the decaying old house that Thomas Capper had described in 1785 as having 'two pair of narrow broken stairs'. This Dola was evidently very much wealthier than those who had preceded him; a former slave who had worked his way up into this position of power and influence, he was a man to be reckoned with and Theodore had taken great care in his dealings with him and managed, by being respectful yet firm, to remain on good terms.

When the Resident and his household embarked aboard the *Durya Beggy*, the Dola was bound to be watching eagle-eyed from the first floor, hidden within the dappled shade of his *rawshan* – a bay window with a pierced screen, or *mashrabiya*, found on the antique façades of most of the grander merchants' houses of Yemen. It is a feature of the elegant architectural style which spread with the Ottoman Empire from Turkey all along the margins of the Red Sea and beyond. Its hinged wooden shutters of geometric lattice were designed to let cooling breezes circulate. Intricately carved corbels and decorated friezes advertised the wealth and status of its owner. But it was more than ornamental; it was commonly used as a retreat from which the master of the house could watch the comings and goings below and identify callers without the bother of going downstairs. Another advantage to the Muslim male was that women of his household could take the fresh air without being seen by outsiders. A house would generally have just one *rawshan*, above the main doorway, but the Dola of Mocha's new mansion had several; as if to reinforce the message that within it lived a man of wealth and power.

The Dola's main *rawshan* overlooked the harbour and faced out to sea towards the setting sun. From it he could see the Island of Perim, the Strait of Bab-el-Mandeb and, on a clear day, the distant coast of Africa. From this vantage point he was able, literally, to oversee all the business of the port without having to descend to the heat and dust of the streets below. His personal income came from commission on the taxes he levied, on behalf of the Zaydi Imam in Sana'a, on all the goods traded in and out of the port. As the family and servants of the retiring British Resident passed below his hideaway they stopped before the sea gate where the Dola's musicians had been stationed to play them out of the city. Around the quay and *Furda* the self-important customs officials strutted about, recording details of people and merchandise. The Dola's *askaris* lounged nonchalantly nearby – deceptively idle – with their dangerously beautiful *jambiyas* sheathed at their waists, and antique matchlocks close to hand, reclining on low couches, smoking or drinking coffee.

As the Forbes household stepped through the sea gate, the emerald expanse of the bay lay before them and beyond it the deep blue riband of the Roads. Though the sun had begun to lose its heat and the sky its brightness, the south-west monsoon was building and the atmosphere was close. The quayside was still thronged with merchants from all along the Red Sea and Persian Gulf and many of them were known to Theodore. Others paused from their earnest conversations to turn and watch his progress, wondering who might he be, this foreigner; this 'feringhi' leaving to the accompaniment of 'the Dola's Musicke'? Shouted greetings and good wishes followed in his wake. Anyone in the vicinity not previously aware of the British Resident's imminent departure, could not have remained in ignorance for very long. Despite the bundles, boxes and baggage sitting in their path, the distinctive little group were soon at the jetty waiting to be taken aboard their ship.

The sandy foreshore, where numerous local boat builders plied their trade, stretched out to either side of the jetty. High above the tideline lay the hulls of nearly-completed craft, scaffolded up for the caulkers and painters. Here and there carpenters were noisily at work; hammering and sawing amongst the quiet sailmakers and patient net menders where they sat cross-legged, beneath their tattered awnings or rough-thatched shelters. The ribcages of half-built boats lay awkwardly by, propped up like emaciated invalids leaning on their crutches and waiting for the longed-for day when they too might be fit to put to sea. Meanwhile a swarm of smaller craft rowed in and out with the rise and fall of the tide, to unload and load people and goods at the dark stone jetty.

Before long Theodore had picked out from among them the *Durya Beggy*'s jolly boat and was helping Eliza and Fazagool down into its belly with baby Aleck. With particular care he handed his precious little girl into the outstretched arms in the bobbing craft below. As the mate cast off from the jetty, the instability of the waves beneath them served as a reminder of the many dangers that lay ahead. Just how vulnerable her young children were now, became ever more obvious to Eliza, as she glanced back at their former home and watched the familiar skyline of Mocha recede. Foreshore and jetty diminished behind them and, when they reached the Roads, the British Factory was barely discernible.

Only three-and-a-half years ago she had come to the old Ottoman mansion as a bride. It had embraced the most important events of her life so far – marriage and the birth of her two babies. Later she would tell Theodore how she wished she could return to the time they had shared in Mocha. They were so young when they arrived and they had been everything to each other. Even now that she is the mother of two young children she is still not much more than a girl herself. In Yemen she became mistress of a household and as Theodore's career flourished she had grown in confidence and managed the running of the British Factory admirably. Theodore would later confide to his letter book that the innocent young Armenian girl he married – his 'dear Betsey' – had developed into 'the very pattern of what a wife ought to be'. They had done well together here, and though they were sailing into the unknown, they had every reason to be optimistic about their future.

Once on board, Theodore took up his letter book to record the event:

'Saturday July 1st 1815. At 5 o'clock P.M. Embarked on board the Ship *Durya Beggy*, Captain Preston Wilson, bound for Bombay.' An entry he made the previous week reveals that with him he had a substantial amount of bullion in gold and silver coinage; some was for Forbes and Co. but his inventory of the coins shows that by far the greater number were on his own account.

– Monday 28th June 1815 –

Account of money shipped by me in the Ship *Durya Beggy*,
On Messrs Forbes & Co.'s Account-viz-
Spanish Dollars – -------------------------------$2,208 –
Venetians – --------------------------------------407 –
        On my own account.
Spanish Dollars – ----------------------------$2,000 –
German Crowns – ----------------------------236 –
Venetians (in Boxed chest No 34) – --------4,000 –
Dutch Ducats – --------------------------------214 –

– and further: 'In a small red silk tray in box', according to Theodore, nestled 37 intriguingly named 'Islamboolees and Furdooklees' and 2 mysterious 'Mahboobs'. It seems that before leaving the Factory, this valuable property was distributed by Theodore amongst the various items of luggage he had to stow on board ship. They would be sold for a handsome profit shortly after he arrived in Bombay, and not long afterwards he would write to his father, asking him to buy the estate of Haddo for him 'if in the market and likely to sell for 10 ad 12,000 £'.

As he waited for Captain Wilson to give the order to weigh anchor, Theodore had the satisfaction of knowing that at a mere 27-years old, he was returning to India in triumph, with a family, and a fortune. During his time in Yemen, he had proved himself in many ways to have been an excellent choice for the post of Resident. The city had served him well, and he in turn had served his masters well. As the household embarked for India, their destination meant something different to each of them: to Eliza it was home; to the servants it was a place of mystery; to Kitty it was just a name at the end of an adventure; to Theodore it held out the shining promise of a prosperous future. He had many friends and fellow Scots in Bombay. Now that the Company monopoly on Indian trade had been removed, he was eager to exploit the opportunities he would find there for more profitable trade. He was confident of building on his current prosperity as long as their voyage was without incident and *Durya Beggy* reached Bombay in safety.

Of course, he realised that their ship would be at risk of attack from pirate raiders for the entire voyage. Large country ships sailed under the British flag when chartered by British firms like Forbes & Co. but the flag did not necessarily confer protection on the vessel – ordinarily neither did native ownership – even a ship like *Durya Beggy*, built in Surat, owned by native merchants and crewed almost entirely by Indian and Arab *lascars*. The Joassime pirates had recently rebuilt their fleet and recruited many more Arab *nakhodas* and their fast dhows. Theodore would not have risked the voyage had he not had full confidence in the convoy system and the competence of Captain Wilson.

The knowledge that they might have to outgun or outrun a pirate dhow was not his only concern; their ship had to be fit to survive the many perils of the open seas. There was the ever-present danger of the unpredictable weather; violent squalls could come upon them in minutes, whipping up the waves and pouring a torrent of rain and seawater over the ship, leaving the crew scant time to lower the mainsails and batten down the hatches. On the other hand there was the ever-present possibility of the voyage being delayed by lack of wind, with the consequent challenge to the provision of fresh food and water. If they were becalmed, they might have to wait, like Coleridge's *Ancient Mariner*: 'Day after day, day after day… stuck, nor breath nor motion; as idle as a painted ship upon a painted ocean.'

While they lay at anchor in the Mocha Roads, Theodore was able to take full advantage of his enforced idleness to catch up with some correspondence. Hussain Hyder in Hodeida and Araby Jallanee in Jeddah were just two of his network of contacts all along the Red Sea into Egypt, and beyond to Malta and Smyrna. These correspondents had enabled him to make good use of advance intelligence of movements in the various markets of Europe. To their mutual advantage they sent each other regular updates on the differential between commodity prices in Europe and the East, as well as political news and the current locations of plague and cholera. His ability to communicate with local merchants and the *nakhodas* of the dhows and *bugalahs* sailing between Egypt and

India provided him with a faster passage for packets to England than aboard a large Company ship by the southern route, via Bombay and the Cape of Good Hope. He would put his letters home under several covers and send them up the Red Sea in relays, rather like a game of 'pass-the-parcel'. When the 'afflicting intelligence' of William's death arrived, for instance, he made a note in his book that he had sent the news 'with a lock of poor William's hair, under cover to Mr S [his brother-in-law, Alexander Scott of Craibstone] by a *bugla* [native ship], undercover to Hussein Hyder at Hodeida, Hajee Chetee Jallanee at Juddah, and Lieut. Col. Missett at Cairo with a most particular request that they would forward the packet with all possible urgency.'

Two days after going aboard *Durya Beggy* and while the ship was still in the Mocha Roads, Theodore took up his pen to write to his father and mother. He was writing in relative comfort and stability, seated at his own desk by an open window in the round house. This generous accommodation, partitioned up with cotton tenting to provide the best cabins, lay immediately below the poop deck. Generous casements encircled the stern and were open much of the time. High above the waves and jettied out from the sides of the ship, the windows made these quarters light and airy. Theodore was able to have his own furniture and other household necessities around him, and his wife and children close at hand, with his confidence in their health assured by the presence on board of Dr Aitken whose friendship and respect he had won despite the difference in their ages. That the two men got on so well together augured well for the time they were about to spend as shipmates.

With William's death being the main reason for leaving Mocha, it was natural that Theodore's thoughts should turn to home. While *Durya Beggy* lay at anchor in the Roads, he took the opportunity to find a ship bound for Suez by which to send his parents a letter that would reach Boyndlie long before any sent from Bombay via the Cape. But the background to his recollections of childhood and memories of his family was not Boyndlie. It was Haddo House by Huntly, in Aberdeenshire. This is where he and William had grown up along with their brothers and sisters; all now dispersed except for the two youngest, James and Jane. The Haddo Estate was leased by their father, John Forbes of Boyndlie, from a distant Forbes cousin. Their mother was Katherine Morison from the next-door estate of Bognie. The Morisons owned several extensive properties in the area apart from Bognie. The fertile farmlands of Haddo lay alongside those of Bognie and the large pleasure grounds and gardens of the house straddled the boundary between the counties of Aberdeen and Banff.

The old house, now derelict, is attractively set amongst its own wooded grounds and gently rolling farmland. It lies some fourteen miles inland from the coast, near the neglected village of Inverkeithny. The landscape that Theodore saw in dreams of home as he waited in Mocha Roads was the rich farming country spread along the coastal margins of the counties of Moray, Banff and Aberdeen. Below his old home the generous River Deveron winds its way northward until it joins the sea at Banff, sometimes running fast and wide over shallows pocketed with ancient gravel and strewn with Ice-Age boulders; sometimes lingering, lazily deep, in eddying pools, or narrowing to meander darkly through shady woods – only to open out again between sunny water meadows fringed with green rushes and dotted with stands of rose bay willow-herb.

The many attractions of the river, evident to the human eye, are equalled for fish by those below the surface of the water – drawing back the spawning salmon year after year to its gravelly bed and providing a rich nursery for their young. It was in 1924 on the River Deveron that Mrs Clementina 'Tiny' Morison caught the 61-pound salmon that still holds the British record for the heaviest fish caught with a fly. It was reeled in at the very end of the season on the Lower Shaws beat on the estate of Mountblairy, still owned by descendants of Theodore's maternal ancestors, the Morisons, just as it was when he was a boy.

When Theodore left Scotland for India in 1808, his parents were still living at Haddo. A few years later the family moved to a house called Ironstone, on the Boyndlie Estate not far from Fraserburgh, while their father was supervising the building of the new family home at Upper Boyndlie. By 1814, just about the time William died in Surat, Boyndlie House was ready for occupation and the family moved in. Their pleasure in the move must have been considerably dampened by the news from India that they had lost another of their sons. John Forbes had built the new mansion on the same site as a much earlier one. Designed in high Regency style and built from the local granite it is well-situated and well-appointed. It is only a mile or two, as the gull flies, from old Pitsligo Castle, seat of the Jacobite fugitive, Lord Forbes of that ilk, and the low grey fishing villages of Rosehearty and Sandhaven, knuckled down by the barren shore of the Moray Firth. With the desolate coastal landscape all around it, Boyndlie House sits there still, comfortably ensconced within mature broadleaved woodland, hidden from public view and shielded from the fierce North Sea winds that beat the bounds of the Firth. To this day it retains a welcoming air of warm security, in contrast to its bleak surroundings. Theodore was fated never to see it, though it would be home to Kitty for a small portion of her childhood. Some of the lavish tree planting was perhaps inspired by the well-wooded 'policies' or grounds of Haddo, which was blessed with a far kinder climate than that of Boyndlie.

The landscape surrounding Haddo is still much as it was when Theodore was growing up there. But the remains of the Inverkeithny he would have known lie concealed now beneath the invasive grip of stout limbs of ivy topped by a wild tangle of briar and bramble. It is barely possible to make out the shapes of the cottages, once so familiar to him, and which would become so too to his son Frederick, whose mother lived nearby, and who was destined to board at the school from 1818. Today he would hardly recognise the House of Haddo that was his childhood home. Both the original house and the distinguished Italianate villa, tacked on to it in the years after the Forbes family left, are now roofless and skeletal. However, the fine situation, though overgrown, is unchanged and the approach to the deserted mansion gives an immediate idea of its former status.

A low neo-classical lodge keeps watch over the wide carriage drive where it leaves the public road in Inverkeithny. After following a shallow, wooded incline, the driveway passes over an imposing broad-span bridge with dressed granite coping and crosses a small corrie with the tumbling Keithny Burn winding along its floor. As the narrow track dwindles its way through the leaf-littered beech groves, glimpses of the ruined mansion flicker infrequently through a screen of trees, until at last the shell of an extensive building appears. Hidden somewhere within the ruins lie interred the collapsed remains of Theodore's beloved childhood home.

Haddo House was built in the first half of the eighteenth century by a Captain John Morison. He was the second son of the family and, as befitted a younger son, Haddo was more house than mansion and on a scale more intimate than intimidating. Many changes of ownership have resulted in fundamental alterations to the structure. Abandonment, neglect and vandalism have resulted in the complete decay of the building and the wilding of its grounds. It is almost impossible now to tell how much of the early house remains or which of the surviving features might have existed when John Forbes brought Katherine Morison home to it as his bride. But this is the home where Theodore was born and where he said goodbye to his family when he left for India. It is his old familiar haunt; the place which must have lived in his dreams and coloured his memories until the day he died.

The surrounding pleasure grounds slope away from the house on the garden side. Mature woodland now shades the slopes where Theodore and his brothers played for hours and hours in childhood's infinitely sunny days. The leaf-littered floor is creased with narrow gullies and the sight and sound of the trickling streams within their gloomy depths is all that is left to recall the tumbling rivulets and sunlit glades of his boyhood. The wildness of this romantic playground was mitigated by ordered beds of vegetables and flowers, enclosed within an unusually large oval brick-walled garden, said to have been designed in the eighteenth century by Linnaeus, the famous Swedish botanist. Not a trace now remains of the cultivation of flowers and vegetables. The encircling brick walls have been breached in several places to make a way in for tractors when the whole area within was ploughed up and sown to a grass ley. The remnants of spacious hot-houses, where melons and exotic fruit once flourished against the south-facing sections of the wall, can barely be distinguished. A tragic heap of rubble and broken slate is all that remains of a handsome lime-washed stone doocot, ornamented with a fine heraldic stone tablet bearing the date 1694, and carved with a crown and thistle and a lion rampant carrying a sword.

Theodore's parents, Katherine and John Forbes, had thirteen children of whom two daughters and six sons survived to adulthood, so it is not difficult to imagine how the wooded slopes and rocky gullies of Haddo must have rung with the shouts of children at play. His sister Catherine was the oldest. George was next, then Alexander and William who were twins. Theodore was also a twin, but his twin brother, John, is said to have died in infancy. Alexander, aged 20, was imprisoned in Denmark in the autumn of 1807, after the Royal Navy bombarded Copenhagen. He had been travelling back to Scotland from Riga where his brother George, the oldest of the Forbes boys, had recently drowned, aged 23, whilst bathing in the river Daugava. They had both been working for Baltic business associates of their uncle, John Morison.

The bombardment of Copenhagen by the Royal Navy had been ordered with the intention of preventing the Danish fleet from assisting the French in their attempt to cut off British trade. Much of the fire fell on the civilian quarter of the Danish capital and the supposedly neutral Danes, understandably indignant, arrested any British nationals in the country, including Alexander. He had already been accepted by the Honourable East India Company to go to India as a writer but, unsurprisingly, his keenness for foreign travel was blunted by being 'unavoidably detained' in Copenhagen and unable to take up his position and so,after he was freed, he decided not to go to India after all. His twin, William, had taken his place. Alexander's decision seems to have been a wise one for he stayed on to farm at Haddo. He outlived both parents and all his brothers and inherited the Lairdship of Boyndlie.

Theodore's father was factor to his brother-in-law, John Morison of Auchentoul, laird of the nearby estates of Auchentoul, Cobairdy and Drumblair, and from 1827 MP for Banff. The Forbes family frequently used estate names as a sort of nickname or patronymic even in the absence of an associated title, as in 'Bognie' for Theodore Morison and 'Edengight' for their uncle Sir Malcolm Innes. In a letter dated 1819 and written from Frendraught, another Morison house, Catherine makes unflattering reference to their uncle John Morison. She tells Theodore that their father has been suffering from gout in his foot, which she hopes:

'Will be of use to him,' [as an excuse to stay at home] and continues, '...He has been a good deal vexed with Auchentoul's business' – for 'He [Auchentoul] does not seem satisfied and yet will not settle with him nor appoint anybody else to do it for him – and he is never almost a week at home so that he cannot attend to it himself.' She goes on to admonish her brother: 'I hope you shall not stay so long out of your own country, nor yet make as much money, for he [Auchentoul] seems to have too much for enjoyment either to himself or other people, goes hunting after the great people and treats his relations and equals with a kind of superciliousness which few people choose to put up with.' It seems that Catherine may have lacked a full knowledge of the facts. Her uncle had only one legitimate child by his wife Jane, daughter of Alexander Fraser, of Strichen; but he had at least eleven more who were illegitimate and by four or five different women. So he evidently had a great deal more to occupy his absences than 'hunting after the great people'. He made provision for all his children in his will but died on the verge of bankruptcy, luckily before his succession to the entailed estates of Bognie, left vacant by the death of his older brother Theodore Morison, could be proved.

By contrast, though he was not laird of a great estate, Auchentoul's brother, their youngest uncle, James Morison, seems to have been judged more favourably within the family. Catherine continues: 'Poor Uncle James came down to Scotland in the autumn but we happened to be from home at that time & Auchentoul carried him off to England when he had only been a fortnight in the country, so we did not see him and I do not believe he will return before he go out again to the West Indies.'

Theodore's Uncle James was destined to become quite a celebrity; though Theodore would not live to hear about it. From about 1825 he began manufacturing and selling 'Morison's patent vegetable pills' far and wide – to the delight of contemporary cartoonists and the persistent irritation of the medical profession, who bluntly labelled him a 'quack'. More than twenty cartoons were published directly aimed at him and he published several in response, satirising the medical establishment. Nevertheless, he made a huge fortune.

Like his Uncle James, Theodore was a younger son and had to make his own way in the world. In common with so many of the Aberdeen gentry of the day, he chose to seek his fortune in India. And a fortune is what was required if he was to realise his ambition of eventually becoming Laird of Haddo. In July 1815, as he prepared to leave Yemen he had good reason to be pleased with the outcome of his trading account from his three and a half years there. During that time he had laid the foundations of the fortune of his dreams. He was taking a considerable quantity of cash back with him to Bombay, on which he expected to realise a handsome profit. At barely twenty-seven years of age, his future held out the prospect of great achievements in any sphere he might choose to enter. He was evidently possessed of great charm, and all who met him seemed to fall straight away into an easy familiarity with him. At this point there was no hint of the duplicity that was later to debase his character.

Chapter 6

Return to Bombay, 1815

The old Portuguese convent at Gorabunder where Thomas Dickinson and his
family lived, and where, in 1815, tigers still prowled.

6

The Arabian Sea, July 1815

Waiting for the start of a journey is almost as tedious for a child as waiting for it to end. Going aboard *Durya Beggy*, Kitty would have been bouncing with excitement and overflowing with artless chatter. She was a little over two-and-a-half years old and described as 'high-spirited'. Everyone on board must have been eager for the convoy to get under way but during their days of enforced idleness Kitty would have plenty of new sights to occupy her attention. She would have new people to get to know; her possessions to stow; a new routine to settle into. It was her first sea voyage and she was aboard a spacious vessel with all her family nearby. Happily, she could not foresee the long journey which, in just four years' time, was destined to carry her away from all she had ever known, with only Fazagool to comfort her. For the moment she had both her Mama and Papa, almost to herself, as well as Fazagool when she was not attending to Aleck. She would share their excitement at the ships' farewell cannonade and the answering boom from the South Fort as the massed vessels hoisted their mainsails and manoeuvred to catch the wind and head out of the Roads.

A country ship such as *Durya Beggy* might take anything from two to four weeks on the voyage across the Arabian Sea from Mocha to Bombay, depending on the winds. They needed to carry enough supplies to feed passengers and crew and would call in at ports along the way to take on fresh food and water. There would be animals on the poop deck above the family's quarters, where Kitty might be taken to watch the chickens being fed or a goat being milked. The cuddy was close by, where their meals would be served, and she was sure to become a favourite with all on board.

The first navigational challenge for Captain Wilson was the perilous Bab-el-Mandeb, the narrow strait which lies within sight of Mocha and separates the continents of Asia and Africa. The name has been variously translated as the Gate of Lamentations, or Tears, Sorrow or Grief. Whatever the chosen translation, the name makes clear that the turbulent currents in the restricted channel between the Red and Arabian Seas had been infamous through the centuries for the loss of countless ships and their crews, dashed to pieces on the rocks. The distance from Yemen to Cape Guardafui on the east coast of Africa is about 20 miles. The rocky island of Perim sits between the two shores and cuts the strait unequally in two, making it all the more dangerous by the unpredictability of the tidal surges that build to one side or the other. The larger the sailing ship, the less room there is to tack, and the more dangerous is its passage through the narrow strait. James Silk Buckingham gives a good nautical account of the passage of the much smaller and more manoeuvrable *Sufeenut ul Russool*, concluding: 'We had a good ship, that stood well under her canvas, sailed fairly for a merchant vessel, and answered her helm quickly… It was a time of breathless anxiety; but when we got through we gave relief to our feelings by a loud and general cheer.'

Safely through the Bab, ships bound for India mostly sailed along the southern coast of the Arabian Peninsula, across the Gulf of Aden, dropping anchor for fresh supplies at ports such as Aden and Makullah. Buckingham, though challenged by sailing against the contrary wind in February, seems to have found the whole experience exhilarating, and took a heightened pleasure from the spicy aromas he describes as wafting out to his ship from the shores of the Aden Sultanate and the reaches of Muscat: 'The morning dew being evaporated by the early warmth of the sun… so diffused through the whole atmosphere that it becomes redolent of balm.'

The *Sufeenut ul Russool* had taken twelve days just to reach Aden, sailing against the wind. Fortunately, when *Durya Beggy* sailed at the beginning of July the winds were more favourable. However, they still had to cross the most dangerous tract of the Arabian Sea. They would have to keep a constant look-out for raiders all along the southern coast of Arabia as far as the Gulf of Oman, the entrance to the Persian Gulf. This was a favourite spot for the predatory pirate dhows to lie in wait, not far from their bases, ready to intercept and plunder any vessels that might be carrying valuable cargo. Only when they were within sight of the coast of Gujarat could Eliza begin to believe that she really might be on her way home and Theodore trust that they were safe at last.

The constant rolling motion of the ship; the querulous complaining of her timbers; the grumbling of her rudder; the whipping and flapping noises of her coarse rigging and wet canvas soon became familiar accompaniments to the routine of shipboard life. Once these irritations could be ignored, there were sights and sounds enough to fascinate and delight everyone on board, and particularly to occupy the mind of an inquisitive child. But while Kitty might enjoy feeling the sun and sea spray on her face, and tasting the salt on her lips when her father took her up on deck, he would have been anxiously scanning the horizon for suspicious looking sails. It was only three months since he had sent a report to Bombay about the loss of the 600-ton *Fath-al Rahman*, close to the Bab-el-Mandeb, and the grisly murder of most of her crew. It was nevertheless an opportunity for him to enjoy having his little girl to himself.

As they watched from the fore deck, they would often see pods of swift dolphins slipping easily through the clear water to ride the bow wave, or spot the occasional sea turtle lazily basking on the surface. Theodore might point out a slithery sea serpent to the child and hold on to her tightly as she leaned out to catch a better view, or laugh at her surprise as a shoal of flying fish suddenly appeared from the depths, to glide with outstretched wings and flash across the face of a wave, scattering showers of rainbow droplets, only to disappear again like magic. For Theodore it would have been a time to treasure; a time with his adored child that he would remember until his dying day; a time which would fix his determination to do everything in his power to smooth her path in life.

By night, as the ship pitched and rolled and the passengers in their berths dozed fitfully, the muffled sounds of the ship's bell ringing out every half hour of the four-hour watch broke in upon their slumbers, until eight-bells and the reassuring cry of 'All's well'. Day after day, they would wake at dawn to see the sun rise up from the horizon ahead in a golden haze above the bowsprit, and at the end of the day sink astern in flaming splendour, leaving a fiery path rippling in their wake. Then, when the last lingering sunbeam had died away, some might stay to watch the afterglow bloom and fade above the horizon in fleeting layers of pink and purple, green, gold and indigo. They would marvel at the sudden darkness, as the deepening sun dropped below the ocean's rim and the black of night brought the stars bursting into startling life. Then the microcosm of the ocean would be revealed in streaks and spots of flickering phosphorescence, dancing attendance on their passage and playing on the surface of the water in ever-changing patterns of ethereal light.

As they sailed ever closer to their destination, any excitement Theodore felt at the prospect of meeting his Bombay friends again must have been tinged with sadness at the loss of his brother. When he first arrived in India he had been resigned to not seeing any of his family again in the near future. William had reported for duty in London barely six months after Theodore, at the very end of 1808. So, when he turned up in Bombay only eight months later, it was a great surprise and a joyous reunion. Once in India though, he did not fare as well as his younger brother; he ran into trouble in his work, and within six years of his enrolment as a writer, he was dead. On arrival he had been appointed 2nd Assistant to the Commercial Resident in Surat, responsible for Company cotton purchases. At first he seemed to be doing well – so much so that he was left in sole charge of the post when his superior resigned.

By May 1810, after scarcely a year, William had been promoted to First Assistant. So far, so good; but only one month later a report was sent to the Court of Directors in London that: 'Mr Forbes had so far neglected his duty as to cause your Government to record a minute that his cotton was in part very inferior.' The cotton at issue was referred to as 'such trash'. He was held responsible and received a warning. He was also given permission to leave Surat and go to Bombay to plead his case. Unfortunately his unrepentant attitude at the hearing infuriated his superiors and he received an official reprimand for 'his unbecoming language and the impertinence of his address'.

Theodore's friend and former boss, Rickards, did his best to defend William, noting in his minute of July 5th 1811 that: 'Mr Forbes was in sole charge of the [Surat] Residency between the resignation of Mr Christopher Wren and the appointment of Mr Corsellis.' And further mentions: 'The risk to which the Company's concerns were liable by trusting so important a charge as the whole Commercial Department for so long a time to one assistant, and that the youngest writer in the service.' Presumably the service referred to was only the Commercial Department – Theodore was younger, and Henderson and Wedderburn, Theodore's companions on the voyage out, were even younger; but at that time they were all occupied in different departments of the Civil Service. Theodore had plenty of time to hear of his brother's problems before he married Eliza and sailed for Mocha. On 18th November 1811, only seven months after his promotion, poor William was demoted back to 2nd Assistant. A month later Theodore's appointment to the post of 'British Resident in the Arabian Gulph' was announced from Bombay Castle and he left for Surat to marry Eliza.

Long after Theodore left for Mocha, William's troubles rumbled on. It was over a year before his appeal against demotion was heard in London. It did not help his case that he had clearly antagonised his superiors in Bombay. His boss, Corsellis, was notoriously bad tempered. The Court of Directors returned a directive to Bombay that: 'It would be a merited retribution for such misconduct were we to dismiss Mr. Forbes from our service.' This is something that Theodore, far away in Mocha, would not necessarily have known. Reports from Bombay could take five months or so to reach London via The Cape, then there had to be time for the Court of Directors to convene, set their response down in the records, then send their orders back to Bombay. It is not surprising then, that not until January 1815 do the commercial proceedings in Bombay record the London Directors' decision... that if there should be any 'repetition of his misdemeanour' he should forthwith be 'suspended from the Hon Company's service, and sent to England by the first ships'. The caution proved to be unnecessary – William had been dead for two months.

Fortunately, the last memories Theodore had of his brother would have been happy ones. When he and Eliza embarked from Surat as a newlywed couple William no doubt teased his younger brother affectionately, clapped him on the back and wished him well. Only a few days after Moozroo's dhow brought the sad news from Surat, Theodore received a copy of the eulogy which, as convention dictates, was highly complimentary. Despite William's well-documented 'misdemeanours', his chief, John Romer, the magistrate in the Adawlet Court of Surat praises 'the zeal, activity, and intelligence of Mr Forbes... his highly respectable attainments as an oriental scholar... [and] ...the integrity, diligence and ability, with which the duties of the late officer in this adawlet were performed.' The obituary in the Bombay courier of November 26th 1814 reads:

'Death at Surat of a fever on the 16th instant, William Forbes Esq. Late assistant to the register and to the Magistrate of that station. – Cut off in early life, the premature death of this promising young man is sensibly felt as a public and a private loss. – The service to which he belonged has to regret the short career of one, whose distinguished abilities, high professional attainments, and honourable conduct held out the fairest hopes of future eminence, while the circle of his friends, so endeared to him, will long lament his untimely fate and cherish the remembrance of his many virtues.'

While Theodore had time on board ship to reflect on past events, and dream of those yet to come, Eliza had the day-to-day care of a lively toddler and a babe in arms to engage her attention. It is not difficult to imagine what a challenging task it must have been aboard a merchant ship under sail, to occupy and exercise an energetic child like Kitty in safety, even with Fazagool's help. After more than a week at sea with her two young children, the sight and sound of sea birds wheeling overhead must have been especially welcome to her, with their shrill cries anticipating a shout of 'land ahoy', or the *lascar* equivalent, from the masthead. Though the gulls might call out that land was very near, the sandy beaches of the Rann of Kutch, the northernmost extremity of Gujarat were usually hidden from the deck by a veil of mist. In July, the flat salt marshes, creeks and seawater channels lie hidden beneath the morning haze until the summer sun has risen high enough to evaporate it – and then the land begins to bake.

Here, Captain Wilson set a more southerly course and *Durya Beggy* sailed closer in to the shores of the land Eliza called home. The great sails flapped and filled with the gusts driving them towards the Indian seaboard. She listened for the *lascars*' joyful shouts and looked out to port to catch her first glimpse of India in more than three years. The coastal desert of the first part of the voyage had been succeeded by misty deltas flanked by flat wilderness. Close in, a ragged line of khaki marshland and the salt plains of the Rann of Kutch underscored the purple and blue of the distant hills, far away to the east. As they sailed further south, Captain Wilson could point out the port city of Porbandar, a fact which Dr Aitken might now acknowledge casually, ignorant as yet that it was to be his next, and his last, posting. If it was unremarkable then except for its cotton market, today it has become revered as the birthplace of the great Mahatma Gandhi.

The next landmark was the Island of Diu, with its massive fortress facing defiantly out to sea on the northern shore of the Gulf of Cambay as Khambat was then known. This well-defended Portuguese colony was only grudgingly ceded to India by Portugal after a brief conflict, along with its twin Daman, in 1961, fourteen years after Indian independence from British rule. These two forts lie facing each other on either side of the Gulf of Cambay. Daman is the southern sea gate to the state of Gujarat. In 1815 all the great cotton trading towns on which the East India Company depended for its purchases were to be found along the shores of the gulf, and it was from these ports that almost all its annual cotton purchases were shipped to Bombay. In only two and a half years' time, Theodore would visit these ports as part of a supposed 'trip to the Northward about Cotton affairs' – though in reality his trip would have a far different purpose.

The old Mughal stronghold of Surat lies deep in the throat of the Gulf of Cambay, sixty or more miles north of Daman. It was built upon the left bank of the river Tapti, as the Tapi was then called, upstream from where the great river disgorges into the salty waters of the gulf. This was where the 'griffin' Theodore shared a house with his brother, William, met his future brother-in-law, 'Agah Aratoon', made his first trades and fell in love and married Eliza. Surat was a decaying but picturesque antique city then; so very different from the ultra-modern and prosperous commercial centre it is today. As Captain Preston Wilson negotiated the treacherous tides and currents across the wide mouth of the gulf, it would have been hard for Eliza not to let her thoughts turn to her home city and the family she had left there. Though 'out of sight', they could not have been 'out of mind'. As the sails filled to speed them past Daman, she knew she was near to the warm familiarity of home.

The passengers on *Durya Beggy* were given proof of their imminent arrival in Bombay when they began to see first the rugged heights of Bassein followed by the palm-fringed beaches and the gentle hills of the large island of Salsette with its rocky islets cloaked in mangroves. Here, drawn up above the tide-line of sandy coves, they could see the boats of the original inhabitants of the island; the indigenous Koli fisher-folk, who have lived along this stretch of coast since time immemorial. Tidal channels formerly isolated Salsette from the Indian mainland to the north and east and from the island of Bombay to the south. It is bounded to the west by the Arabian Sea from which, day after day, the aboriginal Koli draw their livelihood in nets glittering with fish to dry and sell in the markets of Bombay.

New causeways, the building of bridges and the construction of a railway viaduct to the mainland, have encouraged the growing population of Bombay to encroach upon the isolation of Salsette. As one by one her watery defences have been circumvented, the island and its satellites have been gradually swallowed up by what has become the modern metropolis of Mumbai. Fortunately, a large central area of 40 square miles has been preserved away from the reach of modern development. This is the huge Sanjay Gandhi National Park which, though it is now overlooked on three sides by tower blocks and high-rise buildings, remains an oasis of green forest, hills, lakes and streams, still supporting an abundant native flora and fauna.

In 1815, the density of the widespread forest on Salsette hid from view the few buildings that dared to exist there. Its jungle provided a safe haven for snakes and tigers, and only a few farmsteads were scattered as yet amongst the pre-existing Portuguese monasteries and Hindu temples. As *Durya Beggy* came alongside the island Theodore was happily ignorant of the morbid associations with his own life and death that the island held in store for him. At the very moment that he was sailing past with his own young children, the lady who would attend his deathbed in five years' time was no more than a few miles away, on the other side of the island, in the home she shared with her husband, the surveyor and cartographer Captain Thomas Dickinson of the Bombay Engineers, and their children, Sebastian, Fanny and Eliza, who would all too soon become beneficiaries of Theodore's last will and testament.

Somewhere in the jungly forest the tigers still prowled, who only a few months before had frightened those same children in their home 'at Gora Bunder, on the narrow arm of the sea, which divides Salsette from the Mahratta coast'. Their parents were entertaining James Silk Buckingham, recently arrived from sharing Theodore's table in Mocha.

'The house', writes Buckingham in his autobiography, 'had been a Catholic convent in the time of the Portuguese dominion. It was seated on an elevated rock, for the double enjoyment of pure and cool air and a fine prospect, and evinced the good taste of its founders. The ascent to it was by a long flight of steps cut in the steep sides of the rock itself.'

He continues: 'After dinner, the company retired to the drawing room for music... just as some of the party had commenced a vocal quartet, the ayah, or Indian nurse, came running in with the greatest affright, dragging a little child after her, and exclaiming, "A tiger on the steps! A tiger on the steps!" On rushing to the outer door, two immense tigers were seen stealthily creeping up the flight of steps with noiseless feet and crouching bodies; and we were only just in time to slam the glass-door in the very face of one, who, in a moment more of time, would have had some victim in his jaws, carrying him or her off in triumph, as young Hector Munro was seized by a tiger, while in a picnic party at the Island of Saugor, and killed before the very eyes of his companions.'

Even further into the future, Salsette would figure again in Forbes family history when, in only thirteen years' time, Theodore's youngest brother, James, while on a picnic with friends, would be tempted by the picturesque view from one of the island's ruins to climb to the very top of its crumbling walls and fall sixty feet to his death. Fortunately, this association was yet to become reality and it was a reality which Theodore would never know.

From the deck of *Durya Beggy*, the first living sign that the infant metropolis of Bombay was not far away was a column of large birds indolently circling on the thermal currents above the headland of Malabar Hill. These languid creatures were Indian vultures. On the rocky outcrop below, and scarcely visible above the wilderness, lay the focus of their activity: the Parsees' Dakhmeh or 'tower of silence'. On closer inspection, anyone might be forgiven for at first mistaking the stout round tower for one of the coastal Martello towers, still being built across the world by the British to defend their colonial interests and ambitions.

The vultures perching in the surrounding trees or soaring lazily above were waiting for the arrival of a fresh corpse. It was the Parsees' custom to lay out the bodies of their dead on the top of the tower for the avian scavengers to pick clean; it is an efficient way of disposing of the dead in the tropics. Each new arrival is soon divested of its flesh, until only a skeleton remains. Over time the ligaments perish and one by one the sun-bleached bones detach themselves and roll, or are swept, down the open centre of the building into the depths of an ossuary pit where a fast-flowing stream gurgles through a soak-away channel of sand and charcoal, catching up the last crumbs and carrying the remaining particles out to sea until the last purified speck has been reduced to atoms. The practice had evolved to safeguard the purity of the sacred elements of air, earth, fire and water from being polluted by the residues resulting from other methods of disposal. By following their ancient tradition the Parsees could also ensure that the remains of their dear-departed would continue the journey back to their atomic genesis in a far less violent and sudden manner than that practised by other religions.

In 1815, Bombay had a vibrant and prosperous population of Parsees. Today their descendants still contribute hugely to the overall prosperity of the city and of the whole nation of India, though regrettably in severely reduced numbers. The vultures have also suffered a devastating reduction in their numbers. They are now critically endangered due to poisoning by a veterinary NSAID, diclofenac, consumed by them in the carcasses of cattle.

Today Malabar Hill is the site of some of the most expensive and exclusive developments in Mumbai, but in 1815 it was very sparsely populated. On the southern side of the headland only a few villas and bungalows had as yet been built – mainly on the lower level of the headland. From the deck of *Durya Beggy*, the low lime-washed buildings, with their shady verandahs and shallow-pitched roofs showed themselves only intermittently above the shoreline of the gently undulating ridge, winking out for a moment from among the coconut palms, only to be lost to sight again in a blink as the ship dipped within the swell. Lachlan Macquarie, the first Governor of New South Wales relates that in 1797 he 'dined... with Mr. [Charles] Forbes, at the Sans-souci club, at Sorabjee's Bungalo on Malabar Hill.' In 1801, Arthur Wellesley, the future Duke of Wellington, and victor of Waterloo, as yet distinguished merely with the rank of colonel, had lodged in the nostalgically named 'Surrey Cottage'. Nearby was Randal Lodge, the country house of Major-General John Bellasis (1744-1808), Commander

of the Forces and Colonel of Artillery at Bombay, who in 1793 raised a
public subscription to build his eponymous road from Malabar to
Mazagaon, 'to give employment and sustenance to... the poor driven
from the City of Surat in that year of famine'.

At the time of Theodore and Eliza's return, Randal Lodge was let to
John Stewart the managing partner at Forbes & Co. During his brief time
in Bombay, Buckingham reports that he attended 'the most agreeable
parties given by Mr. and Mrs. John Stewart, at their villa, near Malabar
Point'. Stewart, who was shortly to feature significantly in Theodore's
life, was an enthusiastic Scottish dancer and a close friend of William
Marshall, the famous Scottish fiddler and composer. Though a great
number of the British residents of Bombay were Scottish, it is still
strange to think of the strains of Marshall's strathspeys and reels
wafting through the darkest of nights across an Indian shore, while the
waves lapped at the sands of Back Bay, overwhelming the last embers of
its Hindu funeral pyres. But it is stranger still to think of those Hindu
souls quitting this earth to the sounds of a merrily animated fiddle or
the mournful accompaniment of the bagpipes.

After passing the sandy curve of Back Bay, whether by day or by
night, all those on the deck of *Durya Beggy* would see the last landmark
before the harbour of Bombay: the 150 foot lighthouse at the tip of
Colaba Point. The beam from it was said to be visible at night from 20

miles away, warning ships' captains to steer well clear of the peninsular outcrop known as Old Woman's Island, and the submerged chain of treacherous rocks by which it was linked to the island of Bombay. Colaba marked the southernmost point of the harbour. This is where new arrivals would be greeted by the Company frigate; here Captain Wilson might take a pilot on board to see them safely into harbour.

On going about and rounding the point, they had to change tack. No sooner was this hairpin manoeuvre accomplished than they could at last see the panorama of lush green islands and clusters of shipping, which always impressed first time visitors to the bay. James Silk Buckingham, had written of his arrival just a few months earlier:

'The entrance to Bombay is very imposing. On the right or south side of the passage is the continent of India; and in the background, trending away to the north-east, rise the noble hills called the Ghauts, which form the buttresses or bulwarks of the higher land beyond them... The ample expanse of water... presents a harbour capacious enough to shelter the whole navy of England, while the several smaller islands dotting its surface, including that of Elephanta with its celebrated Cave Temple, form objects of picturesque beauty, and afford good shelter as breakwaters against the strongest gales.'

Like Buckingham, the passengers of *Durya Beggy* would be landed at the Fort Stairs, below the old British fortifications known as Fort George, the seat of British government in the Bombay Presidency, with the sixteenth-century Portuguese Castle as its centrepiece. Island and castle had both been ceded to the British in 1662 as part of the dowry of Catherine of Braganza, Infanta of Portugal, on her marriage to Charles II and they and the docks were still owned by the Crown. Through the years that followed, close-packed residential development began to radiate out from this hub. Some was built by Parsee and other native developers and some was built by the fast-growing European merchant community. The fort rapidly became the commercial centre of the great city, and it has remained so to this day. In Theodore's time, there were numerous private houses inside the area now known simply as Fort, many of them owned by wealthy Indian merchants and let to Europeans, but some were owned by the residents themselves. These were mainly established British merchants and bankers with settled business interests or family commitments in the city.

On board ship there would be little time to 'stand and stare' at the unfolding panorama of the harbour. Theodore had to gather family, servants, bags and baggage in readiness for their arrival. The passengers, who had been living so close to each other and sharing the enforced intimacy that all shipmates must endure, were making ready to disembark, free at last to travel onwards to their different destinations. Theodore and Eliza must have felt some regret at having to part from Dr Aitken who had been such an important part of their lives in Mocha. But after several weeks under sail together, all on board looked forward to leaving their 'sea-legs' behind and finding their feet once more on dry land. And so it was, that the couple stepped confidently out onto the Fort Stairs of Bombay, full of optimism for their future prosperity and happiness, but passing once more from the familiar into the unknown.

Portrait of the adventurer and author James Silk Buckingham
in Turkish dress, by John Jukes.

Painted in Bombay in 1815, shortly after his arrival from the Red
Sea, where he had stayed with Theodore for a week at the British
Factory in Mocha.

Buckingham's letter of thanks is quoted in his
Autobiography, published in 1855.

Private collection. Photo © Christies

The Explorer J.L. Burckhardt, 'Haji Ibrahim'.

Buckingham met him in Jeddah in 1814 and, though he claimed that
they had developed a close friendship, the Swiss explorer later wrote an
excoriating critique of Buckingham's character and behaviour.

Credit Wikimedia Commons

Colabah Lighthouse.

Randal Lodge on Malabar Hill, where John Stewart and his family lived and Theodore's younger brother would later lodge.

View of Charles Forbes' dwelling from Apollo Green.

© British Library Board

Forbes & Co. Offices. Theodore worked here from April 1816 until August 1820.

© British Library Board.

PART II

1815 – 17

TRADE & EMPIRE

Chapter 7

Bombay, 1815

Bombay Green. Engraved by Charles Heath.
From Pl. 23, in Forbes, J. *Oriental Memoirs*. Volume 1. London: 1813.

7

Bombay, 1815

If the servants of the Forbes household had thought Mocha busy, the bustle of Bombay must have astonished them. None of them had ever seen such a great assemblage of fine vessels – or so many white faces. Ships great and small clustered around the 'Fort Stairs' while they shipped or unshipped passengers and cargo, all beneath the watchful presence of the imposing Customs House and Company Warehouse or 'godown' at the head of the Stairs. Massive East Indiamen and ships of the Royal Navy, country ships and China Trade clippers, as well as native craft from all across the Indian Ocean and beyond, lay spread out around the bay, bobbing confidently in its safe anchorage against the backdrop of its green patterning of well-wooded islands. The ships lay close together with their sails lowered, those farthest away showed as dark patches of stubble on the smooth face of the water. The ever-changing crowd of tall ships, the furling or unfurling of their great sails at each arrival or departure, the hoisting of colours, fixing of pennants and the boom of their guns gave the safe haven of the bay an air of constant excitement.

Eliza had been accustomed from her earliest days to seeing lesser shipping in the constricted reaches of a tidal river port. Recently, looking out from Mocha's harbour and bay she had become used to the sight of large ships lying at anchor in the Mocha Roads against the wider vista of the Red Sea and the distant coast of Africa beyond. Her first sight of the density of bristling masts on the extensive anchorage of Bombay's harbour could not have failed to impress. Theodore was familiar with the view but would have noted with approval how the number of British trading vessels had increased since his departure, especially merchantmen from provincial English ports, all of them over 350 tons. It was a change that was certain to be welcomed by such a man, ambitious as he was for material success; the breadth of the merchant shipping advertised a multitude of possibilities for profitable trade. But the acquisition of a fortune seldom comes without sacrifice; Theodore was to find that the opportunities about to be put before him were destined to test his loyalty to his wife and young family and threaten the domestic bliss which they had so recently enjoyed in Mocha.

The sudden increase in trade from Britain had been brought about by the passing of the 1813 Charter Act. The East India Company held its territories in trust for the Crown, its continued possession of them depended on the charter it received by Act of Parliament, which was reviewed and amended every twenty years. While the couple were absent from India, the British Parliament had completed their review of the Act of 1793 and in 1813 had passed revisions to it by which the Hon. Company's monopoly on Indian trade was removed. Though the Company retained their monopoly in the markets farther east, it had opened up new avenues for British merchant adventurers to trade in the markets of all the Company's Indian territories. Gradually, The Hon. Company would be forced to relinquish control of licences for Britons wishing to enter British India. Even though the first private ships did not set sail for the East Indies until April 1814, single females, anxious to find a husband, were quick to take note of the imbalance of the sexes within the expatriate communities in India. Before long every ship bound for the east carried a fair complement of the fair sex. This brought a speedy end to the relaxed way of life previously enjoyed by the British bachelors of Bombay, for this growing city was often the first landfall on the Indian subcontinent for British merchantmen.

If Theodore had hoped to renew his acquaintance with James Silk Buckingham when *Durya Beggy* docked, he was to be sadly disappointed. Two months earlier, the Cornishman had been sent for by the new Governor of Bombay, Sir Evan Nepean. On hearing his rich West Country accent Sir Evan had suggested that he might be American. Buckingham later speculated that this may have been an attempt to save him from being deported – his authority only extending to British subjects – however, as he relates in his autobiography, he was ignorant of this nice distinction and held to being a true-born Englishman:

'I was born and brought up an Englishman,' he said, 'and I wish so to continue.'

'Oh, very well,' rejoined Sir Evan, 'if you will not be an American, I cannot, of course, make you one.' Consequently, on May 10th 1815, Theodore's colourful new friend received notice from the Company's solicitor to quit India 'in such ship and at such time as may be appointed by Government', for not having obtained the necessary permits, before leaving England, to enter Company territory. He had endured a very long voyage from Mocha, against the prevailing wind, and been in Bombay little more than a month. However, instead of deporting him and sending him back to England on a forced passage, via the Cape, the Chief Secretary to Government, Francis Warden, Theodore's old boss, allowed him to embark on the Company's cutter, *The Prince of Wales*, bound for Mocha. So by the time Theodore arrived in Bombay, Buckingham was on his way back to the Red Sea. But luckily, as he later explained, he had managed to avoid being shipped out via the Cape and the 'horrors of a "charter-party passage" as a convict – the scorn of the men and the contempt of the officers in whatever ship I might be transported'.

Buckingham had left Bombay on the 27th of June, just three days before Theodore and his family sailed from Mocha. Although they were under sail simultaneously on what might appear to be the same route, there was no chance of an encounter at sea. Buckingham, aboard *The Prince of Wales*, was once again battling against the contrary winds, while *Durya Beggy*, with the wind at her back, was making good speed. Buckingham may have looked forward to availing himself of the warm hospitality Theodore had previously provided at the Factory. If so, he too was to be disappointed. In his autobiography he describes how: 'having been nearly two months in making the long round of the Southern passage, with its variety of heavy gales and tedious calms,' *The Prince of Wales* arrived on the 18th August, but 'Mr. Forbes, with all his establishment, having left Mocha for Bombay, we found the British Residency without occupants.'

Some weeks before leaving Mocha, Theodore had made a note in his book: 'Wrote to Wedderburn, told him I expected to be in Bombay about the month of June – said I should live with him but that as I had some incumbrance I would trouble him to procure for me a large, commodious house, the nearer his so much the better.' At the beginning of their respective careers in the Honourable Company's service, Theodore had shared a house in Mazagaon with John Wedderburn and James Henderson, fellow Scots and near contemporaries, who had travelled out with him from England as 'griffins' or new boys. By the time he returned to Bombay both his friends had been promoted to posts of some considerable importance: Wedderburn had become Paymaster General and Henderson was now Assistant Secretary to the Bombay Government.

Theodore's reference to Eliza and the children as 'an encumbrance' in his letter to Wedderburn should not necessarily be taken as a slur. However, in the light of later events, it may be looked at with some foreboding. For the moment though, all was well with the couple, and Theodore was set to capitalise on the commercial and political reputation that had preceded him. It is unlikely that Wedderburn would have known of the marriage ceremony in Surat or the subsequent births of Kitty and Alexander. None of these events would, or even could, have been registered. Theodore would not have felt the need to enter into lengthy explanations; all would become clear as soon as they arrived.

Eliza and the children, were to have the 'large commodious house' as close as possible to the property where Theodore was to lodge with his friends at Mazagaon. His servants, Walloo and Old Antoon, would accompany him. Fazagool and Markar were to stay with Eliza and the children. Eliza's church would give her an immediate entrée into the close-knit Armenian community of Bombay and bring her a new circle of friends among a congregation far larger than that of Surat. According to the census there were more than a hundred Armenian adults living inside the Fort at the time she and Theodore arrived in Bombay. There were also many others living outside the bounds of the city proper in different settlements around the island. The area around Bycullah for instance, reclaimed from the sea by the construction of the Hornby Vellard in 1784, had already been the subject of widespread development.

Only nine years after the draining of the marshy ground within the new causeway, General Bellasis was able to build his west-east road from Malabar Hill to Mazagaon. It seems that some Armenian families were living in Bycullah even before the building of the road. But in 1815 and well into the middle of the century, the area was still considered as 'country'. Such a large flat area of land, suddenly made available, had been a natural choice for the race course and the Bombay Turf Club had made its home there from 1800 onwards. Bycullah would serve Theodore's purpose admirably; it was only a short ride from Mazagaon. He wanted to be able to be with Eliza and the children whenever he chose and still enjoy the company of his two oldest and closest friends.

Much of Bycullah was still open country when Eliza and Theodore took on a house owned by a well-to-do Armenian lady called Khumburzeefuh. The matriarchal Khumburzeefuh also had several houses in the Fort. She was happy to welcome the couple as tenants and introduce them into her family. The area was still onlysparsely developed, with villas and bungalows sparingly distributed along the length of the road and safely sited within their own walled and gated compounds. Each had its own *chowkidar*, the gatekeeper and night watchman, to guard against thieves and wild animals. According to a contemporary source, jackals were 'always heard at night'. In the cold weather the beasts were well-known to 'wander past the houses and go towards Malabar Hill'. The marshes enclosed by the Hornby Vellard provided plentiful opportunities for 'gentlemanly sport'. Wildfowling on the flats between Bycullah and Mahim, which were teeming with water birds and waders, would provide heron, goose, duck, golden plover, bittern and snipe for the table.

Amongst the Armenian community, Eliza's new landlady was not unique in being a lady of means who had taken advantage of the early property boom in the Bombay Presidency. In 1821, the estate of another Armenian landlady called Rose Nesbitt was advertised for sale at auction. Rose died in October1819, aged seventy-five. According to the *Bombay Gazette* she was the widow of Commodore Andrew Nesbitt, the Harbour Master of Bombay, who had died in 1791, but she had inherited her vast estate from her parents, named Catchick. The *Bombay Gazette* recorded that the auction 'on 10th April and succeeding days' comprised '11 houses, 3 stables, 13 warehouses and 1 office within the Fort; an extensive house and grounds at Bycullah; the estate and village of Mattawady, another house at Bycullah and a piece of land with a stable at Mahim.'

Theodore needed to stay in Bombay for a time to submit his

accounts from the Mocha Factory and take over as executor of William's will. He also needed to sell the bullion he had brought with him. Only after attending to these concerns could he sail for Surat with Eliza and the children. Six weeks after they left Mocha, he sold the gold ducats, dollars and crowns he had so carefully stowed on the *Durya Beggy*. It seems that he made a large profit, not just on the rate of exchange, but because, he notes with some satisfaction, on August 18th, oddly, some of the coins weighed rather more in Bombay than they had when he bought them in Mocha.

Next on his agenda was to take over the administration of William's estate from John Romer, magistrate in Surat and his friend John Wedderburn, Paymaster General in Bombay. Theodore sent his brother's remaining papers to England by the Hon. Company's Ship *Bombay* and notes: 'The letter to my father addressed John Forbes Esq, Upper Boyndlie, by Fraserburgh.' Theodore's special mention of the address to which he sends the letter shows the significance to him of the family's recent move from Haddo to Boyndlie. The plans for the new house must have been a frequent topic of conversation at family mealtimes while he and his siblings were growing up. After Theodore and William left for India, the work on the house had continued steadily. Now finished at last, his parents and the last two of their children still living at home – his younger sister Jane and the youngest brother James – had all moved into their new house. William's twin, Alexander, had stayed on to farm at Haddo.

In Bombay, Theodore, ever congenial, was soon welcomed back into the upper levels of society, where he had so many friends already and was bound to make more within the rapidly expanding British population of the city. His friends' letters make clear that he was a 'party animal' and would have flung himself into the social round with great enthusiasm despite Maria Graham's opinion that: 'The parties in Bombay are the most dull and uncomfortable meetings one can imagine. Forty or fifty persons assemble at seven o'clock and stare at one another till dinner is announced, when the ladies are handed to table according to the strictest rules of precedency by a gentleman of a rank corresponding to their own… if there be any newly arrived young women, the making and breaking matches for them furnish employment for the ladies of the colony till the arrival of the next cargo.'

This new wave of young and not-so-young ladies was accompanied by ever stricter enforcement of 'the rules of precedency' referred to by Mrs Graham. The old hands were reluctant to move over for the interlopers and the parvenus were anxious to enforce their rights. Theodore's friend Thomas Fraser writes to him of an episode which encapsulates the petty-mindedness of some of the female socialites:

'Recollect this is to be known only t'you... a pretty tale has come up here about Miss Draper & Mrs Moyle at a dance; I understand the Spinster placed herself above the married Woman. When the latter seeing it went up to the former, and said "It is usual for the married ladies t'take precedence of Spinster", to which Miss D. I understand made some reply that drew the attentions of the assembly – perhaps you were there and may have heard of it so I shall say no more than this: Miss D must have been much rattled at the idea of married Lady & 10 years younger than herself talking to her in the style she did. They were bosom friends before this took place & are now scribbling away to all their friends tooth and nail.'

At this time the 'cargo' of 'newly arrived young women' who had travelled so far to find a husband, was already beginning to be known as 'The Fishing Fleet'. But the same hopeful ships, sailing in to Bombay harbour, their cabins replete with British spinsters, carried other just as eagerly awaited 'Europe goods' in their holds – and with them the expectation of a profitable sale for the supercargo and the owner of the vessel. Every new arrival was attended by a buzz of anticipation as the cargo was unloaded. That the feverish excitement was soon spread by word of mouth, and that Eliza shared in it, is evident in a letter she later wrote to Theodore from Surat in September 1817:

'I have heard that many Europe ships & 2 ships of French have arrived at Bombay – therefore the all Europe articles being cheapest rate, Laces, Vails, Cloths &ca. and also I think you may [be] occupied in Europe ships &ca Affairs.' The numerous bazaars and shops to explore when she first arrived from Mocha would have been a magnet for her. She could never before have seen such a dazzling array of European and Far Eastern merchandise and, as ever, she would have found it difficult to resist overspending her household allowance. For his part, still passionately in love, Theodore did not even try to prevent himself from indulging her cupidity. An additional source of gratification to her was her entry into an Armenian community new to her, but with a language, culture and, possibly, friends or relations in common. Meanwhile, her marriage remained at the centre of her existence and she held herself ready to welcome her husband at the house in Bycullah whenever he chose to visit 'with full affection to embrace each another'.

As Buckingham had so recently discovered, Theodore had a wealth of advantageous contacts among the merchants of Bombay as well as the Civil Service – but partying with his old chums Wedderburn and Henderson, Erskine and the Mazagaon social set, and rejoining the Bobbery Hunt with its 'jaunts and jollities' were his favourite diversions and tempted him into staying in Bombay much longer than he had intended. A letter he wrote to Aratoon at Surat on behalf of their landlady, Khumburzeefuh, places the couple still firmly in Bombay at least eight weeks after their arrival from Mocha: 'Bombay, September 26th 1815. Wrote to Aratoon at Surat, principally of Khumburzeefuh's intention to ask his eldest daughter Johanna in marriage for her son Agah Zdr-.' [Possible spelling of Tsedur.]

That Khumburzeefuh wanted her son to marry into Eliza's family and asked Theodore to arrange the match shows her respect for her new tenants. It is unlikely that she, a lady of property, would have considered the match to be suitable had she thought that Eliza was of lowly birth or that the couple were unmarried and their children illegitimate. At the time of writing to Aratoon, Theodore had evidently begun planning his return to Surat with the family because in the same letter he asks his brother-in-law to 'take for me Chellabee's house in the Durya Mahal from the 1st November rent'.

Four days later on September 30th came welcome news: 'This day,' wrote Theodore, 'Mr John Stewart informed me of Mr Charles Forbes' direction to receive me a partner in his house of Forbes & Co.' He was delighted; he had arrived back in Bombay with his diplomatic successes well-known, his trading record unimpeachable and his personal wealth so conspicuously increased that now, within two months of his return, he had been invited to join the most prestigious firm in Bombay. This was a great opportunity for him, even though it would mean resigning from the universally respected Bombay Civil Service and joining the merchant classes. However, Theodore had no need to fear any loss of social standing despite Buckingham's observation that: 'The Civil Service constitutes a caste of aristocracy, within whose barriers the military officers are only sparingly admitted... merchants only of the first class, and merchant-captains and traders never.' His family background was well-known and well-respected by the multitude of Scots in all departments of the Company's service in Bombay.

Forbes & Co. was one of the oldest, most successful and most highly regarded of the merchant banking houses in Bombay. Charles Forbes, the Head of the House, was held in high regard in both India and Great Britain. Back in England he was shortly to become a Member of Parliament and would later receive a knighthood. Although he and Theodore shared a surname, they were only distantly related, so it seems that Theodore's appointment was largely due to merit, not to nepotism. His trading success in Mocha was the principal reason for Charles's decision to ask the Acting Head of House and managing partner, John Stewart, to headhunt him from the Bombay Civil Service.

Forbes & Co. were bankers to the British government as well as agents to the Hon. Company for much of their business in the east. Charles Forbes and John Stewart were able to see for themselves how well Theodore had handled everything during his time in Mocha. He had already been entrusted by 'the House' with sizeable cash transactions and with issuing notes of credit, as well as with goods to sell on their behalf. These transactions had turned out well for them. He had, by now, safely delivered to them the considerable sum of their cash he had brought back on board *Durya Beggy*.

James Silk Buckingham describes Theodore as a 'diplomatist' and acknowledges that without letters of introduction from him he would not have been able to step as quickly as he did into the 'élite circles of Bombay society'. He also comments that, on presenting Theodore's letter of introduction to William Erskine, his fellow lodger in Mazagaon: 'By this gentleman I was most cordially received, and invited to take up my abode with him at Mazagong... Nothing could be more fortunate for me than this first step, as it brought me almost immediately into personal intercourse with the elite of Bombay society.'

How easy then for Theodore, on his return, simply to turn up at the shared house in Mazagaon and be 'cordially received' himself. Buckingham had left the house but Henderson and Wedderburn were still sharing with Erskine and he was able to take up immediately where he had left off. This bond among the many Scots in Bombay was important in all aspects of their life abroad. They relied on each other for news from home and for sending letters and parcels back with returning friends. It was not just in their social lives that the two-way exchange of favours was important; in any commercial undertaking in British India 'networking' was the most important ingredient in a recipe for success.

During his time in Mocha, Theodore had maintained a wide-ranging correspondence with both native and British contacts in the Red Sea area in the spheres of commerce and politics. It was Theodore who had brokered the agreement mentioned by Burckhardt, between Mehmet Ali Pasha, Viceroy of Egypt, and Forbes & Co. to allow the House's goods to be shipped direct to Suez and then in supposed safety across the desert to Cairo. Fortunately, no blame seems to have attached to him when the Pasha reneged on the agreement and *Durya Beggy* was to Theodore's 'great surprise and regret... stopped at Juddah and entirely prohibited from proceeding to Suez'. However, it is not impossible that his ill-judged communication with Burckhardt, supposedly travelling incognito as 'Haji Ibrahim', may have had something to do with that unfortunate incident.

Theodore was frequently called upon to oblige a friend by carrying out some small task, such as forwarding a packet, or paying a bill, confident that he could ask to have the favour returned when needed. Perhaps he was too keen to please and placed too much weight on the good opinion of his social equals and superiors. Certainly it was peer pressure that before long would challenge his commitment to his marriage.

It may be that Forbes & Co. invited him to join them solely because of his business acumen but his prospective partners would certainly have counted his breeding and contacts as an additional advantage to the House. He was moulded from the same seam of landed gentry in Aberdeenshire as Charles Forbes and John Stewart, and his social credentials within the Scottish community in Bombay were impeccable.

During his absence in Yemen, his equally well-connected friends, Henderson and Wedderburn, had both risen in rank in their respective departments of the Civil Service. He could therefore be counted on to bring new banking and brokerage business with him through his contacts.

Unlike an upper-class Englishman, Theodore's entry into the field of commerce would have only a positive effect on his standing among his compatriots. The Scottish landed gentry and aristocracy did not have the same snobbish reservations, as many of the English did, about being in 'trade'. In English society only the professions of the Law, Medicine, the Church, or the Armed Services, were considered to be appropriate for well-born but impoverished younger sons. The enlightened Scots, though, had been quick to appreciate the money-making opportunities offered by the private trading concessions hitherto allowed only to the Company's own servants. Many who sailed to India in the service of the Honourable East India Company found an early grave and never returned, but enough of them survived to come home with fortunes, acquired either through trade or military booty, and inspire others to follow in their footsteps. Unhindered at that period by the blinkered social attitudes of their English counterparts, or today's narrow nationalistic constraints, Scottish influence had grown apace and the nation had benefitted accordingly.

As soon as he took over as William's executor Theodore began to hear the distressing details of his brother's death. A letter to Wedderburn from the secretary's office, records that: 'He had been for nearly 30 hours previously in a state of insensibility, & latterly speechless – He had only one sharp attack of fever – but a total derangement of his whole system to have taken place – no medicine of any description had the slightest effect, even from the first.'

Their fellow Scot and friend, Dr George Ogilvy of the Bombay Medical Establishment, 'attributed his complaint to the effects of the land wind', stating that he was 'extremely imprudent with regard to sleeping – which he always did almost in the open air – His house was in the midst of the city much surrounded, & at the time he was taken ill the early part of the nights was extremely sultry, when about 11 a sharp cold land wind used to set in, against which, poor fellow, he seems to have been unprotected and incautious.'

Only on his return to Bombay would Theodore discover that, though the Court of Directors there had demoted William for dereliction of duty, he had not been wasting his time in Surat. It seems that he had made such rapid progress in his command of the Gujarati language and writing that he had been compiling a useful grammar, dictionary and mercantile lexicon.

Theodore deemed it important enough to submit it without delay to the Company and it was later published as *A Grammar of the Goozrattee Language: by the late William Forbes*. It was later extended *With some Additional Dialogues, Letters, &c. by Rustomjee Sorabjee*. Had he lived to see its publication, this remarkable achievement of Oriental scholarship within the space of barely five years' residence in India might have been some consolation to Theodore for the circumstances in which 'poor William' died. Their sister Catherine Scott was surprised and pleased to receive a cheque from the publishers some years after the dictionary was printed. Though she had known of its existence, she had not 'been aware', she wrote in 1841, that it was 'a work that merited publication'.

Theodore himself seems to have had literary leanings. Very soon after his arrival in India he joined the newly-formed Bombay Literary Society. He and his Mazagaon friends regularly attended the society's meetings. William Erskine had been one of the founders, along with his future father-in-law, Sir James Mackintosh, and Charles Forbes. Some years after Theodore resigned as Resident, he arranged a grant from the Literary Society for the benefit of Nathaniel Pearce in Abyssinia, for which Pearce expressed his warmest gratitude. During his time in India, Theodore had managed to build up a considerable collection of books, which were left in Bombay when he embarked on the *Blenden Hall*, a fact which reinforced his brother James's belief that he intended to return. After the news of his death at sea reached Bombay, his library was sold by auction on Bombay Green on the orders of his executors, Forbes & Co., much to the regret of his younger brother James, who arrived in Bombay after the sale. It was extensive enough to merit a separate sale catalogue – as James commented, 'English books being among the scarcest and most desirable of imported commodities.'

Having written to Aratoon in September about renting Chellabee's house, Theodore prepared to leave Bombay for Surat – a distance of about one hundred and seventy miles overland. They would take a passage on board one of the many coasting vessels which regularly plied the route between the two cities or perhaps aboard a larger ship stopping at Surat on its way north to the Red Sea or Persian Gulf. The duration of the voyage was very variable. Neither the vagaries of wind and weather nor the performance of the vessel and her crew could be predicted. But November and December were considered to be the best months in which to sail along the west coast of India; the monsoon winds and dangerous squalls of the rainy season having abated. The Forbes family would probably be at sea for no more than a few days.

Chapter 8

Sacred Port of the Mughals, 1815 – 1816

Part of the title inscription of the large-scale map surveyed by Lieutenants Adams and Newport, during the monsoon of 1817.

8

Surat, December 3rd 1815

The day dawned at last when the family set out for Surat. It was the beginning of December. Eliza would have preferred to have left Bombay much sooner, to arrive before Kitty's third birthday on the first day of the month. She was impatient to show off the children to her sister and her aunts. It was in Surat that she had met Theodore, fallen in love with him and married; her family had taken him to their hearts immediately. Her brother-in-law, Aratoon, was already a friend, referred to in a letter by Dr George Ogilvy to Theodore as 'Your Armenian Protégé'. The couple had embarked for Mocha so soon after their wedding that there had not really been much time for Theodore to get to know all of Eliza's wider family. Now he would be welcomed, not just as her husband, but as the father of two new family members. He was looking forward to living in comfortable domesticity again with Eliza and the children and had asked Aratoon to rent Chellabee's house for them from the 1st November. In the end the family did not arrive there until the first week in December, five months after they left Mocha.

Theodore would be amply compensated for leaving his friends in Bombay by catching up with the many he still had in Surat, both his own and William's. The brothers had shared many good times together with friends amongst their fellow Company Servants and officers of the garrison. When Theodore was given his first posting here on his arrival from England, the city had been under direct British rule for less than a decade. The city was the old 'Sacred Port' of the Mughal Emperors. Though its population was, by this time, principally Hindu, for centuries it had been the main port of departure for ships carrying Muslim pilgrims on the Hajj from the northern Indian provinces. The point of departure in Surat for these pilgrims was still its aptly named Mecca Gate. From here they would embark for the Red Sea, often calling in for supplies at ports along the way, until they reached Jeddah from where they would continue overland to Mecca. When they entered the Red Sea, many of the pilgrim ships used to stop at Mocha to re-provision. So Theodore would have already known many of the Surat *nakhodas* and merchants from his time there and would lose no time in taking up any useful business contacts. Now he was a partner in the prestigious House of Forbes & Co. he would be seen as a man of some importance, both in his own social circle and within the native population. Eliza too could take a vicarious pride in his appointment and bask in the light of her husband's achievement, to which she knew she had undoubtedly contributed. All seemed perfect.

When Eliza and Theodore returned to the 'Sacred Port', it was still an imposing, fortified citadel, built on a semi-circular plan and guarded by two massive concentric walls. The Castle was at its axis, facing west across the river Tapti. The towers and bastions, positioned along the battlemented ramparts of the city walls, dated from the days when it was in the possession of the Mughal Emperors. But their impressive fortifications were already falling into disrepair by the time it was ceded to the British. Of the great city of old there is very little left today that either of them would recognise. Though neglected, the scale of the city's defences in 1815 still trumpeted its importance within the Mughal Empire, as well as its historic anxiety about the threat of Mahratta incursions.

In Surat, Eliza was able to step straight into her own community just as Theodore had in Bombay. He would have the best of both worlds; a stable home life as well as the freedom to take up the many cultural, sporting and social opportunities on offer within the British expatriate society of a city, considered by many to be the best posting in India. It had been the cradle of trade between the major powers of Europe and the Mughal Empire and the site of the first European factories to be established there in the early sixteen hundreds. Over centuries it had expanded into a great centre of trade, particularly of jewels, fine fabrics, wood carving, and cotton 'piece goods'. But by the time Theodore and Eliza returned, the great city was already being nudged into economic stagnation. In the 1790s, crop failures had brought famine to the region. The Industrial Revolution in Britain and a global increase in cotton production had affected the profitability of the trade in India. This had forced many of the Surat merchants to move away to start afresh in Bombay and centres further to the east.

In 1815, the complete destruction of most of the city's ancient ramparts and walls was only a few decades away. The British presence had greatly diminished the threat of Mahratta raids and there was now little incentive or enthusiasm to repair the ancient defences. The disastrous effects of both fire and flood over the years had eaten into them and bite by bite they disappeared. Most of the buildings that once testified to the city's former glory have long since disappeared. Of all the thousands of European, Armenian and Jewish merchants, traders, statesmen and soldiers who once lived, worked and died here, only their stately tombs in the city's impressive cemeteries remain as monuments to their presence.

Today Surat has reasserted its industrial and commercial importance within the growing economy of India. Though the capital of the State of Gujarat is now the modern city of Gandhinagar, about fifteen miles north of Ahmedabad, Surat is once again its commercial hub. The city had been built on the left bank of the River Tapti, where its ample waters flow across the level seaboard towards the open sea. It was well-situated for easy access through the Gulf of Cambay to all the ancient trade routes of western India. Visitors coming from Bombay invariably travelled by boat, except during the most violent monsoon storms when the mouth of the gulf was too treacherous to admit any shipping. At the start of December the sea is at its calmest along the coast of western India, giving sailing ships a smooth passage from Bombay. And so it was that in the balmy days of December 1815 Eliza and Theodore took to the sea again and returned to the great cosmopolitan city where they had met and married.

In his *Oriental Memoirs* James Forbes writes that when he visited Surat at the end of the eighteenth century, the venerable river port was still a hub of cosmopolitan activity: 'The bar or sand bank where the ships anchor and discharge their cargoes is generally crowded with merchant vessels from the commercial nations in Europe and Asia. The city exhibits a busy multitude of Hindoos, Mahomedans, Parsees, Jews, Turks, Armenians, Persians, Arabians, Greeks and other

Asiatic strangers besides the Europeans... It is also frequented by merchants from Malacca, China, Abyssinia, Mosambique, Madagascar and the Comorro Isles and by numerous traders from the sea ports and inland provinces of Hindostan.'

When the great merchant vessels reached the Surat Bar, their passengers transferred to smaller boats with a shallower draft to speed their progress up the river with the tide. Any attempt to interest three-year-old Kitty in the few landmarks, such as the monumental 18th century Vaux's Tomb or the tall village trees by which the pilot navigated the dangerous shoals and channels, would have been futile. James Forbes describes the landscape of the estuary as being flat and uninteresting, but December at least can offer a colourful display of bird life. This is the time of year when great flocks of wading birds arrive from Europe and Northern Asia. Clouds of flamingos rise up from the boggy margins and marshy flatlands along the river bank, only to descend again and colour the shallow waters pink with their reflections. Flocks of these elegant birds, far greater then than now, return annually, taking flight from the cold of a northern winter to feed on the plentiful food in the warm estuarine waters of the Tapti, along with storks, stilts and pelicans. This wonderful avian spectacle must have made everything else seem very dull to the little girl from Mocha.

Suddenly, as they rounded the wide bend of the river, the outermost of the two great city walls, the city's first line of defence – known as the Mota Kot or Alampanah – the 'Safety of the World' came into view. It was tangible evidence of Surat's turbulent past. Looking along the river bank, the newcomers would soon discern battlements and bastions, towers and gun batteries keeping watch over the river and interrupting the outline of the wall which now loomed over their heads while the waves slapped noisily against the sides of their boat. The Alampanah enclosed all the outlying suburbs and fortified outer gates of the city and it was divided into administrative areas called *pooras* or *puras.*

In 1815, the wall was under siege, not from the invading Mahrattas against which it had stood firm for centuries, but from armies of weeds and bushes which took immediate advantage of every opportunity to colonise any small fissure as soon as it appeared. But, despite the creeping degradation of its outward face, in the survey carried out by the Revenue Department the following year, this first part of the wall would be described as being 'in tolerably good repair throughout' – Its gun batteries though, were declared to be 'unserviceable'.

At the southernmost tip of the city, the first buildings which came into view were the administrative and commercial offices, such as the Jail, the Court House and the Post Office. Here, the new arrivals were greeted by the Adawlet flagstaff bearing the Union Flag of Great Britain, to advertise to all comers that the city was now under British jurisdiction. If that message needed any reinforement, by 1816 several regiments of the Bombay Native Infantry, as well as the British regular army's 47th Regiment of Foot, were garrisoned in the city to provide a speedy response to the Mahratta forces to the northward. The following year would see the start of the third and final Mahratta War.

Several of Theodore's military friends were stationed in the city when he arrived from Bombay; one of whom was an old childhood friend, Lieutenant William 'Bob' Ogilvie, who was to play a significant role in forthcoming events. Will Ogilvie was Aide-de-Camp to the Commanding Officer of the Native Infantry in Surat, General Laurence. Ogilvie was slightly older than Theodore. He was a fellow Aberdonian, from the Ogilvie family of Ochiries. Like the Forbes family of nearby Boyndlie, the Ogilvies of Ochiries had suffered for the Jacobite cause in the 1715 and 1745 rebellions, but like the majority of the lowland Scots, they were now stout pillars of the Union. They had given their children Protestant names such as William, after the Royal House of Orange, and George, after the reigning House of Hanover. Will Ogilvie was an exact contemporary of Theodore's twin older brothers William and Alexander. Soon news would come from Scotland that the two families were to be further connected by marriage.

Another Scot, Dr George Ogilvy, was surgeon to the Surat garrison on the East India Company's Bombay Medical Establishment and was destined to attend Eliza and the children. He enjoyed a good professional reputation amongst the Europeans but most of the native population preferred to put their faith in the Hakim. Though their names were spelled differently, the identical pronunciation had meant their close friends had given the soldier the nickname 'Bob' to distinguish him from his 'namesake' the doctor.

Theodore's priority, when he arrived from Mocha, was to take over the handling of William's estate from the Surat judge, John Romer. One of the first things he did, as executor was to write off Will Ogilvie's 'trifling' debt to the estate. Later he personally paid off other debts for him at Surat, and stood surety for yet more, receiving interest on the loan. Ogilvie was now under a considerable obligation to Theodore and would feel honour bound to return the favour when he could.

As the boat carrying the Forbes family came alongside the landing steps by the courthouse and jail they were abreast of the houses and bungalows rented by Theodore's friends. Though they were concealed from sight, just inside the Alampanah, where a small stream tracks the south-west boundary of the suburb known as Nan Poora, Theodore would have known that his friends' substantial detached residences were only a short distance away. The proximity of the suburb to the jail and courthouse had been convenient for the first British administrators. Subsequent development by prosperous native landowners was tailored to British taste. Their houses were elegantly situated right on the green margins of the city, surrounded by their own gardens, productive orchards and gravelled driveways. Theodore had rented a house and garden here from Hurgovindass when he first arrived in Surat in 1810. This enclave had been the scene of many convivial parties in the past and Theodore anticipated that it would be so again.

Christmas was fast approaching. Generous leave was allowed at the festive season, and so the parties and social activities of the garrison were many and lavish. In the Forbes household it was bound to be a time of great jollity for everyone. As soon as they arrived they had Kitty's third birthday to celebrate because it had been on December the first, while they were travelling. In only a few days time on December 9th it would be Alexander's first birthday. Eliza's family reunion, the children's birthdays and their own house-warming would ensure that Chellabee's house would be a scene of almost continuous celebration until January 6th, when the Armenian Christmas is celebrated

To Antoon and Walloo, as well as to little Kitty, the place was strange and exotic. The sloping Alampanah rose from its broad base at the river's edge to its parapet and narrow walkway above – in some parts built up from below the surface of the tidal waters, in others emerging from the rocky scrub of a narrow foreshore or spit of land where small boats could be pulled up for repair. Only as they passed the gaps where gates or stairs and little channels pierced the great defensive wall, were they able to catch tantalising glimpses of the buildings within.

As the family continued upstream from the Adawlet Court they passed by the 'Dutch Bunder', where the very first Europeans in Surat, the servants of the Dutch East India Company, or VOC (Vereenigde Oost-Indische Compagnie) established their trading base in the 17th century. Today it is the site of a public park and formal gardens whose name 'The Dutch Gardens' keeps alive the historic significance of the place. The mouth of a small tributary of the river marks the end of the Alampanah and the beginning of the inner defensive wall known as the Nana Kot or Sheherpanah – 'Safety of the City'. Within this lay the citadel and almost fifteen thousand households.

The centre of British administration, the Castle, sat at the centre of the arc defined by the Sheherpanah. Marianne Postans in *The Moslem Noble* describes the situation of the Castle in the days when her husband Thomas was stationed there: 'The most considerable building on the banks of the Tapti... is the Castle, which takes up a prominent position on the wall of the city... and may be considered in local position as the centre of a chord of which Surat and its suburbs include a semicircle of some six miles in extent. The castle has angular bastions and a dry ditch but in old times could hardly have been well adapted for defence... the Reveille was played upon a flageolet from this castle.'

Just as the area inside the Alampanah was composed of *pooras*, the area within the Sheherpanah was divided into fourteen districts called *chuklas*. Theodore and Eliza were heading upstream for the Moolna Chukla, which lay alongside the river bank, just to the north of the Castle. Saleh Chellabee's house in the Deriah Mahal was situated beside the river, within the Moolna Chukla, in part of the quaint old quarter referred to by the British as 'The Old Mughal Serail'. Chellaby or Chellabee was a member of a large and well-established

Mohammedan family of Turkish origin; he had been a rich and powerful merchant and ship owner, active in the late eighteenth century. Within the same *chukla*, and close at hand, were the factories of both the French and the Portuguese companies, as well as the Armenian and Portuguese churches. The proximity of their church was one reason why the Moolna Chukla was home to most of the Armenian population of the city.

When their boat drew level with the Castle, they were only a few hundred yards from their new home and the ghats or steps where they could disembark. The northernmost boundary of their *chukla* was some distance upstream from their new home past the godowns of the British Factory, away past landing places, piers, dwellings, gardens, private *masjids* and burial grounds, where the Sheherpanah turned sharply away from the river to cast a protective arm around the eastern suburbs. Further away still, beyond the Sheherpanah, within the north-west angle of the Alampanah, were all sorts of properties, villages, smallholdings and steadings, criss-crossed with lanes and studded with trees.

It was here in the Moolna Chukla that Eliza's sister, Guyane, or 'Khayanee', as Eliza's scribe writes it, lived with her children, and it is probably safe to assume that her aunts and cousins lived not far away. According to John Romer's census taken around this time, 'Mughals, Armenians, Jews and a few Europeans' were the main groups of inhabitants living within this *chukla*. The list confirms Mrs Postans' description of how 'the proud Moslem, the stately Armenian, the crafty Jew, the bustling Parsee, the daring Arab and the cautious Hindoo all mingled' in the streets of Surat. In Mocha, the Forbes household had been used to the racial and religious tolerance of a great cosmopolitan trading port. No matter how visibly different their present surroundings appeared to be, the ambience was familiar.

As they drew near the ghat where they were to disembark, Eliza, looking eagerly among the bathers on the steps for a familiar face, might be hoping to spot a young woman, just a little girl four years ago, who would call out a greeting to her and send one of the playful urchins racing through the narrow streets to Aratoon's house with a cry of 'They're here, they're here. Hey, Aratoon, come quickly, they're here!'

Mrs Postans paints a colourful picture of these landing places, which she says were daily peopled by: 'The Brahmin repeating the Mantras of his morning service and laying aside as he does so his turban of striped cloth and all the items of his upper dress; the handsome wife of the Banian merchant laden with jewels and attired in silks of the richest texture and brightest colours, stooping to fill her polished vessels from the sunlit waters; the bright eyed little bullock driver filling his skins for the city's use; the washerman, surrounded by heaps of garments the colours of the rainbow, beating them on the smooth stones as he laughs and sings and chats to every fresh arrival at the Ghaut; the little children, singing, playing, and weaving fresh necklaces of jasmine flowers; the Hindoo girl, slight and handsome, the fruit seller of the bazaar or the flower dresser of the temple, her shining hair heavily braided and adorned with gold coins and fresh pomegranate blossoms; all these from time to time descend to the banks of the blue Tapti and render the landing places of Surat the long remembered spots of interest and of beauty that they are.'

The travellers did not have far to go once they reached the ghats and the tindal, or boatman, had thrown a line to make fast the boat and handed them ashore. Chellabee's property was situated right beside the river. Alongside their new lodgings the defensive wall was almost thirteen feet thick and rose to a height of forty feet from the bed of the river. The old riverside houses, lying just behind the wall, looked out to the west only from their upper storeys; to the east they looked towards the jumble of densely packed houses close to their own. Some of these dwellings were attached to their neighbours; many were loosely linked with dark passageways between them, some had their own private courtyard, for some the only outlook was fronting the large central area they all shared.

When the family arrived just a week before Aleck's first birthday, he was still unable to walk without support, but Kitty was at an age to be running about confidently, chattering and showing a lively interest in everything. There was still plenty of time for Eliza to settle the children and prepare for Christmas. She was naturally keen to show her children off to her family and friends, but most of all she wanted to go to her home church where she and Theodore were married a mere four years earlier. The Armenian Church was not more than five minutes' walk away from their new lodgings. For the past month the Armenian community had been fasting in preparation for their Christmas festivities on January 6th and everyone longed for the approaching feasts

To Antoon and Walloo, who had come from Mocha only five months earlier, their new home was of an entirely different order from anything they had known in Yemen, with its hot dry sand and dazzling white buildings, where all but the Dola and his guards went on foot, and where the wide expanse of the Red Sea formed the backdrop to all the activities of the port. They had experienced the contrast of Bombay Fort's dusty streets, full of horses, hackerys, palanquins and carriages, relieved only by the esplanade with its sea vista; the tented encampments and open spaces, where the military drilled; or by the sight of outlying areas of green, as yet undeveloped, and glimpses of distant blue mountains across the island-studded bay.

Now only Eliza could have been prepared for the claustrophobic atmosphere of the 'Mughal Serail' of Surat. The thousands of homes jumbled throughout the network of narrow lanes of the Mughal Serail were contained within an area of fewer than ten acres and its busy thoroughfares were consequently crowded with people on foot, on horseback and in palanquins with all the attendant noise and bustle. Occasionally everyone would have to make way for elephants and camels. The meeting, mixing and merging of styles in its ancient houses, the teeming life in its streets and their noisy hubbub might have made the area fascinating to some; but to the British, the closeness of the houses and the general stuffiness of the atmosphere meant that the whole of the Old Mughal Serail was regarded as insanitary. A building not far from the family's new lodgings provides a good illustration of this. Near the Nawab's racket court, behind the old buildings fronting the street, was a large square courtyard, described by the officers of the survey as 'an old suraee fitted up as an invalid barracks' but, they add, 'the men do not reside in them due to the unhealthiness of the place'.

To move away from the miasma of overcrowded humanity was frequently the only medical advice given to the chronically sick in the

Mughal Serail. But the Armenians, who had come to India by way of Persia, and were familiar with Farsi, the Persian language, and Arabic, still felt more at home here in this Muslim enclave than in any of the other districts of Surat. Despite its many disadvantages, this is where they had usually preferred to settle and this is where they built their first church. So it was little wonder that Eliza was drawn to bring her young children to live here, despite its reputation for unhealthiness. With the English Factory close by and the precincts of the Castle little more than 400 yards away, the situation was undoubtedly convenient for both Theodore and Eliza.

In 1817, The Revenue Survey Department undertook the comprehensive mapping of Surat. The work of producing a huge scale map in pen and ink and watercolour fell to Lieutenants Adams and Newport and the survey was carried out 'during the monsoon' of that year. The *pooras* inside the outer wall were numbered in large numbers; the *chucklas* of the inner city were labelled with large capital letters. A manuscript key to the whole map was drawn up. The key to each district was headed by a brief description of the mix of inhabitants and their ethnicity or religion. The height, thickness and condition of the walls were recorded and the condition of gates and gun batteries described. A thorough census of the population had been carried out in the previous year by John Romer, who had concluded that the total population of Surat at that time was one hundred and twenty four thousand four hundred and six souls.

Eliza's home city of Surat c. 1825

Panorama of buildings within the Sheherpanah from across the Tapti River
by Thomas Postans. © British Library board

Buildings on the banks of the Tapti, south of the Castle.

Castle and environs.

The old Mughal Serail, north of the castle.

Western portion of the city of Surat.

Eastern portion of the city of Surat

The Moolna Chukla and environs: The House of Saleh Chellabee is no. 27, opposite the 'P' of 'Taptee'.

Detail of the Revenue Survey Map of Surat 1817

© British Library Board

WITHIN THE INNER WALL.

MOOLNA CHUKLA

1 Syud Wara, is inhabited chiefly by respectable Moosulmans

2 Meerza Samee's Mehla D.° D.° D.° and Arabs some Hindoos also

3 Rooel Wara, is inhabited chiefly by the poorer description of Moosulmans

4 Arab Faris Khan's Mehla, is inhabited chiefly by Arabs, Moghuls, and other Moosulmans some Hindoos also.

5 Moghul Sieraee is inhabited by Moghuls, Armenians, Jews and a few Europeans.

6 Ungrez Chukla, is inhabited by Moghuls, Armenians, Jews and a few Europeans.

7 Moolna ka Kirkee or Lally Gate.

8 Tower, name unknown, Pentagon, 6 Portholes, 1 Gun mounted, Roof fallen in, Platform decayed, its length F.° 26.4 breadth F.° 18.5, Wall hereabouts, is F.° 4.5 thick, its height outwards F.° 17, Parapet is F.° 5 high being 1½ thick, it has fallen down in several places, Bottom of the Wall is ... much decayed and washed away by high Freshes in the River.

9 Tower, name unknown, fallen down and overgrown with bushes.

10 Tower, D.° Parapet fallen down, Wall of the curtain on both flanks much decayed, Height outwards F.° 20.10.

11 Inner Verow Gate, flanked by 2 Septagonal Towers, each 25½ Feet wide, 3 Embrazures in each, no Guns, without Roofs. Height outwards above the Street F.° 28.4 tolerably good repair.

12 Circular Tower 33 F.° wide, leaving an open space of 4 F.° between the wall and Minaret which it nearly encircles. The height of the top of the railing on the balcony from the Ground at the base of the Minaret within the Tower is exactly F.° 60.10, the extreme point of the Minaret may be about 13 F.° more, giving F.° 73.10 as the extreme height of the Minaret. The wall of the Tower only 4 F.° thick, but the wall of the Curtains F.° 9.4

13 Tower, called Bhooteea Boory. much decayed, Height of the Wall of the curtain (outwards) is F.° 20. the Parapet south of the Tower has fallen down in many places.

14 Tower, name unknown, much decayed.

15 Tower, D.° D.°

16 Syud Poora Gate, flanked by 2 decayed Towers, each F.° 32 long by F.° 25 wide, the height outwards is F.° 28.4 from the top of the Parapet over the Gate. Parapet much decayed here, but in better condition on the Curtains, the whole wall, however, is in a state of ruin beyond repair.

17 Musjid and Burial Ground of Syud Ulee Vedroos

18 D.° D.° D.° Syud Mahomed Vedroos

19 D.° D.° D.° Meerza Samee

20 The Lally and Warehouses.

21 Portuguese Church

22 D.° Factory

23 French Factory

24 Armenian Church

25 The Racket Court, in an old Sieraee the property of the Nawaub and Pereau Shah.

26 An old Sieraee, fitted up as an Invalid Barrack, from the unhealthiness of the place the men do not reside in them.

27 Derria Mehl, belonging to Saleh Challabhee, the wall here is F.° 12.9 thick and F.° 50 high, above the bed of the River.

28 Bukshee's Residence

29 Jootee Bazar

30 Moorghee Bazar

31 Peer Bala's Durgah

32 Khan Sahib's House

33 Hulkarra's Musjid

34 Rooel Wara Musjid

35 Shaik Fakier Mahomed's Musjid

36 Meer Hyder's House

37 Hur Kishundas' House, he is Dallal of the Arabs

38 Temple of Mahadeo, a small one.

39 Hukeemjee Meah Unwur's House.

Manuscript Key to the Revenue Survey Map of 1817

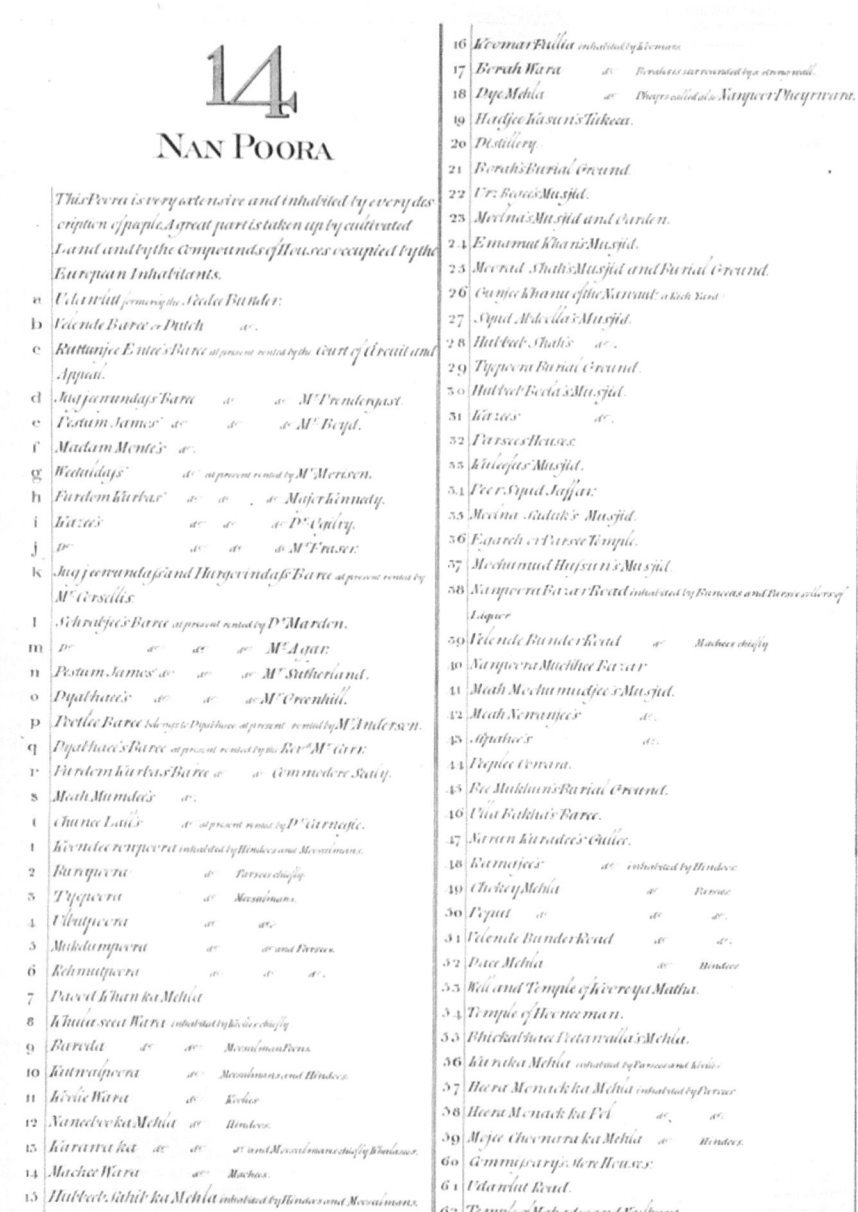

Manuscript Key to the Revenue Survey Map of 1817

Nan Poora, where Mr and Mrs Fraser, Dr Ogilvy, the Morisons and other high-ranking Europeans lived. Detail of the Map of Surat surveyed in 1817.

© British Library Board

Chapter 9

Power and Peoples, 1816

Surat Castle, and the old quarter within the Sheherpanah, seen from
across the Tapti River from the English Factory to the Dutch Bunder.

From an engraving published in *Oriental Memoirs* by James Forbes.

9

The Deriah Mahal, Surat, 1816

The Deriah Mahal, was a grand or palatial conglomeration of buildings, described in the 1817 survey as "belonging to Saleh Chullabhee", built around a large open space, probably with a tree or two, if James Forbes' well-treed prospect drawn in the 1780s and that of Thomas Postans twenty years later, are to be believed. Saleh Chellabee, to use Theodore's spelling, was the richest merchant in Surat in the eighteenth century and it was only one of his houses that Aratoon had taken for Theodore and Eliza. Not far away, across the Mughal Serail Street, just over the boundary of the Moolna Chukla, according to the survey, the rich merchant owned another 'house, musjid and burial ground' in the Muchleepeeth Chukla. This was presumably where he lived latterly with his family.

The old house to which the couple brought their young family was situated close beside the river. In the *View of Surat from across the River* at the head of this chapter, drawn by James Forbes for his *Oriental Memoirs* some years earlier, the union flag marks the position of the British Factory, the position of the Portuguese Factory is pinpointed by its flag according to Forbes's note. The Armenian Church lies beyond it and slightly farther away to the right. The buildings of the Deriah Mahal lie along the same line of sight in Forbes's sketch, closer to the artist's view point and are mostly hidden behind the wall. Farther south along the wall is the Castle, farther still is the Dutch Bunder.

Though the Forbes family's new lodging was in a courtyard of old houses tucked in behind the wall, it was by no means isolated from the vibrant life of the city. The calls of the busy boatmen on the river, the cries of street sellers and the jumbled voices of a dozen families living close beside each other, enlivened every daytime hour. Each evening as the sun sank below the parapet of the Sheherpanah the Deriah

Mahal was overcast with the gloom of twilight. The lucky few, blessed with two upper storeys, could look out across the sparkling river Tapti and watch as her silvered ripples blushed pink and hid themselves beneath a cool grey veil of mist. Then they might turn to look across the court to the jumbled roof tops of the Mughal Serail and see the tops of the surrounding buildings still suffused with tints of rose and old gold. Dusky evening shadows and the spicy smoke of charcoal braziers and open cooking fires soon cloaked the lanes and dimmed the lower floors of the neighbouring houses. A dense darkness would steal into the empty streets. Pin-sharp points of the stars above and a dull glow from scores of candle lamps being lit below were the only constant sources of light in the darkened alleyways, while the noises of the day faded to a whisper.

Very occasionally a rich man returning late in his palanquin would pass by, and the flaming torches of his *mussauljies* might flickeringly illuminate the walls and light up the glittering casements of the surrounding houses, casting huge shadows, as if of fleet-footed giants, and frightening the children. Gradually the raised voices, footsteps and the barking of dogs tailed off. In the depth of night the Mughal Serail slept. As the sun prepared to break free from the eastern horizon and light up the topmost points of the minarets, the first cool light of dawn would begin to creep across the hollow courts and empty cloisters to light the inner face of the Sheherpanah, and just before the sun's foremost rays pierced the network of paths and passages, the muezzin's rich tenor calling the faithful to prayer awakened the quiet streets instantly to noisy life. This was the ambiance that surrounded little Kitty Scott Forbes at an age when she was just beginning to make sense of the sights and sounds of the world outside the domestic confines of her home, but while she was still too young to remember them later.

The streets of Surat were made for commerce. Whereas in Mocha the goods had been kept out of sight in the cool and dark of the merchants' ground-floor rooms, and business was conducted on the light upper floors; in provincial Gujarat all trade was carried out at street level, from dwellings which doubled as offices, studios, workshops and emporia. Goods of all sorts could be found displayed on platforms built at the front of the venerable family houses known as *havelis*. Raised just above the level of the dusty streets, coppersmiths, weavers, dyers and ivory carvers pursued their crafts; and haberdashers, spice merchants, fruit and vegetable sellers displayed their wares – in short, all sorts of tradesmen conducted their business from their own front doorsteps. At their backs, great iron-bound doors of teak stood fast – the 'safety' of the home, skilfully jointed and panelled, and strengthened with serried ranks of rose-headed iron studs. A good number of the houses boasted carved wooden columns, which rose up at either side of their doors to support first-floor balconies, jettied out above the street and running along the full length of the houses. Even regular customers who stopped to chat or haggle would have had little idea of the domestic world concealed behind these stately portals: a private domain of secret courtyards; of colonnades and balconies and aged wooden façades, facing inwards but often ornamented with richly detailed carvings.

The bare grey bones of the wood carvers' art protruded from beneath a faded palette of dusty colours, applied in years gone by to mask the grains and knots of the raw material. Finely carved birds and animals peered out from amongst a sharply-cut tracery of flowers, leaves and scrolling vines, to bring a fond reminder of the world outside to the sequestered world within. In these homes the women of Indian Muslim families and even some Hindu households, could observe purdah. Here, whole extended Hindu families built their homes as close as possible to each other and to the heart of the property – the courtyard and family shrine – where the revered household gods received their daily *puja*.

Whenever Eliza walked from Chellabee's house to the Armenian Church, the people she saw in the narrow streets were still mostly Muslim. Mrs Postans unequivocally attributes the many charms of Surat to the Muslim inhabitants of old, who had settled there as the city grew in importance within the Mughal Empire:

'The Moslems loved Surat. Its capabilities were all such as delighted their peculiar tastes; the fine river with its refreshing breezes; the great sea which making this port the readiest highway to Arabia, gained for it the title of the port of Mecca; the bright gardens full of gay flowers; the rich mango groves; the beautiful position of the city; and thus this great and powerful people sought to embellish it, as they did all places which came into their power, so that the palaces and wells, tombs and terraces, Ghauts and pleasure Kiosks of Surat charmed the eye of every traveller who lingered there.'

Citizens of old, subjects of the Mughal emperors, had built their houses in the Old Mughal Serail on plots awarded through imperial or local *zamindari* patronage. The first householders in the Serail had been a mixture of immigrant families from Persia and Arabia along with native Indian converts to Islam. While these residents, who came from such differing backgrounds, still carried on their own traditions, over the years each had exerted their own peculiar influences on the other. The long Gujarati tradition of wooden house construction and figurative carving bestowed on the buildings an organic richness; the Islamic marble masons' carved repertoire contributed elegant geometric patterns and sinuous lines to that of the indigenous wood carvers. Eventually the two styles merged into an idiosyncratic North Indian Mughal style. As more and more houses were crammed into the available space the blend of styles began to create its own homogeneous texture.

Over the years, the effect of the climate and weather was to give these dusty dwellings an air of muted grandeur and faded antiquity; a dilapidated but romantic quality which was not universally admired by the British. The bends and twists of the alleys; the overhanging upper storeys; the glint of coloured glass in the old casements; the washed out colours lingering in the depths of the carved façades; their fitful illumination by the inconstant sunbeams: all these helped to transform the bustling city into a magical theatre of light and shade. Mrs Postans describes these streets as dirty and distressed, but had they survived fire and flood they would today be preserved as a precious record of India's rich multicultural heritage.

When Theodore and Eliza returned to Surat after nearly four years abroad, there were many who had an interest in their arrival: from the Garrison Commander to the Armenian Vartaped; from Parsee scribes and merchants to the Muslim and Hindu shopkeepers; from door-to-door *wallahs* to local landlords; and from servants to sahibs and their ladies. News of the return of the newly wealthy young sahib and his family would have diffused through the streets of the old city like a dyer's tint and through the languid drawing rooms of the British like a breath of fresh air. They were all connected; everybody knew everyone – and everyone knew everybody else's business. All who stood to profit financially or socially from Theodore would take a keen interest in the new arrivals. For Eliza's close family and friends though, it was simply a long-awaited reunion, and now it was party time and a time to catch up on the latest gossip.

Eliza's letters convey the impression that great fun was had by all at these family celebrations. When she later describes Markar's wedding party to Theodore she lists some of the guests: 'The Vartapeth Padrey, Avaness ter Marteeross, Estephanoos, Karapett Pethkaum, Ageenah and her daughter,' and continues that 'Aratoon and his family, had given them a small supper,' then 'after 10 o'clock... boys, girls, Ageenah, her daughter and Aratoon's family played with dholukree and song.' 'Dholukree' may refer to the beat of the Indian drum called *dhol*.

Tellingly Eliza adds, 'As well as usual, which you know very well', so it is certain that Theodore had taken part in these celebrations too, perhaps she was reminding him of their own wedding. Shared meals; going from one house to another with a drummer to beat time, through the winding streets of the old Mughal Serail, music, dancing, singing and children's games; no wonder that Theodore writes not of his agent but his 'friend Aratoon' whose wife Guyane, writes of her 'brotherly love' for him.

Once Eliza had been welcomed back into her own community she was quick to establish herself at the centre of the devotional and social activities of her church. The Armenian community in Surat, already in decline when she left, was dwindling rapidly at the time of her return. The British administration still paid a stipend for a *vartaped* and contributed towards the upkeep of the church, but that was not to last indefinitely. Eliza was a generous benefactor of her church; something for which Will Ogilvie would later criticise her. For some time now, the city had been losing its long-established Armenian population to other burgeoning centres of commerce; the opportunities for profitable enterprise had become far greater in Bombay and even further afield in Calcutta. Many of the families who had been there when Eliza was growing up had already left Surat for good – and the drain on its mercantile establishment was set to continue for many years to come.

The Armenians are a nation in diaspora, and of necessity have always been sensitive to changes in trading conditions or in the political climate. They are found scattered throughout the world but, like the Jews, wherever they have settled they have retained their cultural identity and are proud of their nationhood. The close-knit Armenian community in Surat grew out of the very earliest beginnings of their Indian diaspora. Well before the Hon. Company began its military forays into the farthest recesses of the subcontinent, like the Zoroastrian Parsees, these Christian migrants from Persia were already well-established and well-tolerated within all the Princely courts and Mughal cities of India.

Though the historic homeland of Armenia has suffered throughout the centuries from its geographical situation at a cultural and political crossroads, the dispersal of the Armenian population in modern times can be said to date from 1604 when the citizens of the old city of Julfa in present day Azerbaijan, were forced, under threat of death, by Shah Abbas I of Persia to abandon their homeland and settle in his country. This forcible relocation brought them closer to the Indian subcontinent and opened up new trading possibilities just at the moment of Christian European expansion into Asian markets. Following the arrival of the dispossessed Armenians in Persia, occasional episodes of religious persecution occurred which caused spasmodic waves of migration to the south. Western India – and Surat in particular – became the destination of choice for the Shah's reluctant citizens.

One version of the story of the 1604 exodus describes how Shah Abbas, leading his mighty army through Armenia, came upon the magnificent city of Julfa. At the time it was home to between three and four thousand Christian households – a huge population in those days. The Shah coveted the wealth generated by the Armenians' silk industry and realised the economic benefit they might bring to his own country. So he simply gave the whole population of the city three days to pack up their belongings, then he destroyed their homes and marched them back to Persia. According to some sources as many as 300,000 Armenians were taken into exile.

Another version makes the Armenians the victims of the Shah's rear-guard scorched-earth tactic against the pursuing Turkish army – dispossessed of their lands, taken into exile and dying in thousands from starvation along the way. Whatever the truth of the matter, what is certain is that when they arrived in Persia, the Shah granted his new subjects good land at Isfahan. Here, on the south bank of the Zayandeh Rud, they founded the city of New Julfa where, ever since, they have been allowed to practise their religion; most of the time without interference. The new city prospered and it still exists today, populated by Armenian Christians within Muslim Iran. It has an Armenian school and a dozen or so Armenian churches. The citizens dress in accordance with Iranian law but they have otherwise kept their Armenian culture and language – a Christian population, living and thriving within the Islamic state in an admirable example of tolerant biculturalism.

During seventeen centuries of tribulation the Armenian Apostolic Church, the world's oldest national church, has been the glue that has held their nation together, despite their homeland having long been dissolved within the fluid borders of the younger nations of the region. Much of the historic Armenian homeland is now located within Azerbaijan, Iran and Turkey. Since the break-up of the Soviet Union, a new, independent and democratic Republic of Armenia has emerged. But unfortunately, over many years, within the wider region of historic Armenia, a rich heritage of beautiful ancient art and centuries-old architecture has been deliberately destroyed in systematic and organised acts of state-sponsored vandalism motivated by jealousy, ignorance and guilt. Very recently, despite an international outcry, the vast cemetery of old Julfa (Jougha, in the Azerbaijani exclave of Nakhichevan), which contained tens of thousands of beautifully carved *khatchkar* (cross stones) and ram-form tombs, dating from the fifth to the seventeenth century, was razed to the ground and the memorials smashed to pieces. The ravages continue.

Through the years and across a global sweep of nations the Armenians have been respected for their mercantile, medical, musical, linguistic and artistic achievements. Over time the descendants of those early captives of the Shah began to spread out from their city of New Julfa; many Armenian families followed pre-existing trade routes to settle in western India, in and around Surat. It was in Surat, in 1608, that the 'Company of Merchants of London Trading into the East Indies' set up their factory. During its early years in Mughal India the Armenians were the most highly valued and trusted contacts of 'John Company', as the East India Company was beginning to be commonly known. A common religion, their well-established trading contacts, their linguistic talents and their literacy, all made them immediately compatible with and valuable to the *'feringhis'* of John Company. Under the later Mughal Empire, many more Armenians moved from Persia, either to escape persecution, to follow family and friends, or simply to seek their fortunes in the expanding markets of the subcontinent. Their arcane alphabet and written language, together with their trustworthiness, enabled them to set up a closed circle of reliable and responsible contacts which soon developed into an extensive banking network; they can justifiably claim to be the originators of the first merchant banks. Being able to transact business confidently with paper promissory notes instead of heavy coin proved invaluable to the cash-deprived 'Merchant Adventurers of the British East India Company'. The Company allowed the Armenians equal pay with Europeans as well as other special privileges and concessions, including an undertaking to fund the building and maintenance of an Armenian church in any British territory where their number 'exceeds forty souls'.

That Theodore chose an Armenian to conduct business on his behalf was not unusual among Company servants. It happened that the man he engaged was his future brother-in-law, Aratoon Baldassier, married to Eliza's older sister Guyane. When Theodore and Eliza met at Aratoon's house she was an orphan, as she mentions several times in their later correspondence. In 1817 Theodore would still be referring to her as a 'girl'. His description of her in his will as 'my housekeeper' would appear to imply that she was originally engaged for household duties, but given the ease of obtaining cheap domestic labour, and the number of servants usually allocated to each specific task in India, it is unlikely. In 1818 she reminds Theodore that she has been 'under [his] protection since 8 or 9 years'. Back in 1809 when he arrived in Surat, she was more than likely a very young girl, living in Aratoon's household as a dependent minor. Her exact age is not recorded but one thing is certain; had Eliza been older than about sixteen, Aratoon would have found her a husband by then to spare himself the expense of keeping her. He was not a wealthy man. Her date of birth could therefore be reasonably calculated as being between 1793 and 1795.

Eliza was literate, and her letters reveal that she taught the young Scot Farsi, 'Persian language' as she called it. Farsi was then the second language of India, a relic of the recent rule of the Mughal Emperors and still widely used in the old sacred port of Surat. This hints that a more likely beginning to their relationship is that he fell in love with her over the language lessons begun in her older sister's house. Whatever the case, they clearly met in Aratoon's house and she was young, exotic and very attractive. Theodore had the family talent for languages and Eliza may have offered to teach him Arabic or Farsi.

It is easy to picture the young Scot, finding himself once more in the family atmosphere he has missed since leaving his parents and siblings, becoming a frequent visitor and seeing Eliza often enough to kindle a desire that would not go away. Aratoon realises that the well-connected and intelligent young merchant has a flair for business as well as for languages and must have good prospects. It is definitely a match to be encouraged. At a stroke the marriage would remove a drain on his own purse and provide him with a close contact in the British establishment. The relationship between the two men changes from one of business to one of friendship. Theodore confides to him that he fancies Eliza. Aratoon passes the compliment on to the girl who is flattered and excited. The knowledge proves to be a powerful aphrodisiac and soon she is in love with Theodore. Marriage offers her the best chance of escape from her dependent position in her older sister's household.

Theodore must have realised early on that if he wanted Eliza he would have to offer marriage, if not one sanctified by the British Padre or another company official, then at least one celebrated in the Armenian Church. Though he was genuinely in love with her he may also have known that, in John Company's Indian territories, such a marriage could not be registered or legally binding. On their wedding day, Eliza left from Aratoon and Guyane's house, veiled, attended by her nieces, also veiled, as well as other relatives all in their traditional Armenian dress and accompanied by music and dancing through the narrow streets. Her maternal great-aunt, Mariam Khatchatoor, and another aunt, 'Khalah [maternal aunt] Ageenah', with a daughter, were also living in the city at the time. And most of the close-knit Armenian community would have turned out too, to take the bride on the short journey to meet her groom at the Armenian Church. The ceremony would have been followed by music and feasting.

Did William act as best man for his younger brother? We shall never know, but there was no shame or secrecy attached to such a union. It was a Christian church so there is no reason why he should not have attended the ceremony. The story of the capture and ransom of Robert Taylor's Armenian wife Rosa was still current news and Theodore would know that a marriage that might have been looked at in some quarters with disapproval was clearly well tolerated within the diplomatic service. Taylor's mixed marriage certainly did his career no harm; he was to rise within the service to become Political Resident in Baghdad, with an outstanding reputation for scholarship. His story may have inspired Theodore to apply for the Mocha posting.

When Eliza returned after almost four years, on the arm of her widely admired young husband, with two healthy children, she must have been very proud; she was now a married woman and very wealthy by local standards. She was living in one of the grandest houses in the Mughal Serail; her position in the community had been fundamentally altered by marriage and motherhood. She had a lot of catching-up to do. Aratoon and Guyane had at least three daughters, of whom the eldest was Johanna. Now Eliza's own 'little ones' had the chance to play with their cousins while she was chatting with her sister and her aunts. Many years later in Aberdeen, Kitty would christen one of her own daughters by the unusual name of 'Johan'; was this perhaps prompted by the stirring of a dim memory, of Johanna, the big cousin she had looked up to and loved, half a lifetime away in distant Surat?

One of the attractions of the city for Theodore, was the opportunity for doing business in the money-changing shops of the famed Surat *shroffs*. He had already turned a good profit on the specie he had brought back with him from Mocha. Now he was also savouring the prospect of the profits to be made from making forward purchases of commodities in the busy local markets. But the opportunities for pleasure and relaxation in Surat, within the lively British community and military garrison were an additional attraction, especially so after Mocha, where Buckingham had considered a party of seven Englishmen to be extraordinary.

Though Theodore had asked Aratoon to take a house for him and his family in the old 'Mughal Serail', most of his British friends were residents of Nan Poora. Their houses lay along the semi-rural southern boundary of the city, only just inside the Alampanah, and set back from the area where the courthouse and jail were situated. This locality consisted of a belt of well-cultivated land reaching back about three quarters of a mile to the east of the river. The houses were mostly detached bungalows with shady verandahs and spacious compounds. They boasted courtyards or blocks of separate servants' quarters and stables and were set within neatly ordered gardens. The landlords were a diverse mix of wealthy Hindus, Muslims, and Parsees.

Theodore's closest friends, the very sociable and popular couple, Thomas and Eliza Fraser, lived in Nan Poora in a house situated in a sizeable compound. Thomas was from a family well-known in British India. His father, Major General Fraser had defeated a large Mahratta force at Deeg in 1804. The general himself had been mortally wounded in the action. Thomas and his brothers grew up in the Sussex village of West Ashling. Whether because of their father's untimely end on land or because of their boyhood proximity to the sea, apart from Thomas, all the brothers chose to enlist in the Royal Navy. He chose the East India Company Civil Service and in 1816 was the Inspector of Sea Customs for Surat.

Mr and Mrs Frasers' house is shown on the Revenue survey map in the centre of a generous plot. It has an enclosed courtyard of buildings to the rear, probably consisting of stables and servants' quarters, a paddock to one side and orchards to the other. In front of the bungalow is a turning circle around which carriages and palanquins could circulate to drop or pick up guests right by the front door of the house. Next door to the Frasers, in an adjoining compound, lived Dr George Ogilvy, the garrison surgeon. He was another Scot and good friend, who Theodore would later call upon to attend Eliza and the children. Both these houses were owned and let by the Cazee, or Mufti, the Mohammedan judge of Surat. On the other side of the Frasers was the house owned by Hurgovindass, which Theodore had shared with his brother William in 1810. The key to the survey map identifies the trees at the rear of these properties as a 'thick jungle of custard apple trees'. Little more than two hundred and fifty yards away, through streets mainly inhabited by Parsee families, other Scottish friends, the Morisons, rented a large property from a Hindu landlord named Weetuldass. This too had a driveway with a turning circle to the front, an 'in and out' carriage way to the rear and was situated within neatly laid out gardens.

The only one of the seventeen 'garden houses' identified on the map by the letters A to Q and not rented by the British was listed simply as 'Madam Monte's'. It sounds like a gambling den or a brothel, but it turns out to have belonged to the very respectable widow of the late Dutch Resident. Some 600 yards or so farther to the south lived the Rev. Thomas Carr, still only a short walk away from the others but whose house appears on the survey map to have been a much more modest establishment. He was destined to be installed later as the first Bishop of Bombay. In 1816 though, he was simply a young Company chaplain to the Surat garrison, living in the city with his wife and growing family. The following year, as disclosed in Eliza's letters and documented in Company records, he would be called on to christen Kitty and Alexander in the garrison chapel of Surat Castle.

It was hardly surprising that East India Company Servants who had their wives and families with them preferred the greener *pooras* between the walls to the crowded *chucklas* within the Sheherpanah. Most of them came from minor landed gentry and would have been brought up in the well-treed British countryside. In Nan Poora, the spacious residences of the British mostly faced south towards the outer wall and open countryside but, because of their well-tended orchards and gardens, they could not have enjoyed far-reaching views. However, to the British community, including Mrs Postans, the shade provided by the trees was just as important as a fine outlook. In *Western India in 1838* she describes 'the rides around Surat' as 'delightful' and continues: '...long pleasant lanes, sheltered and woody, adorn the neighbourhood, while the open country, studded with villages, farms and plots of useful enclosure, affords constant interest and refreshment to the eye.'

Even the busy thoroughfares of the inner city had their shady byways and back alleys where a graceful tree or climbing shrub would occasionally outgrow its confines to peep over the top of a high wall and betray the tantalising presence of the hidden gardens within. Among some of the most densely populated *pooras* between the two walls, there were still many green areas of pleasure gardens, family burial grounds and farmland. Beyond the curving inner-city wall of the Sheherpanah, these eastern suburbs formed a wide crescent-shaped tract, clinging intimately to the back of the inner city and shielding its dusty buildings from the more exposed hinterland. Here lay a motley assembly of hamlets, farms and dwellings, all forming a defensive ring to the east, sparsely populated but all within the safety of the Alampanah.

As soon as Surat was ceded to them in 1799 the British lost little time in taking over the whole of the Mughal administrative structure of the city. In his diary for Monday April 28th 1800, Lachlan Macquarie, later to be first Governor of the Australian colony of New South Wales, records that: 'The Honble. The Governor having received orders from the Earl of Mornington Governor General of Bengal to proceed forthwith to the City and District of Surat for the purpose of new modelling the Constitution and Government of that Town and its Dependencies, the present System in both being found very defective and inadequate; Governor Duncan... intended Setting out tomorrow for Surat, and would embark very early in the morning at Mahim on board the Bombay Frigate.'

It seems then, that vigorous constitutional reform was among the very first changes to be made by the British in Surat. They were careful to preserve the right of her citizens to choose to be tried under Muslim law, administered by the Cazee and to fly both flags at the Adawlet Court. Unfortunately they were not so conscientious as to preserve her beautiful architecture. Already deteriorating by 1816, this would be further neglected over the ensuing years and subjected to the ravages of fire and flood. This is one of the things that led Mrs Postans to the opinion that the academic interest in Indian culture shown by earlier Company servants was not shared by those of her own day, or by the influx of free-traders bent solely on making a profit. In *Western India in 1838*, she laments the disappearance of Surat's polyglot population and with it the city's mercantile heritage: 'Now, in common with all the cities of Western India which were famed for oriental commerce in olden times, Surat is humbled to the dust. Her palaces are crumbling remnants of the past, her gardens are tangled with the weeds of desolation, her revenues are decreased and her population is scattered among distant lands.'

In another of her books, *The Moslem Noble*, Mrs Postans is fulsome in her praise of the Mughal cultural heritage, and she deplores the ruinous effect of British rule: 'The Mahomedans had ever taste for the beautiful; the sites of their cities and the exquisite delicacy of their architectural decorations are proofs of this... But as the Moslem power gave place to the British we find ruin and devastation.' The decay of much of Surat's Mughal architecture had actually begun long before the city was ceded to the British, but evidently the British did little or nothing to halt the decline. However, in 1822, through the phenomenal combination of fire and flood, natural forces were to accomplish a more rapid demolition of the ancient city's buildings and commerce than could ever have been made possible by man.

Within the Bombay Presidency of Theodore's day, all the Europeans seem to have enjoyed a very generous Christmas break. He was in Surat for the whole of December and January and it was not until the very end of January 1816 that he started looking for accommodation for the family's return to Bombay. He wanted to rent a two-storeyed house in the Fort, with accommodation for Eliza and the children. A note in his letter book dated Saturday 27th January 1816 records that he had written to Boyce, his wine merchant, about the matter but he stresses that he needs a 'good comfortable house' which is not too small. At this point he is clearly planning that they should be in Bombay on or just after February 15th:

'Wrote to Boyce – to take me a good comfortable house in the fort, at a moderate rent, if possible not to exceed 100 Rupees per month, but did not limit him to that – his answer must reach me by the 8th of next month by which time at latest I should leave this – an upper roomed house preferable, and rent to commence on the 15th Proxime – Baxters house would not do being small and the rent high.'

It seems that Boyce did not come up with anything suitable. By Friday February 3rd, time is running out; they really need to leave Surat soon and so he turns to Eliza for help: 'Eliza wrote to Khumburzeefuh about taking a house for us in the fort – one of her own if vacant – requested an answer immediately with particulars of rent &ca &ca.'

Theodore uses the first person plural, 'us'. He needs to be near his new office in the Fort and he wants his family with him. Besides arranging for their accommodation in Bombay, there is still some 'Company' business to be attended to before they can leave. On Wednesday 8th, he writes a letter about Factory expenses to Ramsay, the new Resident, and sends it 'Per Salim Musood's Dow about to sail for Mocha'. On the following Saturday he asks Forbes & Co.'s agent, Dinshaw Eduljie, to advance Aratoon four thousand rupees on 'the mortgage of his *pattamar Mary*'. Theodore is a guarantor for the loan, and it is to his credit that, four years later, even as he lies dying aboard the *Blenden Hall*, he does not forget his friend and brother-in-law, Aratoon. At his dictation Mrs Dickinson would write:

'It is my wish that the bond dated Surat 10th February 1816 for Surat Rupees 4000 lent by me to an Armenian there by the name of Arathaon Buldaseer on the Mortgage of his Patamar *Mary*, may be considered as null and void, as it is my belief that the poor man's circumstances can never enable him to discharge it. The amount having been advanced at my desire by Dunshaw Edelga, my estate is of course responsible to him for the same.'

Four thousand rupees was a considerable sum of money then – more than four hundred pounds sterling; when he lent Aratoon the money, his 'Armenian protégé' became considerably indebted to him – and like Ogilvie would feel obliged for friendship's sake to return this favour in any way possible. The following day being Sunday, Eliza had an opportunity to pay a last visit to her church and take leave of the *vartaped* and her friends in the congregation. Having said their warm farewells to her family over the weekend, the Forbes household were ready to quit Chellabee's house. Within a matter of days they would be setting up home in the Fort area of Bombay, and Theodore would be starting work at the widely respected House of Forbes & Co.

Chapter 10

Forbes & Co., 1810 – 1816

Town Hall and St. Thomas's Church, Bombay, c.1820.

10

Bombay, 1816

On 10th February 1816, Theodore, Eliza and the children left Chellabee's house and embarked for Bombay. Amid a storm of hugs and kisses and shouted goodbyes they waved farewell to Eliza's family in the Old Mughal Serail. The conditions were still pleasant for sailing along the coast to Bombay and they would have come in to the harbour of Mahim, which was nearer and much more convenient than the Fort Stairs for small country ships arriving from the north. In Mahim, naval cutters, frigates, Company *pattamars* and other country ships could come and go freely. From there the family and their servants would travel on to Bombay in a variety of carts, carriages and palanquins. It was not far to Bycullah from Mahim and, should the children be tired there was sure to be a friendly welcome from Khumburzeefuh. She would happily take in the weary travellers, before they travelled on to their accommodation in the Fort.

Theodore's new office was in Forbes Street, close to the centre of town. Wherever the family found lodgings within the Fort he would not have to walk very far to work in the morning. He was already well-known and well-liked; at almost every turn he was likely to see a familiar face and receive a cordial greeting. When he set up home with Eliza and the children, Charles Forbes was in Europe but Bombay was buzzing with trade. Three years after the passing of the Charter Act, free merchants and their ladies were flocking to the Presidency. Under the management of the senior partner, John Stewart, Forbes & Co. was profiting from the increased business coming their way. For the enterprising, the opportunities for rapid enrichment were many. The sudden growth in the British population had resulted in a soaring demand for 'Europe goods'. They arrived on ships inbound from the Cape, and were attended by a flurry of selling and buying. Some supercargoes would be selling goods they had brought with them and then buying local goods to carry farther east to Bengal, or even to China and the Far East. Others would be bringing Chinese goods from the east to send home in their recently emptied holds and some would advertise London-bound passenger berths for the return journey. The House of Forbes & Co., with interests in shipping, as well as banking, was ideally placed to take advantage of any of these new opportunities.

Forbes and Co. still conduct business from within the Fort area of modern Mumbai. It is the oldest registered company in India, and one of the oldest anywhere in the world. Theodore rightly felt honoured to be asked to become a partner, and it seemed to him that he was arriving at an opportune moment when the general increase in trade might bring about a corresponding increase in his own wealth. It was an offer that he felt he could not refuse. When he accepted the appointment, he was living in Mazagaon with Henderson and Wedderburn; Eliza and the children were in Khumburzeefuh's house in Bycullah and so the question of the suitability of his wife and family had not been raised. It was not until now, six months later, when they returned from their Christmas break to live together in the Fort that his domestic arrangements had come under scrutiny. While the proximity of Theodore's new lodgings to the offices of Forbes & Co. was welcomed by his partners, the presence of his mixed-race family was not.

Forbes & Co. acted as bankers to a great number of civil servants and army officers who deposited their monthly pay 'hoondies' with the House, confident that a bill drawn on their Forbes account would be acceptable to any number of merchants throughout the Presidency, to obtain cash from the native *shroffs*, or remit a bill to family at home for monies to be drawn on Forbes & Co. in London. Bullion or coin was always in short supply in India, and so trustworthy bills of credit were extremely important to the viability of the whole economy. This part of their business was vital to the success of Forbes & Co. as a whole. When banking business from the wave of new free merchants began to contribute substantially to the profits of the House, the new value of the new arrivals became increasingly important. The good opinion of the recently arrived merchants and their ladies was eagerly sought by the companies competing for their business. Any hint of louche behaviour or impropriety on the part of one of the partners could affect the profits of the House, to the detriment of all their pockets. This change in social attitudes was so rapid that it was destined to take Theodore by surprise and force him to reassess the likelihood of building a prosperous mercantile career alongside his happy marriage.

Enthusiasm at home for the newly freed trade to the East Indies had been growing rapidly and the enthusiasm was not confined to the Port of London. Soon, provincial ports also began sending ships out to Bombay and beyond. *The Asiatic Journal and Monthly Miscellany* reported that: 'In the year 1814 Liverpool dispatched only one [private] ship to the East Indies and that ship was of 512 tons. In 1817 however we find her sending to the same quarter no less than twenty-six ships of which the tonnage was 10,876 tons.'

The article goes on to describe the extraordinary public interest in the success of these ground-breaking provincial enterprises: 'The first ship fitted out for the East Indies direct from Hull returned to that port with a valuable cargo. On entering the New Dock the spectators, who were exceedingly numerous, gave three cheers and the bells rung the whole of the day.' Many of the spectators would no doubt have made spectacular profits from investing in the enterprise. The dangers which might be met with at sea, the lack of communication and the suspense of waiting for the first sighting of sails on the horizon were all forgotten in a joyous celebration of the success of the enterprise. The origin of the optimistic saying 'When my ship comes in' is plain to see.

Forbes & Co. had been founded in 1767 by Charles Forbes's uncle, John 'Bombay Jock' Forbes. Their father was Bombay Jock's younger brother, an impoverished clergyman. Their Uncle Jock never married and had no heir. His namesake and eldest nephew, John, was tragically drowned in the China Sea in 1787 and a few years later Jock invited the next brother, Charles, to come out to Bombay and help him in the running of his burgeoning business. Charles took up his uncle's invitation and set sail for India. When he joined the firm he was an impecunious young bachelor.

Before long, Uncle Jock realised that Charles was more than capable of managing the firm without him, and so he retired to Britain, leaving his nephew in charge. Back at home the ageing *nabob* busied himself in spending the large fortune he had amassed during his years in India. He was generous with his wealth and, like so many of the wealthy entrepreneurs of his day, his new-found riches inspired him to share his fortune with those less fortunate than himself. Bombay Jock originated from Bellabeig by the banks of the River Don in Aberdeenshire. In Scotland he repurchased and improved the family estate of Newe in Strathdon, Aberdeenshire, and generously endowed a number of Aberdeen charitable institutions, including donating ten thousand pounds, almost the entire cost, to the building fund for the new asylum for the insane. When in London, he still lived in some opulence in his house in Fitzroy Square.

Meanwhile in Bombay, Forbes & Co. was prospering under Charles's management; the House bankrolled many of the British Government's military undertakings in India, and in the closing years of the eighteenth century had advanced huge sums for their campaigns. Amongst other adventures they helped to fund the pursuit of the second Anglo-Mahratta War, in which the interests of the Bombay Presidency were involved. Soon Forbes & Co. was perceived as being part of the Bombay establishment, and its head was admired and respected by British and native populations alike; Charles had amply rewarded his uncle's faith in him.

Though not blessed with conventional good looks, Charles Forbes was dynamic and personable, with good friends across the divides of race and class. He must have been considered to be the most eligible bachelor in the Bombay of the time. But out of all the pretty young ladies who were pushed in front of him to tempt him into matrimony none seemed to suit. As the new century dawned however, the young managing partner of the House of Forbes was in love; not with one of the young belles of Bombay, but with a widow, three years his senior and mother of four young children.

Elizabeth Cotgrave was the widow of William Ashburner, a barrister and editor of the *Bombay Courier*, who had died suddenly, aged twenty nine, on September 7th 1798. Mrs Ashburner was beautiful, sophisticated and accomplished, a devoted mother and only twenty-seven-years old. It is not surprising that the twenty-four-year old Charles soon fell under her spell. When her husband died Elizabeth already had three young children and a fourth was expected. She returned to London to place her oldest son in school. There, the following year, her fourth child, William Ashburner's posthumous daughter Elisabeth, was born.

Two years later, back in India to oversee her late husband's estate on the Island of Salsette, Elizabeth accepted Charles's proposal of marriage, and within a year the couple had produced their first son. They named him John, after both her own father, killed in action at the Battle of Cuddalore in 1783 and Charles's late lamented older brother. Charles's Uncle Jock, in his house in Fitzroy Square, must have been delighted at the news from Bombay, and the choice of name for the little Forbes. Charles had produced a male heir, his namesake too, a great-nephew who would ensure that the name John Forbes would be carried forward onto the next page of the familial balance sheet. He must have been more than pleased with his nephew; not only had the profits of the family firm increased under Charles's management, but so had the stock of family members to ensure its future.

Charles's prestige and status increased as the House prospered. He became a leading member of Bombay intellectual society. In 1804, together with that eminent man of letters Sir James Mackintosh, Recorder of Bombay, and his son-in-law, William Erskine, he founded the Bombay Literary Society, to which Theodore and most of his circle of friends later belonged. He was also instrumental in raising a public subscription to fund the publication of James Horseburgh's hydrographical observations and marine charts, so vital in the age of sail. The two men were to remain close friends well into old age and retirement.

Mr and Mrs Forbes regularly attended the races at Bycullah and Charles became an enthusiastic and generous sponsor, putting up prize money as well as keeping a stable of winning horses. He could always be relied on to support worthwhile local charities and public appeals. It seems that he was respected – even revered – by both the European and the native populations of Bombay, not merely on account of his wealth and generosity but also because of his innate kindness. Respect for him among the natives of Bombay was such that he was widely known as 'Farbes Sahib'.

In 1829, James Silk Buckingham dedicated his *Travels in Assyria, Media and Persia* to him, describing him as 'the warm and steady friend of our Asiatic fellow-subjects in India, as well as the benevolent advocate and promoter of the freedom and happiness of man, without distinction of colour, caste or country' and many years after his death a book about him, *Forgotten Friend of India, Sir Charles Forbes, 1ˢᵗ bart.* was written by Ruttonjee Ardeshir Wadia, a member of one of the families of eminent Parsees of Bombay who were so closely involved in the early success of Forbes & Co. and still are to this day.

Wealthy, respected and contented, there was little to unsettle Charles Forbes's comfortable private life in Bombay until 1810, when the troubling news came from England that his thirteen-year-old step-daughter Mary Ashburner had been abducted by her guardian, a Mrs Morgan, and taken to America. Luke Ashburner, brother of Elizabeth Forbes's late husband William, was married to a Sarah Price Morgan and her family had connections in Massachusetts. It seems that the girl's 'kidnapper' may have been a member of her Aunt Sarah's family, but what is certain is that Charles and Elizabeth Forbes had not given their permission for the girl's removal from England. It was widely rumoured that Mrs Morgan intended to marry the young heiress into her own family in America. But since the Morgan family were staunch Methodists, it may have been more of a custody battle to do with continuing Mary's education within a dissenting household, rather than abandoning her to what they may have considered to be the malign influence of the established Churches of Scotland or England.

Elizabeth Forbes's meek looks in her portrait by Sir William Ross evidently belie her strength of character. As soon as she heard of her daughter's abduction, she rushed to book the first available passage to England. When she sailed she took the two youngest children, George and Katherine, with her. Suddenly Charles was bereft of his family. He was left in their large house in the Fort with dozens of servants to wait on him, a company to run, but little companionship to enjoy. Elizabeth had the needs of her two children to occupy her on the voyage. In the absence of any further news, she also had the whole of the long sea voyage to worry about her oldest daughter and to plan her course of action. As soon as the ship dropped anchor off Deal, she hurried to London, to Number Nine Fitzroy Square, where her older boys had been left in the guardianship of Bombay Jock. Fortunately, funds were instantly made available to her to follow her daughter across the Atlantic.

Emotional as Elizabeth's reunion with her boys must have been, it was not long before she had arranged for the two younger children to be taken care of in London. She soon picked up the trail of Mrs Morgan and Mary and, for the second time, embarked aboard one of the great ocean-going sailing ships; this time, one bound from England to America. She arrived safely. It did not take her long to track down her missing child and obtain custody. She wasted no time in once again crossing the Atlantic under sail and by the middle of 1811 had returned to Fitzroy Square with Mary, now nearly fifteen-years old. Excepting short sojourns between voyages, Elizabeth had been constantly under sail for a total of almost fifty two weeks – a full year.

Whether it was because he had always planned to return to England and enter parliament, or whether it was because his house in Bombay had lost its warmth without Elizabeth and their little ones, Charles decided to quit India.

On October 16th, shortly before he embarked for England, He was accorded a stunning send-off with a huge banquet and 'entertainment'. It was attended by all the leading lights of Bombay society. At the 'entertainment' in the Bombay Theatre, illustrated here on page 255, General Malcolm, presiding over the occasion, declared Charles to be 'a fine representative of a British Merchant' and continued that 'everyone who did business with Forbes made money'. This was less than two months before Theodore's appointment to the Mocha Residency was announced. As a young man of evident promise and as a relative of Charles, as well as a fellow member of the Bombay Literary Society and the Bobbery Hunt, he must have attended the banquet. On board the ship *Caroline* with Charles went his favourite horse, John Bull, Peninsular war veteran and famous mount of his outings with the Bobbery Hunt. The horse's portrait can be seen on the right hand wall of Rowlandson's depiction of the interior of the Sportsman's Hall in the *Adventures of Qui-Hi? In Hindostan*, illustrated here on page 176.

When Charles arrived in England he had not seen Elizabeth or his younger children for more than eighteen months. It must have been a great relief to them all to be reunited at last. By this time he was wealthy enough to buy a seat in parliament and almost exactly a year after he left Bombay he was elected MP for Beverley in the East Riding of Yorkshire. The Reform Bill would not be passed until twenty years later and Beverly was still, by modern standards, a notoriously corrupt constituency; Charles had to pay out ready money for his seat. While

Uncle 'Bombay Jock' attended to improvements on the family estate at Newe in Strathdon, Aberdeenshire, Charles and Elizabeth took up residence in his house in Fitzroy Square until, in 1813, they moved into nearby Number Three, just in time for the birth of another son, James Stewart Forbes.

Charles had left John Stewart in charge of the House, and accepted with relief the resignation of another partner, James Kinloch, whom he had described in a letter to his Uncle Jock as 'malade imaginaire'. With both Forbes brothers away, John Stewart 'of Belladrum' had been left as managing partner and was living in Randal Lodge, the Bellasis family house on Malabar Hill, mentioned by Buckingham as being the scene of Mr and Mrs Stewart's many 'convivial parties'. Stewart was yet another of Theodore's Aberdeen connections and was now his senior in the House. He came from Banffshire, close to Haddo, and his family were connected by marriage with Theodore's mother's family, the Morisons of Bognie.

Very soon after his return with Eliza, Theodore could see that Bombay was beginning to shake off the liberal tenets, by which its largely masculine British population had formerly been self-regulated. In their place a new feminised wave of social conventions and order of precedence was beginning to be introduced. He could not have handed Eliza to table or partnered her to a ball anywhere in the Presidency; it is unlikely that any well-bred English woman would even have deigned to sit in the same room with her, let alone be handed to the same table. Here he was then, with impeccable social connections, plenty of money and brilliant prospects; yet he was unable to take his wife to any of the dinners, dances and private parties taking place almost daily. How could he bear to see either his dear Betsey or his darling Kitty snubbed and shunned by people who were his social inferiors? Yet these were the very people on whose patronage the success of the House now depended. Theodore was living openly with the woman he loved and their growing family. Although he might be happy with this domestic arrangement, his partners were not.

The unpleasant duty of cautioning Theodore about the provision he had made for his household fell to the lot of John Stewart, who agreed that his current arrangements reflected badly on the House and wrote to Theodore asking him to conduct himself 'with due propriety' and to behave always with 'a view to the House's reputation'. This meant that he should not continue to keep Eliza and the children with him in the Fort. It is tempting to speculate as to whether such an edict would have been issued by Charles, who had always championed the rights of the native residents in the Presidency. 'The more I see of my own countrymen, the more I like the natives of India,' he would declare in an address to the House of Commons on May 4th 1830. But despite his charm and his talent, it was soon made clear to Theodore that he must give up either his beloved Betsey or his new career, and with it his hopes of making a fortune. For the moment he was undecided. He had already invested a large amount of money to buy into his partnership in the House. Considerable sums that could not be realised at short notice were already laid out in ventures from which he could not withdraw.

Happily for him, he was given a temporary answer to his quandary; by June 1817 Eliza knew that she was pregnant again. The couple agreed that it would be better that she should return with the children to her family in Surat for the remainder of her pregnancy and 'confinement'. Theodore promised that he would join her there at the beginning of December for his annual leave. A letter from his secretary, Jagunnanth Wissvananth, reveals that on July 17th 1816 Eliza took out a loan of five hundred Rupees for her personal use, borrowed on Jagunnanth's security at the time of her return to Surat. Almost a year later he complained to Theodore that 'Since her Ladyship proceeded to Surat' she had not paid him anything – the full amount, plus interest was still outstanding. He was desperate, he said, because he was in imminent danger of imprisonment for the debt. This is the first hint of Eliza's extravagant habits, which Theodore seems to have countenanced in the early years of their marriage, but which would later exasperate him and become a constant source of worry to them both.

After Eliza had decamped to Surat with the children, a good number of the servants – and the cash borrowed from Jagunnanth – the large 'upper-roomed House in the Fort' must have seemed very empty. As soon as they had gone Theodore assured his partners that after spending the Christmas holiday with his family in Surat, he would return to Bombay unencumbered. After their departure he jumped enthusiastically onto the merry-go-round of British expatriate society. 'The dinners, balls, and concerts it were endless to recite' recalls James

Silk Buckingham of the time when he had been thrown into the midst of Theodore's circle.

According to his friends, Theodore was never short of female company and was an enthusiastic participant in the dinners, dances and balls, which were an almost daily occurrence, but he also enjoyed the more masculine pastimes on offer. These were the glory days of the Bobbery Hunt, of which he was a keen member. The hunt was described by Robert Grenville Wallace: 'The word bobbery in the Hindostannee language signifies noise and the members of the bobbery hunt are true to their designation, spreading wherever they go the loud tones of well-tuned uproar.'

The Bobbery Hunt was more than just a pack of hounds and a few hunt servants. It was a well-attended men's club with a mixed pack of hounds, a clubhouse equipped with bathing pool and dining facilities and a good wine cellar. The members were notorious for their riotous behaviour and daredevil escapades. Kitted out in cream linen coats with blue silk-velvet buttons done up to the neck, and sporting matching blue velvet caps and collars embroidered with the emblem of a running fox and the words 'Bobbery Hunt' embroidered in silver thread, the young writers of John Company and budding *nabobs* of Bombay found an outlet for their high spirits in riding to hounds in the pursuit of jackals and wolves or the dangerous wild buffalo or boar. However, according to James Douglas in his *Glimpses of Old Bombay*, at the time that Theodore re-entered Bombay society even the races at Bycullah were being tailored to the wishes of the newly-abundant females of the Presidency:

'In 1816, for the purpose of attracting the fair sex, the Bombay Races were held no longer in the morning, but in the afternoon.' They had formerly started at 4am to avoid the heat of the day. The prospect of early rising did not apparently appeal to the 'ladies lately arrived from England'. Some years later, the *Bombay Gazette* published a little ditty entitled 'Lost Gaiety of Bombay'. The poem tells how in 'olden times our Bombay Races commenced at daylight, spite of fog and dew', it was not for gain in the old days but 'gentlemanly racing for amusement' and, declares the poet, 'people little cared who won the plate'. The departure of Charles Forbes for England in 1811 might also have had something to do with the gradual decline of the Hunt and the races. He was such a generous patron and enthusiastic supporter of both events that his presence must have been sorely missed.

It was during this time of freedom from family ties, when Eliza and the children had gone to Surat without him, that Theodore was able to engage enthusiastically in the wider circles of Bombay society. There is no doubt that he still loved Eliza and he was devoted to his children, particularly to Kitty, whose first years in Mocha had so enchanted him. But he realised how he had missed the company of his British friends. They were quick to point out that his marriage to Eliza was not legally binding and advised him to find a new and legitimate British spouse. At first aghast at the suggestion, under their influence his loyalty to Eliza began to be eroded and by the time he left for his Christmas break his mind was firmly made up to heed Stewart's warning and conduct himself 'with due propriety' for the sake of the House's reputation.

By the beginning of December, when he set out for Surat on his annual leave, he had already formed a plan of withdrawal from a marriage he was now persuaded was at best an inconvenience and at worst a stumbling block. He would be with Eliza for the birth of their third child, but after that he was determined to put an end to their marriage, and he resolved never to bed his 'dear Betsey' again. This resolution was easy to make while he was living alone in Bombay, but it might prove difficult to keep once they were living as a couple again in Surat.

Chapter 11

Return to Surat

19th century engraving of an old house in Surat, built of teak.
Reproduced in Sir William Hunter's *History of India*.

11
Surat, December 1816

Eliza was halfway through the third trimester of her pregnancy and, knowing nothing of Theodore's intentions, she was looking forward excitedly to the Christmas holiday, and had been holding the old house in the Deriah Mahal in constant readiness to receive him. As soon as he walked through the door he was greeted excitedly by Kitty. Suddenly, here was all the affection and comfortable domesticity he had missed during the last few months. Eliza was overjoyed to see him, eager to discuss when the baby might arrive, and to know how long it would be before they could all go back to Bombay together. He did not have the heart or the courage to tell her the truth. After nearly four months without him, she had welcomed her husband joyously. In the face of such innocent reaffirmation of her love, his resolve began to slip away. How could he desert the three people he loved more than anyone in the world and who still needed him so much? How could he give up his stout, dark-eyed little son, 'a fine chubby little fellow' – according to his friend Will Ogilvie – just beginning to shuffle about on bottom or knees? And how could he not be there to enjoy his little girl's artless chatter and take pride in her progress? As soon as he arrived he was straight back in their world again, and part of it; a world of warmth and light and laughter; of music and feasting; of play and teasing and above all of tenderness. What a contrast to the world he had left behind in Bombay; hedged about by convention, cleverness, coldness and conceit.

Eliza was happy. Theodore's very presence seemed to fill the old house to bursting. But with him he also brought Antoon, Walloo and Tippoo the dog, along with a multitude of mysterious parcels – which were quickly hidden away. Everyone was laughing and smiling. They would shortly be celebrating Christmas, but both children had December birthdays too. There is no record of Kitty's fourth birthday present from her 'Papa', but only a few months later, Eliza mentions in a letter to him, Kitty's 'small scrutor' – Kitty's small *écritoire*, where she kept her personal possessions, and which nobody else was allowed to touch without risking her fury. Was this the present her Papa brought from Bombay in December 1816? If so, it would very likely have been one of the intricately engraved ivory boxes in the form of western furniture, produced in Vizagapatam on the Coromandel Coast, and sold throughout India for the sahibs to send back to their families in England; beautiful and costly examples of craftsmanship, as highly valued today as they were then.

While he was enjoying being once again at the centre of his loving family, the impending separation began to prey on Theodore's mind. In a letter written not long after his return, he makes an oblique reference to his unhappiness. He had written to his brother, Alexander, and he records that he '...congratulated him on being finally settled in life as a farmer – a station although not probably leading to the acquisition of a large fortune was nevertheless a very happy & enviable one – in short preferable to mine notwithstanding all its apparent advantages – requested he would write me frequently & always mention my brothers Andrew & James, to whom I had almost become a stranger, not having heard of them for a long time past.' The description of his own 'advantages' as 'apparent' gives more than a hint that he might already have been regretting his decision to accept the partnership with Forbes & Co. His doubts had evidently come flooding back as soon as Eliza rushed into his arms. His struggle to renounce his love for her was already beginning to wear him down.

The Anglican Christmas and New Year came and went, and the Armenian celebration on January 6th passed by with all the usual celebrations of a family happily together again. As the due date for Eliza's delivery approached, increasingly Theodore found himself seeking entertainment away from home. The social scene in Surat may have been less populous than that in Bombay but it was much more relaxed, and life there was generally thought preferable. There were just as many sporting, theatrical and social diversions for him to enjoy and now he had the added pleasure of his family around him. He was bathed in the warm friendship of Aratoon and Guyane and their wider family, to whom the door of Chellabee's house was always open.

He dined often in Nan Poora with his good friends Thomas and Eliza Fraser. Mrs Fraser would frequently impress on him that before long he must send Kitty to his parents in Aberdeen. It was not too soon to make arrangements to have her baptised into the Church of England.

Her passage should be booked so that she might arrive 'home' before her sixth birthday. The Frasers' own daughters had only just returned to India after a long absence in England and they were a credit to the system. Their friends the Morisons' little girl was due to leave within the year. What future would there be for 'dear Kate' in Surat, playing barefoot in the courtyard of the Deriah Mahal, brought up to speak a mix of Armenian, Hindi or Farsi with just a smattering of broken English? Their next-door neighbour, George Ogilvy, was a doctor and he warned of the ever present danger of smallpox; Theodore had seen the pock-marked faces of some of the local girls hadn't he?

When he dined at the Castle with the commanding officer of the garrison, General Laurence, the General's Aide-de-Camp, Lieutenant William Ogilvie, would often be there and he fully agreed with the Frasers' arguments. It seems that all his best friends and closest companions were of the same opinion, that it was only right that he should continue to support the mother of his children financially – but he really should consider himself free to find a British wife. Theodore accepted the proposition, but he worried to think of how bereft Eliza would be. She was his own 'dear Betsey'; a devoted mother and passionate lover, and with a self-confessed hot temper. He could not imagine how he could break the news to her that he must abandon her, and that eventually she must give up their little girl for ever. She would plead with him, telling him what he already knew, that she had married him: 'Not to love of Jewels money, riches etc but ...only heartly affection.'

He could not bear her hurt or her anger; surely the best course of action would be simply not to tell her for the moment? He could leave Surat on business while she was preoccupied with the baby and go back to Bombay alone. Everything had seemed so simple back there, when he was free of domestic distractions. He had planned to write her a tactful, even a loving, letter explaining why they must part. But he now began to formulate a plan to invent a business trip 'to the Northward about cotton'. He had already been in regular contact with John Stewart about the price of cotton in ports around the Gulf of Cambay and he could use the trip as an excuse for leaving Eliza and the children in Surat.

In the weeks after Christmas he idled the days away in Chellabee's house, playing with the children, sharing a loving but abstinent time with Eliza and became ever closer to her extended family. The occasional financial dealing with the Surat *shroffs* and dinner with his European friends passed the time pleasantly enough and distracted him from his plan to return to Bombay without his family. On January 27th, three weeks after the Armenian Christmas festivities, Eliza gave birth to their third child, another boy. Theodore had not yet thought of a name for the baby, and the household quickly fell into the habit of calling him simply 'baba' or 'Chotabhoy' – Hindi for little boy. Chotabhoy had arrived late in the evening by candlelight. Eliza was delighted with the precious child whom she was later to describe as 'like a diamond'. Fazagool took charge of the infant and by the time she had swaddled him and handed him to Theodore for his approval it was nearly midnight.

As soon as he could, he scratched a record of the happy event in his letter book under the date Monday 27th January 1817: 'This night at a quarter to eleven P.M. my dear Betsey was safely delivered of a boy.' Despite his resolution to leave her, she is still his 'dear Betsey' – as indeed she is six weeks later when he makes the next mention of her in his book. Had she read that entry, dated March 14th 1817, and been able to comprehend it, her happiness would have melted away in an instant: 'Returning rather merry from General Laurence's,' he writes, 'I was this night so imprudent as to know my Dear Betsey, being the only time since her confinement, and which I am firmly resolved shall be the last.'

Poor Eliza! Oblivious to his plans, she must have looked upon his drunken love-making with relief at the return to normal relations between them after the birth of the baby. All seemed to be going well for them and the pleasure she feels at the 'heartly affection' which once more exists in their marriage is reinforced just one week later as Theodore's 'resolve' falters again and, he writes, that he 'was last night again so imprudent as to have connection with my dear Betsey,' adding in a moment of sudden anguish, 'As the time approaches for the melancholy separation my spirits become more and more depressed.' So there it was – dispirited and depressed as he is by the prospect of a parting to which he is a reluctant party, he does not consider, even for a moment, putting it off. He is convinced that his only option is to put head over heart and break the bonds of his happy marriage.

The senior partners of Forbes & Co. had felt no compunction in compelling their new partner to abandon his Armenian wife and young family. This demand would have been considered outrageous had Eliza been fair-skinned and British. In British India at this time, only marriages conducted by a minister of the established Church of England or Scotland were registered and legally binding. It is easy to see why doubts were later expressed about Kitty's legitimacy. The practice of keeping a *bibi*, formerly widespread and well-accepted among Company Servants, was beginning to be regarded in many quarters with disgust. The resultant Anglo-Indian children's origin was evidenced at a glance by the colour of their skin and they would grow up to be treated with disdain. Mixed-race children in British India seem to have been more or less acceptable according to the depth of colour of their skin. DNA analysis carried out at Edinburgh University has established that Eliza's maternal grandmother was Indian; the likelihood that she herself may have been olive or brown skinned has gained further credence with the recurrence through the years of dark colouring in her descendants.

The diverse ancient religions, languages and culture of India, which had for so long enthralled learned Orientalists from Europe, were now increasingly reviled at all levels of British society and these altered attitudes were creeping into hitherto liberal expatriate communities throughout the whole Indian subcontinent. Founded on an unfaltering belief in British racial superiority and bolstered by the social aspirations of the newly-rich *nabobs* and their ladies, the trend had begun to gain momentum even before the Charter Act of 1813, while Theodore and Eliza were still living in comfortable but isolated domesticity in Mocha. After the passing of the Act it gathered speed and within a few decades it was to reach terminal velocity – universal acceptance.

'The world now has another fashion,' Eliza observes bitterly, when eventually she comes to grasp the reason for Theodore's desertion. She cannot know that the 'melancholy separation' being secretly planned by the man she loves, is shortly to be represented to her as a fact-finding tour of the cotton manufacturing cities of northern Gujarat. Theodore intends to start by visiting Broach [Bharuch] where his friend Henry Barnard is the magistrate and judge. He will go on to visit Cambay [Khambat], 'proceeding from thence to Baroda' [Vadodara], then Jumbooseer [Jambusar], Dollerah [Dholera] and Bhownuggur [Bhavnagar], from where he intends to sail direct to Bombay. Clearly he needs to justify this circuitous route to his new partners at Forbes & Co. At the same time, he does not want Eliza to know that he has no intention of returning for her. First he makes sure that everyone he knows in Surat is under the impression that at the end of his tour he will come back to collect Eliza and the children; the only exception is to be his friend Lieutenant William Ogilvie. For his plan to succeed he needs Ogilvie's complicity to corroborate the information he gives Eliza.

The day before he is to leave for Broach, he writes to John Stewart, and makes a précis in his letter book: 'Mentioned... the intention I had formed of proceeding to the Northward, which I acknowledged I was anxious to do, not with a view to amusement nor the gratification of an idle curiosity, but from the desire of obtaining some information which might eventually prove beneficial to the House... My future progress, from circumstances he was aware of, would not be so dilatory as it had hitherto been – Requested him to address me always at Surat in the care of Lieut. William Ogilvie, Aide-de-Camp to General Laurence.'

The 'circumstances' Theodore says that Stewart is aware of and which have supposedly hindered his return to Bombay, are a reference to his need to comply with the senior partner's demand that he should not bring Eliza and the children back with him. His request that Stewart should address him care of Lieutenant Ogilvie is prompted by the fear that Eliza would read any letters that might arrive addressed to him at home, and so learn of his deception. His assertion in the same letter that he hopes to acquire information 'beneficial to the House' seems somewhat disingenuous for, as entries he is shortly to make in his letter book make clear, the trip has been planned solely as a subterfuge to keep Eliza for as long as possible in ignorance of his plan to desert her. Of course he does not want his senior partner to think his ploy is a sign of weakness, so he has had to invent a sound reason not to go directly to Bombay. It has to be sufficiently plausible to be acceptable both to Stewart and to Eliza – who must not discover his deception until he actually reaches Bombay. He is determined to avoid any painful scenes with her because, as he acknowledges to himself, she just might induce him to change his mind.

Theodore's guilty conscience is made plain in his jottings. A few days before he leaves Surat he turns his attention to Eliza's financial needs. Dinshaw, from whom Theodore draws five hundred rupees for her expenses in his absence, was a prominent merchant in Surat. For years he had been trusted as Forbes & Co.'s agent there, as well as being a general credit broker for transactions between many other European residents and local tradesmen. A member of the extensive Parsee community, he came from a family destined to produce many distinguished scions in later years. Theodore usually records the sums of money drawn on Dinshaw factually in his accounts. But this entry is followed by an unusual aside which perfectly sums up his dilemma and his confused state of mind:

Wednesday March 26th 1817. 'Received from Dinshaw Eduljee the sum of five hundred (500) Rupees which is to be appropriated for the expenses of my dear Betsey and family until I can take measures for making a permanent provision for one possessing so many claims on me, and who is worthy of far more than I fear I shall ever have it in my power to do for her – She has proved a most faithful and affectionate partner to me for the past few years, and nothing but the absolute necessity of the thing can reconcile me to a separation from her – I consider her as a pattern of what a wife ought to be, and of whom few indeed are to be met with in this country, so much so indeed that if I should hereafter be inclined to marry I cannot flatter myself with being fortunate enough to obtain so excellent a permanent partner for life as she (poor girl) has proved to me a temporary one.'

The record of this transaction seems to be at odds with the usual business-like tenor of his entries; it has moved him to an uncharacteristically emotional outburst in which he first describes Eliza's wifely attributes in glowing terms and then, professes himself free to marry. Only five years ago he and Eliza placed crowns on each other's heads and exchanged rings during their wedding in the Armenian Church. He is married, yet this is a direct rebuttal of his wedding vows. It is the first instance of the confessional tone which is set to permeate the entries in his letter book throughout the whole of his trip 'to the Northward'.

On the 27th March he writes that he is planning to leave Surat for Broach on the 31st of the month, and that he anticipates the duration of his trip will be about a month in all. Aratoon is to accompany him, at least on the first leg of his journey. The only problem for him now is how to keep his emotions under control when he says goodbye to Eliza. He needs to convince her that he will be back very soon to collect her and the 'babas' – though he knows very well that he may never see her again.

Chapter 12

Deception, 1817

Baroche on the Banks of the Nerbudda in Guzerat.

From Plate 49 of *Oriental Memoirs* by James Forbes.

12

Surat, March 31st 1817

While Eliza was busy with little Chotabhoy and had her own friends and family close at hand, she was content for Theodore to mix with his British friends and return to her every night. She could never have imagined how often she and the children were the subject of their discussions or that she was now perceived as a problem. She alone remained in blissful ignorance of Theodore's intention to leave her. As far as she was aware, the family would soon be based in Bombay and then return to Surat only for their annual Christmas vacation. So she wanted to make the best of her remaining time in the Mughal Serail with her sister and aunts, and to give Kitty as much time as possible with her cousins. For now, in the cosiness of the old house, with her family and trusted servants around her, and her sister, her three nieces and Great-Aunt Mariam Khatchatoor to coo over Chotabhoy, or to play with Kitty and Aleck, she is in buoyant mood, looking forward to a happy future with an apparently contented husband.

With her help Theodore had prospered in Mocha and he could do so again in Bombay. She and the children would acquire a status that as an impoverished orphan she could never have aspired to, even in her dreams. Her ambition is to live in a 'country house' in one of the salubrious tree-clad residential areas such as Mazagaon, Bycullah or Malabar Hill. Theodore did not discourage these dreams because he wanted to keep secret the real purpose of his trip for as long as possible. As he and Aratoon prepared for their expedition, she still had no reason to suppose that anything was amiss. But it was a journey with one destination and two purposes: one journey in the interests of commerce; the other, an odyssey of deceit, which would only serve to prolong the agony of separation. Both will take him to Bombay without her.

The first step of Theodore's so-called fact-finding journey would take him to the old city of 'Broach', known today as Bharuch, situated on the banks of the River Nerbudda, the 'little journey of thirty-six miles' from Surat is described in Forbes's memoirs as 'delightful'. There is no record of how he travelled to Broach. There was a caravanserai halfway between the two cities, at Khim-Chokee, where travellers of all nations could get a bed and refreshment for themselves and their horses. Forbes describes it as 'a caravansary on the banks of the river Kim about half way to Baroche situated in so great a thoroughfare it is much frequented by merchants and travellers of all descriptions.'

It would be good to be able to say that when he set out on his journey to 'the Northward' he did so in fine fashion, splendidly mounted on the Arab horse, which he had shipped back from Mocha with Buckingham and Captain Boog; it would be satisfying to paint a picture of him cutting a dashing figure on his prancing steed with Aratoon at his side, and a colourful baggage train of peons, straggling in their wake. However, the picture presented by the pair was, more than likely, a very different one; it is probably safer, because most of the northern cotton towns they were to visit were small ports, to assume that they set sail together from the ghats or godowns of the old Mughal Serail in Aratoon's *pattamar*, *Mary*.

Aratoon's *pattamar* would have been able to leave from a landing stage very close to Chellabee's house and, who knows? Eliza and Fazagool may even have taken Kitty along the river bank to wave them off. Theodore had told Eliza that he would be back in Surat to collect them in a matter of weeks. In whatever style, or whatever conveyance he left Surat, the agitation he was feeling at a parting that he alone believed would lead to a permanent separation, and which, as he had so recently confided to the pages of his letter book, he found deeply depressing, must have affected his demeanour. But if Eliza noticed that he hugged Kitty for longer than usual or that his eyes glistened with barely-concealed tears, she could only assume that the unaccustomed display of emotion was further proof of his devotion to her and to the children. As he took leave of her for the last time, the pangs of guilt he was suffering would soon have led him to abandon any desire to prolong the painful moment. Almost certainly he would have wanted to slip below deck as quickly as possible and begin his journey in the privacy afforded by the basic cabin accommodation provided abaft the swift coastal vessel.

Her brother-in-law's presence must have helped convince Eliza of the sincerity of Theodore's promise that he would be sure to return to Surat within the month. As well as being master of the ship, Aratoon would be able to give Theodore many useful business contacts. He knew the cotton ports to the northward and, no doubt, he was acquainted with the merchants there. As soon as the pair reached Broach, Theodore made his way to the old Mughal courthouse called 'The Durbar'; the official residence of Thomas 'Henry' Barnard, judge of the Broach *Purgunnah* (Revenue area). Barnard, a bachelor, lived in some style with his *bibi* and their son, three-year-old Tom. The two men had many friends in common and much to talk about and Barnard would be sure to have given Theodore a hearty welcome and generous hospitality.

While he was staying at the *Durbar*, Theodore's letter book reveals how guilt and the fear of discovery were beginning to play on his mind. As the days passed pleasantly with his friend, he had time to mull over the impending separation and refine the details of his plan. He employed several strategies to deceive Eliza into believing that he had every intention of returning to Surat. He gave her little tasks. In one instance he asked her to find melons and forward them to him in Broach: 'The season for melons almost over but ordered strict search to be made for same & if found should be despatched immediately.' She complied happily, content to help in any way to further the ostensible purpose of his journey and support him in his new career. She bought melons and sent them to him in Broach as speedily as possible as a small contribution to his host's dining table.

The giving out and calling in of favours among fellows, friends and acquaintances was widely practised among the expatriates in the Hon. Company's territories. In this context and perhaps because the subject of their respective children had been a topic of conversation during his stay, within a few months Barnard was unhesitatingly to ask Theodore to take on responsibility for making the necessary financial arrangements for young Tom to be sent back to England. Choosing to send their little Anglo-Indian children to England to be educated was certainly not a cheap option for British fathers in discharging their parental duties; the passage home cost in the region of a thousand rupees or one hundred pounds sterling. Despite the distress of being separated from their mothers, there were thought to be two overwhelming reasons why being sent to England was considered to be advisable for boys and imperative for girls: firstly, it was widely accepted that the climate of India was a danger to the more delicate constitution and fair complexion of a child of European parentage; secondly, it was considered to be better for their prospects in later life that they should be cut off at an early age from the language and culture of their native mothers and servants. Theodore must have had similar considerations in mind when deciding what he should do about Kitty.

Before leaving Surat he asked Lieut. William Ogilvie to act as his intermediary with Eliza during his absence. He had already explained to his friend the importance of keeping secret his plan of returning to Bombay without her. Less than a week into his trip, on April 7th 1817, he wrote to Ogilvie from Broach, with explicit instructions: 'Hoped he would be able to impress her with a belief that I should return in Surat to take her down with me to Bombay – until the unpleasant task of revealing the real truth should come & which [should] be deferred until he hears of my actual departure for Bombay.'

In this one letter he has deftly shifted onto Ogilvie's shoulders the whole burden of the 'unpleasant task' of revealing his true intentions until some unspecified time in the future. Theodore had discussed his long-term plans with Mrs Fraser, but she is not party to his scheme of sailing for Bombay without returning to Surat. She seems to have taken it upon herself to further the project of sending Kitty to England and in this respect she intends visiting the family. So it is vital that she too should believe his subterfuge. Now, in a ploy clearly designed to ensure that she continues in ignorance and does not give his game away to Eliza or the children, he adds, 'Wrote also a short letter to Mrs Fraser... Said I should have the pleasure of seeing them in Surat again in about a week or so.' At the same time he sends 'short general letter to poor Eliza, enclosed in Ogilvie's & in which I said I should be in Surat in a week or so!' On the page, the exclamation mark is tiny but its significance is enormous – it is an open admission of the lie he has just told 'poor Eliza'. He closes with 'Kisses and remembrances to the little ones and love to Sister Khyanee and family'. It seems that his fear of discovery is driving him into an ever wider web of deceit. The involvement of Ogilvie in his deceit would surely be deeply wounding to the trusting Eliza if ever she were to grasp the full extent of their conspiracy.

The following day, April 8th, Theodore records that he has written to the newly married Michie Forbes, Charles's younger brother, recently arrived in Bombay with his bride. Michie had come from London where he had courted and won his step-niece, Mary Ashburner; the very same girl whose kidnap six years earlier had precipitated her mother's sensational dash from India to America and Charles's return to Britain. Mary Forbes was seventeen years her husband's junior. In a self-deprecating but somewhat toadying vein Theodore assures Michie that: 'By being associated with you in the firm of Forbes & Co., I flatter myself I shall possess a firm and sincere friend whose advice and ample experience cannot fail to be of the utmost benefit to so complete a novice as I am in all matters of business.' He goes on to explain his absence from the office: 'I came up to the Northward some time ago, both with a view of obtaining some little insight into the Cotton Trade, as well as for other reasons which I will explain when I have the pleasure of seeing you... You are I trust by this time comfortably settled in your brother's house... & I regret much not being on the Fort myself to give you what little assistance I might have been able in that or any other way.' He asks that should Michie wish to reply to him, he too should address him care of Barnard at Broach and he makes it plain that he does not intend to return to Surat.

Theodore struggles to reconcile his conscience with his actions, until at last the day comes when he and Aratoon are to leave Broach. Now he surely has to tell Eliza that he will not be returning to her. Yet he still cannot bring himself to make a clean break and he decides to tell her simply that he has been delayed. It takes him two days to compose a letter to 'the injured Eliza' along with one to each of the Parsee brothers Dinshaw and Munchershaw Eduljee in Surat: 'The above two letters were post paid, left open and put under cover of the letter to Eliza of this date for particulars of which vide below – with directions after perusal to put wafers in them & deliver them immediately.' This had given him an opportunity to spread further disinformation among the wider community. In the letters Eliza is 'to peruse' he tells the brothers, 'I intend to cross over by Sea from Bhownagghur to Surat, which I expect to reach about the end of this month.' The use of the imperative Latin instruction *vide* [see] is another instance of the confessional aspect of his notes, as if he or someone else might need to refer to it later.

The letter to Eliza he refers to, dated 11ᵗʰ April, is carefully composed to corroborate the information sent to the Eduljee brothers. It is found recorded in detail among other brief business transactions on the crowded pages of his book: 'Wrote also a general letter to the injured Eliza, hypocritically lamented that I could not be back so soon as I wished and intended… Having very unexpectedly received letters from Bombay directing me to proceed to Jumboseer, Dollerah & Bhownuggheer to see how our Cotton purchases are going on there – very disagreeable to me but cannot help it, besides a merchant, must go where ever his business leads him – should set out for Jumboseer with Aratoon early on Sunday morning & thence proceed by way of Baroda to Dollerah and Bhownugghur from which last place I shall proceed to Surat by sea and expected there once again the pleasure of saluting her and the little ones about the end of this month – and if possible before that time as I should get through the journey as speedily as possible – hoped she would not be so foolish as to give herself any uneasiness on account of my being obliged to stay away a little longer.'

The fictional 'disagreeable' orders that are supposedly preventing his return allow him to prolong the deceit; because he was only supposed to be away for a week, he had not packed enough clothes for a longer journey. He now sets Eliza another little task to resolve the problem of his lack of adequate underwear. He asks her to: 'Put up for me a scanty stock of Clothes, but must make the best shift I can with them until I can get back to Surat – Thought it better not to buy Dhoolees or Pantaloons here… I should be cheated to a certainty – she could buy them cheaper at Surat…'

At this point Theodore begins invariably to refer to 'Eliza' always with the additional epithet of 'dear', 'poor' or 'injured'. Never again is she referred to as his 'dear Betsey'. At the foot of the letter he has made a note of the affectionate manner in which he has signed off; he sends:

'Many loves and kisses from Aratoon and myself to herself & children' and to complete the litany of deceit he includes the rest of her family – 'Aunt Mukhanee – Sister Khyanee & family… and Salaams to Rustomjee Cheeneemeenee.' He has cunningly included Aratoon's name, to lend credence to his change of plan. He must have hoped that the warmth of his tender expressions of affection would convince her that he would come back to her –and it worked.

Before dispatching the packet to Surat, Theodore writes a covering letter to Ogilvie, and in it he is quite open about the reliance he places on his friend's discretion: 'Said I would leave this for Jumbooseer for Bhownugghur early on the morning of Sunday the 13th Instant – which intention I had communicated to poor Eliza in the enclosed letter which I requested him to deliver & treat the subject the best way he could – had mentioned to her that I should cross over from Bhownugghur to Surat by sea & expected to be in the latter place in about 15 or 20 days – i.e. – about the end of this month… he should be kept advised of all my future motions – put every confidence in his discretion – was sure he would let neither her nor my dear children want for anything that would make them comfortable – said he might make public my intention of proceeding to Bhownagghur, accompanied always by the assertion that I was to go thence to Surat again.'

After leaving Broach, it seems he makes no more self-recriminatory entries in the letter book. Perhaps the continuation of his journey has given him less opportunity to dwell on his duplicity, or perhaps he is too far from Surat to be within easy reach of postal services. In either case there are no more records of letters to Eliza during this trip and no further mention of his brother-in-law after saying that the pair are to set out for Jumboseer on April 13th.

Aratoon's *pattamar* is invaluable for this kind of port-hopping voyage and just under three weeks pass while the two visit Jumbooseer, Baroda and Cambay. On 30th April 1817, they are preparing to set sail once more, this time they are bound for Dollerah. Before they sail, Theodore dashes off a letter to Stewart at Forbes & Co. Before sealing it and putting it in charge of the captain of a ship bound for Bombay he makes a rough copy of what he has written:

'Merely to say that I leave this for Dollerah and Bhownagghur this afternoon and shall embark… for Bombay direct, where I expect to have the pleasure of seeing you by the 10th of next month.' As he sets down in writing his request that Stewart should impart to Michie 'the family reasons which have obliged me to protract my stay to the Northward so much longer than may appear to have been necessary for any useful purposes', his head, heart and hand seem to collude to punish the paper, and in a telling gesture of frustration and, perhaps, shame, his pen scores a deep line beneath the word 'family', that cuts right through the surface of the paper onto the leaf below. Evidently he has still not come to terms with a course of action which he knows will wound Eliza deeply.

Exactly one week later, on May 7th, he and Aratoon are sailing down the Gulf of Cambay close in to the sandy palm-fringed beaches of the approach to the port of Bhownagghur. This is where the two friends have arranged to part company. From there Theodore will take the first ship sailing direct to Bombay and Aratoon will sail a little farther south to the ancient port of Ghogha, described by Ibn Battuta in his *Travels* and famed for having the remains of an eighth-century mosque, the oldest in India. Aratoon had business to attend to in Ghogha before sailing home to Surat.

As soon as they reach Bhownagghur, Theodore writes once more to Dinshaw, ostensibly to give him final instructions about the financial provision he wants to make for Eliza. He refers to Eliza as 'Mrs Forbes' throughout and instructs his agent to pay her a generous monthly allowance of two hundred and ten rupees per month: 'I leave this for Bombay tomorrow,' he tells Dinshaw and invents a new excuse for not returning to Surat: 'The state of Mrs Forbes's health,' he lies, 'renders it necessary that she should remain in Surat with the rest of my family during the ensuing rains.' There is no evidence that he had received any news from Eliza, or anyone else, that she is unwell. The rest of the letter confirms that it is yet another ploy on his part to spare himself the task of telling her the truth. He knows her well enough to realise how humiliated she would feel if his desertion were to become public knowledge and so he tells Dinshaw that he is writing: 'Merely to recommend them [Eliza and the children] in the strongest manner to your attention, and I have more especially to request that you will afford Mrs F. your best advice on whatever point she may have occasion to consult you. Being confident that these wishes will be most cheerfully complied with on your part, I shall at all times be most happy to receive from you, accounts of my family and more particularly of Mrs Forbes's health.'

As the tortuous plan of deception unwinds through the medium of his guilty scribblings, it is impossible not to conclude that Theodore's desertion of Eliza was due not so much to a vein of cruelty in his nature, but rather to a fundamental weakness of character, coupled with a propensity – a talent even – for deviousness. It seems that financial gain and social advancement were his governing motives and peer pressure was the driver. Before he and Aratoon part company he writes another loving letter to Eliza, pretending yet again that he is suddenly prevented from returning to Surat because he has just received further orders to present himself without delay at the offices of Forbes & Co. in Bombay. He promises that he will come back for her as soon as his work allows. He knows it is a lie, but he seals his letters and hands the packet to Aratoon; the brothers-in-law bid each other farewell and God speed and go their separate ways – Aratoon to Ghogha and Theodore to Bombay.

Inscribed on back, The Parsee Priest's House, Rampart Road, Broach.
By a member of the Bellasis family.

The CASTLE, and HARBOUR of BOMBAY, from the Bunder Pier.   1810.

Presumed portrait of Theodore Forbes HEICS.

Born Bognie, Aberdeenshire April 1788 –
died at sea, Indian Ocean September 1820.

Inscribed 'Theodore?' on the reverse. One of four portraits of Forbes brothers in
one frame; the others being of Andrew, William and James Forbes.
Photographed by kind permission of the Brose family of Boyndlie.

Photo © Susan Harvard

Bobbery Hunt Tunic c. 1820.

Cream linen with blue silk velvet collar and buttons, with lettering and running fox embroidered on the collar in silver thread.

Meet of the Bobbery Hunt. Theodore was an enthusiastic member.

Sportsmen's Hall and Bath.

Bobbery Hunt tented dining on the Esplanade, November 1809. Theodore arrived in Bombay earlier in 1809. He was probably at this celebration.

© British Library Board.

Bobbery Hunt bonfire, June 1811. Six months after this celebration, Theodore was appointed British Commercial and Political Resident in Mocha.

© British Library Board.

'Qui Hi at Bobbery Hall'.
The portrait of Charles Forbes's horse 'John Bull' hangs on the right-hand wall.

'Qui Hi Shews off at the Bobbery Hunt'.

Illustrations from *The Grand Master or The Adventures of*
Qui Hi in Hindostan, 1816.

Engraving and aquatint by Thomas Rowlandson.

PART III

HEARTS & DIAMONDS

Chapter 13

Silence and Tears, 1817

Armenian Girl, from a painting by J F Lewis, Cairo c. 1860.

13

Bombay & Surat, May – September 1817

On Thursday May 8th 1817, Theodore embarked direct from Bhownagghur for Bombay, just as he had promised Michie Forbes he would. As the ship sailed out of the Gulf of Cambay, the mouth of the River Tapti lay open before them on the southern side. He recognised the lie of the land. It was the gateway to Surat; soon they were not far from the Surat Bar, close enough to be able to see the masts of the ships anchored there. Pangs of remorse must once again have assailed him as he imagined all the passengers disembarking into smaller craft to sail on up the river to Surat, just as he and Eliza had done when they first came back to the city. It was still only eighteen months ago. They were so secure then in each other's love; so confident in the strength of their marriage; so careful of their little ones. He could imagine his 'dear Betsey' waiting patiently, still confident of his return but ignorant of his intentions. He could picture Kitty's excited welcome when he stepped through the door. It was not too late to ask the captain to disembark him at the Bar. Soon Aratoon would be back from Ghogha with his letter. In his mind he could see the 'injured Eliza' eagerly snatching it from his hand; he knew she would be bitterly disappointed when she read its contents, but he also knew she would believe his lies.

This was his last chance to change his mind. He was so near, was he not tempted to return to her? It seems not. The opportunity passed and his resolve was firm enough to be able to continue the voyage in pursuit of a glittering future. The enviable offer of being a partner of Charles Forbes, the wealthiest and most widely-respected man of business in the Presidency was too good to refuse. And besides, he was by no means averse to returning to Bombay society, to partying with friends and to playing the field of newly-arrived British spinsters. As the ship breasted the turbulent waves of the Gulf, the ties of his marriage grew ever looser in its wake and the image of Eliza faded from his thoughts.

Aratoon returned from Ghogha alone. After going to his own house, he went straight round to the Deriah Mahal. The court was full of the chatter of women's voices and the rise and fall of carefree laughter drifted from the open windows. Eliza had friends staying in the house – a lot of friends. They were Armenian women but they were not the type that Aratoon could approve of. When Eliza saw that her brother-in-law was alone, her heart must have sunk with fear. Misadventure and accident, sickness and sudden death were all too common amongst the European population of India and there was Aratoon standing in the doorway alone. She took the proffered packet from him and he left her to read the contents in private. Neither of them yet realised that this was just the first stage of Theodore's carefully planned scheme to detach himself from them all.

While she recovered from her disappointment that he had gone to the Presidency without her, Eliza comforted herself that at least her man was safe. She could picture him now; at sea, on board a country ship well on the way to Bombay; he would be up on deck, his face and his hands reddened by the sun and the salt sea spray; the rest of him as white as a lily, just as she had seen him when they married and sailed to Mocha and as she had loved him when they sailed home with the children. As yet she had no reason to doubt his story and took the news that he was sailing direct to Bombay with resignation. They had been apart for a whole month but she was able to recall with some satisfaction that when they parted, 'we were heartly love each another'. She ached for him and imagined that he felt the same. Surely the business that had called him to Bombay must be urgent or would he not have hurried back to her? As yet there was no real reason for her to worry about his loyalty, she knew how difficult it was for him to resist her, and she did not doubt his love for the children. How could she ever imagine that he had decided to set aside their sacred marriage vows and desert them all? If she ever began to suspect his motives, it would be no consolation to know that Ogilvie had instructions from Theodore to 'let neither her nor the dear Children want for anything'. But now his cruel determination was fixed, and this directive, it seems, was enough to satisfy his conscience.

From the day Theodore left Surat Eliza had kept the whole household in constant readiness, expecting to leave again for Bombay as soon as he returned. All her efforts were wasted. She replied to his letter straight away, promising him that, just as he had asked, she would try 'not to vex' herself. But she could not resist describing the children's disappointment when they learned that their Papa was not coming home yet: 'Ketty Baba, and Alexander… cry and says as want to see their beloved Papa instantly.' Her letter reached him shortly after he arrived in Bombay. Ogilvie had evidently carried out his friend's request that he should 'lull the suspicions of poor Eliza' about his 'real intentions'. He congratulated himself that she seemed not to have even the slightest inkling of his deception. Now he had the satisfaction of knowing that the first part of his scheme had succeeded. Already, in his mind, he was single again. Yet, even now, his conscience and, perhaps, a deeper attachment than he dared to acknowledge to himself, held him back from admitting his duplicity to her. This deceit was to continue for months while his British friends would encourage him to court a succession of available Bombay Misses. In the end it would be Ogilvie who had to tell her the bald truth, and then not until after she had discovered it for herself.

Theodore had not decided on a name for the baby before he left Surat and so at three months old he was still called 'Chotabhoy'. Chubby little Aleck had not yet learned to walk unaided, although he was two-and-a-half years old. According to Ogilvie and others, Kitty was as vivacious and engaging as a little girl of four-and-a-half can be, laughing and keeping up a constant chatter and playing the big sister to her brothers. From time to time she is allowed to help her mother or Fazagool with her baby brother, lifting him up to feed or dress him. Occasionally she would whisper or sing a lullaby to him when he was put back in his little cot; the cot that on her return from Bombay, Eliza had draped so lovingly with the finest and lightest white muslin, beautifully embroidered with sprigs of tiny green flowers. Sometimes Fazagool would give Kitty a measure of millet and take her to feed the song birds who lived in a cage on the balcony overlooking the courtyard, from where the tiny prisoners could see the light of unattainable freedom and watch the birds of the city fly across the little patch of blue that answers, in their circumscribed existence, for the sky.

Lieutenant Ogilvie keeps his promise to Theodore, calling in to the Deriah Mahal on his way to the Castle, at least once a day, to check on

Eliza and the children. Sometimes Mrs Fraser sends her palanquin to bring the children across town to spend an afternoon at her 'garden house' in the green suburb of Nan Poora. Eliza waits and worries. She writes to Theodore about the profitable contracts she has made with the cotton weavers, and keeps him up to date with news of the children. As the weeks wear on and the month of May turns into sultry June, the mood of her letters changes with the weather. She begins to brood over Theodore's failure to reply to them. The monsoon clouds build and build, cutting out the sun. It seems as if she is trapped in a world of shadow and she knows that the opportunity of going to Bombay is diminishing daily. It seems that she has become even more of a prisoner than the little song birds: a prisoner of her emotions and of her unquestioning obedience.

All Eliza's letters that have survived have been dictated by her, in her imperfect English, to her Parsee scribe. They are beautifully written, and so faithfully transliterated that her voice rings out from the page, as, for example, when he writes 'thees' for 'this'; Mr 'Goodveen' for 'Goodwin' and when 'Toorinj marmalaut' [th'orange marmalade] and 'cannary bird sheed' make their appearance in her discussion of domestic purchases. Her heartfelt emotions find direct expression at her dictation, and bring her personality vividly to life. Wayward grammar and quaint spelling give her letters an immediacy missing in more carefully composed correspondence. Fortunately, she cannot see that when these affectionately composed letters are delivered to Theodore, they are invariably put aside, marked 'Answer unnecessary'.

These are the very characteristics that, through the years, while her letters lay half-forgotten in Scotland, may have led successive generations to deduce, incorrectly, that she was illiterate, of lowly rank, and possibly heathen. The likelihood that the 'Native of India' perpetuated in family lore might be a middle-class Christian of Near-Eastern origin seems to have escaped consideration. As well as the uncertainty about her ethnicity, the lawfulness of her marriage to Theodore had been always been open to doubt. But there was no room for doubt in Eliza's mind; at the foot of all her letters to him, in the scribe's beautiful cursive copperplate hand, is written, 'Your affectionate Mrs Forbes', and below this line she signs in Armenian script 'Arsayber Forbes' – *Sahiba* – Mrs, Madam or even Lady Forbes. The manner in which she signs these letters sets the seal on her firm belief that she is a married woman – the Sahib's lady – and proud of it.

When Aratoon arrived back from Ghogha, he was surprised to find the house so full of women, and he was worried when he discovered who they were. He lost no time in writing to Theodore about the matter: 'I beg you to excuse me for the liberty thus taken, but if I do not inform you in future you will blame [me] for not informing [you] about this, that is to say that from my coming from Gogah, I found Equinah, her daughter, and all the people from her house stop with your family till this day, & besides this Equinah's daughter this his one month since she begins to send the massages to the deferent Gentlemens acquainting them that she wished to stop with any one who pleased to keep her as a Girl, and amongst those Mr Sandwith who leaves close to your families [wife's] house was the first man that had been acquainted with this. – besides this close there got a messhouse of 5th Battn and when the officers comes there to dine, she use to stop very often close to the window and begin to laugh with them, – and this thing having I understood, I went one day to your family [wife] and inquired her about this news, also I told her not to keep this people in her House because you are an honest woman, & not deserved to keep such peoples company, also the Gentlemens think you are of the same train, & was great shame for you, also if your Mr ear this he will take it for ill, but she never leastened [listened to] me, and she thus [does] what she pleases. – In the same time I request you do not tell her my name that I informed you all this things, only tell her that some Gentleman informed you everything about this matter. – & hope you will give her good advice & get this people out from her house, and mind her in everything, once more I beg you do not tell her my name.' Theodore must have been concerned for his beloved Kitty, worrying that she might fall under the unsuitable influence of a 'loose woman' such as Equinah's daughter. If there was any hint of impropriety, he did not want his little girl mixing with such women.

Kitty was probably too young to comprehend the emotional tension building up around her as the weeks passed by and her Papa still did not return. Eliza managed to show a brave face to the world and to concentrate on looking after the children but she worried. The towering black clouds of the gathering monsoon built up and forecast the arrival of the rains; the deluge might begin any time and treacherous tides would soon close down ports all along the Gulf of Cambay. She knew from her time in Aratoon's house how Surat was more susceptible than most to complete closure. She was right; the rains came in force and on July 4th Aratoon wrote to Theodore: 'You writes me about the Patamary, it is true I wanted to send but the monsoon was very bad to go. I suspended from the river, I hope on God and your kindness to send the above Patamary after the rains over.'

But Eliza's mind is now on other things – suddenly little Chotabhoy has been fretful and off colour. Though the three children are a constant reminder to her of their father and her unhappiness at her separation from him – yet they bring back memories of happier times and they are also her only consolation. Chotabhoy's crying is like a reproach to her – what if she should lose him? The rainy season often brings disease and death, and she is stuck in the Old Mughal Serail without the support of the man she loves. She feels helpless. As ever, Fazagool is an invaluable support and does her best to reassure her, but Eliza's own health begins to suffer.

From Theodore's letter book, it seems that he is already beginning to regret the generous allowance he has arranged for Eliza with Dinshaw Eduljee; an allowance which she appears to be finding insufficient for her needs. His own living expenses have begun to escalate alarmingly. This seems to have outweighed any worries he might have had about Eliza's health or that of their baby. Increasingly concerned about the expense of maintaining two households, he asks Aratoon to advise Eliza not to overspend her allowance. Aratoon replies by return:

'I heard that about three days ago, Agah Jany was been to your Madam to offer his house which would cost her only 20 Rs 12 per month but she rejected... Your Goodness has been pleased to mention me to give a good advise to your family and according to your direction I will perform it as far as it lies in my power... as for my part, I do not think she will hear me if I tell her about this matter.'

Aratoon suggests that Ogilvie would be best placed to settle the issue of her expenses with her and he ends the letter by telling Theodore: 'Whatever you sent by the hand of Dinshaw Parsee I think it is almost over. Your Servant Marcar is going to marry him from there.

You must know what expenses will occur to her, therefore I hope you will write to her about this things and also to diminue her estravagant expenses, but I beg you not to mention my name, nor let her know who gave you this notice.'

He was right to ask that his name should be kept out of the matter; Eliza was clearly irritated by his interference and lost very little time before protesting to Theodore. Her letter leaves him in no doubt that she is not prepared to accept guidance from her brother-in-law on this or any other matter: 'Long while ago I know him,' she writes, 'and being surprize now myself as you can mind his useless word.' She dismisses Aratoon's concerns over the expenses involved in Markar's wedding, stressing to Theodore that at the moment it is only the engagement party, the *'mugnee'*, that has taken place. It seems also that Theodore had already let her know that he disapproved of her friendship with Mrs Rubka's family:

'When you was at Bhownugar, our Fazagool was made the Mugnee of her adopt son Maurkaur with Rubkaus Slave Girl, which I did not acquaint you but Fazagool performed the said Mugnee, by her own request to expence... and you will be sure as I am not so fool to do anything that you can be displease sake of the irregular expence... – I let you know Agah Aratoons family, Khalah Ageenah and daughter except them as no other person I choose to be come to our house... I let you know that I been to Rubka House at all in three times only to visit her, my first visit to her when you was at Surat, the second visit on the day of Markars Mugnee and the latter 3rd visit on account her sickness. If you will issue an order, [I] will never visit to her or any other to whom you may not like.' It is signed, as always, with her married name, in English and Armenian, 'I am, My Dear Sir, your very affectionate Mrs Forbes.'

Aratoon's letter of July 4th is concerned with topics other than his problems with the monsoon and his truculent young sister-in-law; it describes his progress in procuring copies of two texts that Theodore had asked him to find in both Hindi and Sanskrit: *The Chowrasee Assan on 84 Positions* and *The Book of Kook Shastri*. Both are works on the subject of lovemaking and sexual technique. It had been nearly four months since Theodore confided to his letter book that he had been 'so imprudent as to have connection' with his 'dear Betsey' and vowed that it would be the last time. He had already been in Bombay for two months and is evidently suffering some frustration at the lack of a loving and regular sex life. Aratoon tells him that he has engaged a *munshi* to make copies of the texts for him, and will send them to Bombay when they are ready.

Almost as soon as Theodore arrived in Bombay, Eliza had begun to raise the question of the children's baptism. She was anxious that he should 'put up the name of our Chotabhoy' and also 'do the baptism of our belove childrens'. She means, of course, into the Church of England. Theodore himself had certainly baptised Alexander, and probably Kitty too, in the Factory at Mocha, where, as in most East India Company outposts where there was no church or chaplain, home baptism by an unordained person was accepted practice. This was only a temporary measure to make the child members of the Christian faith, and protect its immortal soul. Though regarded as Christian, children were not legally accepted as British subjects and issued with passports until their births were registered when they were baptised into the Church of England or Scotland. Eliza evidently regarded the baptism of her children as vital to their future prospects. In addition, she believed her own status would be enhanced when they were officially acknowledged as British:

'Pray don't now Put off and disappoint me on Account Baptise,' she writes at the beginning of July – 'I pray for God sake you must do the Baptism of our belove Childrens, which will be great Honor for me.'

Though she had given Theodore the impression that she trusted his assurances that he would return, Eliza was no fool. It was easy for a man to stray in a city like Bombay. She was clever enough to understand how important it was to keep a dialogue going if she was to have any hope of winning him back. As ever, she remained true to her mercantile origins, and her perception of an Armenian wife's duty. She continued helping him in his cotton trades. Manufactured cotton goods, known as 'piece goods', destined for England had been scarce recently, 'because', Eliza tells him, 'the Honorable Company not let purchase any sort of English-use Piece Goods to any other Person but to the Honorable Company.' Undaunted by the challenging trading conditions and well placed to visit the weavers and bargain with them, literally at street level, she describes how she has dealt with current problems by seeking out 'musters' of different lengths of cloth from the lesser artisans to make up a worthwhile consignment to send to Bombay. She even organises the finance, asking him to send a bill of hand to Rustomjee Cheeneemeeny, who will then order the cloth, obtain cash from the Surat *shroffs* and pay the weavers. If he pays for them in advance, the goods would be ready in four months' time. Matters of commerce seem to take precedence for a while in her letters over news that Chotabhoy has recently been unwell again.

Shortly after his arrival in Bombay, Eliza had written to Theodore about the possibility of his rejoining the Hon. Company's Service. His professed reluctance to go to Bombay without her; his claims of 'pressure of work'; and possibly her own observations of growing racial intolerance, had convinced her that he might already consider leaving Forbes & Co.: 'If you can think for yourself to enter again into the Civil Service,' she tells him, 'I think it is the better for you.'

Aratoon had been thinking along similar lines and writes that he has heard about a Civil Service appointment available in Ahmedabad. But the aspiring *nabob* had already become too enmeshed in the workings of Forbes & Co. to be able to resign his partnership so easily. A memo in his letter book reveals that he had written and 'requested my father would <u>not</u> act on the hint I formerly gave to purchase Haddo for me… – unless the money could be borrowed at home, on mortgage or by any other means.' He adds that he has funds invested in Forbes & Co. from which he cannot withdraw 'for fear of giving offence'. Some of the money he has deposited with the firm to 'buy in' to the partnership is evidently tied up. Perhaps these are the same investments that will so dramatically reduce the size of the legacies he is shortly to leave in his will. So, for the moment, his hopes of buying his childhood home have had to be shelved.

This raises the question of what his ultimate intention was when he left Eliza and the children in Surat. He had clearly, at one time, envisaged retiring to Scotland as Laird of Haddo, but whether he intended taking Eliza with him is another matter. Since joining Forbes & Co. it had become plain to him that they could never enjoy a normal social life together in Bombay or Aberdeenshire. While they were living in Mocha she had enjoyed the status of 'First Lady' and had been invaluable to him in many different ways. She had provided him with a happy home life and a family when he was a stranger in a foreign land and she had helped him slip successfully into the role of a merchant adventurer abroad, a role that was fundamental to her own cultural heritage within the Armenian diaspora. Even as he was planning to abandon her, her language skills, business acumen and wide range of contacts were still useful to him. A cynic might suspect that this could have been a factor in his reluctance to tell her that he wanted their separation to be permanent, but despite his evasiveness she is already beginning to work out for herself that this might be the case. When she does grasp that changing social attitudes are the main factor driving their separation, she observes bitterly: 'The world now has another fashion.'

However, if she harbours any doubts at this point about his feelings for her, she does not show them, and she certainly never doubts his affection for their children. She mentions them in her correspondence at every opportunity, and must have hoped that this would maintain his interest in her too. Even when he does not reply for months, she carries on writing, giving him details of all her cotton deals as well as news of the children and she seldom fails to remind him that their union is sacred before God, to whom he must ultimately answer: 'My beloved Sir by your pleas[ur]e I remain here but amongst us the Supreme God is still the same, but you must not be off from your God which you know,' adding presciently, 'This world are very short... what more I can say?'

Chapter 14

In Sickness and in Health, 1817

The Bombay Bobbery Hunt in pursuit of a bullock.

Just as Theodore was when he had a bad fall.

From *The Grand Master*, or *Adventures of Qui Hi in Hindostan*, by Quiz.

Engraving and aquatint by Thomas Rowlandson.

14

Surat, July 1817

After Theodore sent word to Eliza that he must go directly to Bombay, she carried on hoping, against all signs to the contrary, that he would return again to Surat or send for her. But the arrival of the monsoon with more than usual violence meant that the ships for Bombay would not risk sailing. The clouds had gathered and the mercury had dropped and dropped, and with the pressure her spirits too had dropped. Then the rains had come. The mountain torrents raced into the plains below, bursting the banks of the streams and rivers of the hinterland, covering the fields and disgorging their muddy waters into the Rivers Tapti and Nerbudda.

Eliza's worst fears were confirmed – the opportunity to go to Bombay had been lost. The citizens of Surat and Broach watched the water levels anxiously. As the days passed with no answer to her desperate letters, her worries grew; she was running into debt and there was still no news from Theodore. The depth and bitterness of her disappointment is almost tangible in her letters. The activities of the British community cannot have helped her mood; they seemed to be as jolly as she was miserable. 'Mrs Fraser gave an Evening party and Ball last Monday,' writes Henry Adams to Theodore on July 17th, 'which went off extremely well considering the scarcity of dancing ladies, all the married women (nearly) are as women wish to be who love their loves, and consequently we may expect a number of young Suraties to make their appearance in the course of a few months or rather earlier.'

Only when Theodore starts to receive bills for cash advances and goods that Eliza has bought on credit does he feel compelled to write to her. She is thrilled to receive a letter after such a long interval but dismayed at its contents. He has written to Dinshaw expressly forbidding him to advance any sum, other than 'Mrs Forbes's' 210 Rupee monthly allowance. From Eliza he demands a full account of her household expenses from the time she left Bombay pregnant, more than a year earlier. She is offended at the implication of dishonesty and, despite feeling unwell, quickly returns a long list to him.

Her list gives a snapshot of her lifestyle. As well as a hefty bill from the *moorjeewallah*, seller of chickens, in the *moorjee* market, close by their house, she lists:

'Paid Palanquin hire on the time of going to Surat' and... 'a cabin lamp bought from Leemjee Bhikajee shop'; this would have been for her voyage back to Surat with the children. Leemjee Bhikajee was a well-known emporium in Bombay where all sorts of expensive imported commodities and goods were advertised for sale. The sum Eliza says she owes to the Parsee merchants Hormajee & Khursedjee is for luxurious silk stockings, bolts of fine satin for her dresses, and expensive imported 'China Trade' ribbon with which to trim them:

3 Yard satten at 2.2.Rs per Yard – 7.2
2 Pairs Silk Stockings...............14.-
China Ribbin.........................10.2-

'May be more than above 32 Rs but I cannot recollect proper,' she says. Overleaf she lists 'Money due to the following person... Old Taylor for sewing my gowns – 15 R.'

In the letters that follow, Theodore's tone becomes more exasperated and Eliza's more submissive. She quickly settles some of the outstanding bills and writes him a conciliatory letter:

'My Dear Sir, you desire me with very angry respecting the Bills left unpaid with considerable amount, which I pray be please to be not pay them without let me know, and send me their proper list then I can return you proper answer, & I think only 1 or 2 bill having unpaid, a bill of Moorgeewalah [chicken seller], & a bill of Parsee Hormajee & Khursedjee. Except these 2 persons have no any others Bills remained unpaid on the time I had been sick. Not know how became so much Fowls in use of my Acquaintance hungry persons, but I do not understand what Play of the Servants passed at that period with Moorgeewalah, and I let you know have paid 50 Rupees to Moorgeewalah by my own separate money which Butler [Caitan] know very well...' She assures him: 'Respecting the Expence, I acknowledge your best advice, you will be sure I will do everything agreeable to your wish.'

That the strong and successful bond of the last five years could completely unwind in such a short time was still unimaginable to Eliza, and confidence in the strength of their marriage seems solid as the letter ends: 'If you will write me a Thousand words to make me uneasy... I will not take it a miss nor I will do less my love on you, and also your love never will be less on me.'

Inevitably, as Theodore sticks to his plan and does not reply to her letters, her confidence begins to falter. She worries about the effect of his absence on her creditors. He has involved Will Ogilvie in regulating her expenses and ordering her accommodation and she becomes suspicious of the motives of all those around her. She knows that Aratoon is spying on her and reporting back to Theodore. She has already snubbed his well-intentioned efforts to find her a cheaper house to rent. Only Ogilvie knows that Theodore plans to make their separation permanent and, though he has said nothing to her, she senses it. The worry begins to make her ill but as usual she ends her next letter to Theodore on an upbeat note, with news of the children:

'Our Ketty, Alexander and Chotabhoy having in Good Health, and let you know the happy news, that thank God our Alexander now walk a little himself without any support. – These letter I would to write you before but I was unwell therefore excuse me.'

Her ill-health persists, and in a letter dated Surat, the 6th August 1817, she tells Theodore: 'I now being 10 days since I am with fever and Ague which made me very weakness and pooshing my whole body like a Bow, our Excellent friend Lieut Ogilvie gives good attend to comfort me & Doctor Ogilvee also supply good medician to me, the said gentlemen daily attend our house by your favor, & of good recommendation to them for me and beloved children. – I requesting the favor to send me some Preserve of arroot & Europe Jelly of 2 sorts which you know very well of the said jelly I like very much, send me few don't charge more money only I want to eat in such fever. – if any different sorts of preserve, Dry Fruit, Honey, Coffee & would be come to present you from Mocah, Europe then you will be so kind as to keep from those fruit &ca for your own use & whatever you may like and remainder send them for me and children use, and I let you know don't trust any servant for those fruit &ca when you choose to send them for me.'

The 'arroot' she wants him to send is *Curcuma Angustifolia*, East

Indian or Bombay Arrowroot, described as being 'used as an agreeable, non-irritating diet during convalescence from fevers... in the form of jelly, variously seasoned with sugar, lemon juice... essences or aromatics.' Plaintively she tells him that she is still so unwell that she cannot move from her bed, and makes the poignant observation that: 'I recollect to Mokha is better than Surat, because I never see myself such fever and Ague.' She may have hoped that mentioning the fruit jellies he knows she likes 'very much' in the context of Mocha would bring to his mind the happy intimacy they once shared.

Despite her bout of fever she manages to send Theodore up-to-date information on the Company cotton purchases. She has heard that no one has yet made a contract with the Honourable Company because they were offering only 108 Rupees per corge [a unit of 20] and the Surat merchants wanted 110 Rupees. Seeing that this might work to their advantage, she tells him: 'In such Objection between the Honorable Company & Merchant, our business will pass easily with less Amount... & will get to us 100 or 200 Corges until [before] the Honble Companys Contract.' On another subject, she cautions him, 'If you can do the business of Rustonjee Cheeneeminee which I informed you in my before letter, and at present you wish to Commission on him for any business, Please you must not do absolutely without let me know.'

Whether or not Theodore did send her the fruit jellies, Ogilvie was soon able to report to him that: 'Your friend's feverish attack... has now left her,' and continues, 'All the children, I am rejoiced to say, are in high health and spirits & I just now left Aleck & Kitty preparing to go & pass the day with our excellent Friend Mrs Fraser.'

By August 21st Eliza was well enough to procure and send a present of rice, chutneys, cheese and pickles to Theodore and tells him: 'Myself, Ketty, Alexander and Chotabhoy are in good health & pray for your honors Long life Health & Prosperity.'

But the very next day there is a sudden change in Chotabhoy's health. Will Ogilvie describes how: 'In the evening I went in my Palankeen – as far as the House where your Family live – & found them all in good health, with the exception of the young boy – who has considerable heat of skin.' But he continues reassuringly: 'On calling again this morning, I found him entirely free of fever – & Ogilvy considered him so much better, that he deemed it unnecessary to administer the medicine which he had prescribed yesterday.' Perhaps the mention of the baby's fever has brought the question of the children's baptism to Theodore's notice again because he writes to tell Eliza he has decided to give Chotabhoy the name 'Fraser' and he hopes that his good friend Mrs Fraser might help to arrange the children's christening. Eliza is thrilled when his letter arrives and overjoyed that Chotabhoy has a proper Christian name at last; now the children's baptism into the Church of England can go ahead. Using Chotabhoy's proper name for the first time she adds a post script to her reply: 'Alexander & Fraser are in health,' she says, but adds worryingly, 'Ketty are now little unwell and I see her day by day grow lean herself.'

The cooling rains begin to slacken off at last but as September approaches Eliza is growing ever more distrustful of members of her close circle. In a letter to their servant, Francis Caitan in Bombay, she tells him: 'The Petticoat [I] have made ready for your daughter, which I shall send again by the boat belonging to Deenshaw or Munchershaw, as soon as possible.' But Caitan has evidently not returned her favour and she suspects his motives:

'I am very sorry that you entirely forget to send me the lavender water, honey water and oil for hair &ca. different small articles which I did commission you... now you may be think, that I can remain at Surat and our Hd. Master are at Bombay, on that account you recon I shall never meet again with Honored Master. You be sure yourself' she warns him [when] 'I should meet again with our good Master in same affection, then I will be same Mrs Forbes.'

By September 11th, the news of the Forbes children's health is, at first, encouraging: 'Ketty, Alexander, and little Fraser are in good health,' Eliza writes, 'and Alexander now begin to walk himself without any assistant, and also I let you know that our beloved little Fraser's one Tooth appearing out.' The letter had come to hand on the 19th. But as he marked it 'Answer unnecessary' and put it casually to one side, Eliza was writing to him again, worried about baby Fraser:

'Since long ago I expect your kindest letter and request your Honor may please to write me often to Comfort me in every respect. – Our beloved Ketty & Alexander are with perfect health; but little Fraser since a month ago are unwell with fever on account Teeth and thank God he now begin to prattling a little as Papa, Papa, & by your goodness favor

Our friend Doctor Ogilvy daily attend to see Fraser... I think you may [be] occupied in Europe ships &ca. affairs, therefore forget me to write some lines, Ketty and Alexander often recollect their beloved Papa, & I myself are not well and happy since Obsolute separation therefore I hope to God may soon restore our visiting with full affection to embrace each another, indeed my beloved Sir, I have wrote several letters to your Honors to intreat the merciful favour, that if should the iron would be soon the water, & you must observe that without any fault no deserve to make burn so hard to me, which our God no please, and this world are of 2 days which I pray you may do your Honors hard heart so soft like was.'

This is the first mention Eliza makes of little Fraser being unwell – and it would prove to be the last.

While she frets, Theodore is having a rumbustious time in Bombay; he is enjoying the social rounds as a free man and carousing with fellow members of the Bobbery Hunt. With his evident wealth and a prestigious partnership in the foremost financial house of Bombay, he is in great demand for any and all of the many balls, breakfasts, dinners and soirées that made up the social calendar and he is much talked about. Still only twenty-nine-years old, he would be a good catch for any spinster who might succeed in ensnaring him. It seems that Mrs Fraser's sister, Miss Charlotte Wrangham, is tempted to try. But any plans that she and her sister might have been hatching are soon confounded. Thomas Fraser receives the unexpected and most unwelcome news that he has been posted to Broach – Mr and Mrs Fraser had already left by the time Eliza writes on September 11th but she makes no mention of it in her letter.

On the same day, Dr George Ogilvy had written reassuringly to Theodore about the children: 'Your youngest little boy has lately been occasionally feverish – chiefly I think from teething – he is now however much better & I cannot see that the little fellow is pulled down one single inch by his illness. – Kate & the other, are perfectly well, thriving, and in high spirits – & you may rely upon it that while I continue in Surat – I shall feel the greatest pleasure in paying them every attention in my powers – not only professionally – but in any other way in which my services may be useful to them.' On the subject of the Frasers, he comments, 'No one can regret their departure more sincerely than I do – for to me they have proved most kind hospitable neighbours – and their absence occasions a very great blank indeed... I should have regretted the circumstance less than I now do – had their removal been more to Fraser's advantage... To your little ones also they will prove a serious loss – for they were most kind & attentive to them. & indeed generally speaking they were most excellent members of society – Alas! poor Surat – many changes are taking place – & in a short time 2/3rds of its European inhabitants will be strangers.'

Whether or not Eliza regrets the Frasers' move to Broach, she is clearly beginning to feel isolated, and that she cannot trust many of the people around her. Worries about the baby's health; the loyalty of friends and family; her finances; her good reputation; and, most importantly, Theodore's commitment to her, begin to build up into a real sense of persecution:

'I am now oblige to let you know before my enemys can write you some words as false & vain,' she writes, possibly referring to Aratoon's letter about the expense of Markar's *mugnee*, 'that our Fazagool, made the wedding of her adopt son Markar on the 14th Instant [September]... She [Fazagool] had no urging [urgency] to perform the same wedding but the family of Rubkhas insisted very much to perform immediately because Mrs Rubkhas are very ill and will depart her life in a few days, also Mrs Rubkhas send message to perform the Wedding as soon as possible she choose to see in her lifetime, then she oblige to do same and on the wedding day was assembly the Vartapeth Padrey, Avaness ter Marteeross, Estephanoos, Karapett Pethkaum, Ageenah and her daughter, Aratoon and his family.'

Soon it is not her own health, or the baby's, or even Mrs Rubka's, but Theodore's, that is to become the subject of her concern. He had not written for over a month when she hears that he had recently had a serious fall from his horse while out with the Bobbery Hunt: '– I informed that you have been falled down the horse,' she writes, on September 16th, 'which news made me very uneasy... I wish God almighty might have preserved you from any hurt thereby.' But Eliza is not the only female with a close interest in Theodore's health. While her sister has moved to Broach, Miss Wrangham has arranged to stay with her friends, the Borchards, in Tannah, not far from Bombay, from where she can remain in regular contact with Theodore. A few days later, when the news of his fall reaches her ears, she too feels it incumbent on herself to write to him:

'My dear Mr Forbes, Most sincerely sorry was I to learn from your letter the cause of your silence. I fear you must have been very uncomfortable while answering my letter, particularly as you had been bled – which must have weakened you very much, I trust by this, however, that you are quite recovered from the ill effects of your juvenile frolic of hunting a bullock – it is really too bad, suppose the animal had tossed you in the air after you fell from your horse, and unable to help yourself, what a dreadful death have you escaped – it really makes me shudder to think of it even. – Pray take care of yourself in future, what would your helpless innocents have done if anything had happened to you? They would have had money no doubt, but what amends would that make for the loss of a kind parent – forgive me for what I have said, but I do not mean to be impertinent – I hope you will not think me so.'

Markar's wedding; the sudden departure of the Frasers; Theodore's accident, had all happened in the space of a fortnight. Dr Ogilvy's letter had been reassuring on the subject of baby Fraser's health, but on September 22nd Will Ogilvie returns to the subject. He tells Theodore that the infant's symptoms are now so serious that the doctor has called in a second opinion: 'Our good friend the Doctor informs me that about ten days or a fortnight ago, he despatched a letter to you – in which he informed you, of the ailing state of health of your youngest Boy, arising from fever incident to teething.

'When he wrote, the fever had considerably abated and [he] was in hopes that it would soon yield entirely to medecine. – Within the last two or three days however, the poor little fellow has suffered very much, & Ogilvy has lanced his gums – with the view to assist nature in those parts – but the fever has recently increased & with such serious symptoms, that O told me this morning when we went together to your House – that change of air is in his opinion indispensibly necessary – He is however to call again this afternoon with Marshall – when I shall meet them and receive their final opinion, which shall be acted upon without an hour's unnecessary delay. –

'Such, My dear Forbes, is the Doctor's opinion – but let us hope that a favourable change will soon take place – & I have the gratifying consolation of assuring you that Kitty, Aleck and their Mother are in excellent health – altho' the latter as must be expected is under great uneasiness of mind on account of the poor little boy, who, I most sincerely trust will yet do well.'

The faith Ogilvie places on the doctor's intervention is not to be rewarded. Two days later, on September 24th 1817, Fraser Forbes dies, aged eight months and three days The loss compounds Eliza's feeling of isolation. At a time when she desperately needs her husband at her side, he is not there to give her the comfort and support she needs. Beside herself with grief she immediately makes arrangements to move out of the Deriah Mahal, no doubt bitterly regretting that she had not removed the children from the insalubrious area sooner. The busy streets, once so familiar and so pleasant, now reproach her at every turn and the old house holds a score of painful memories in its very fabric. The circumstances of baby Fraser's death are painful to read in Ogilvie's letter; how much more painful then for Eliza to have to revisit her desperation, as she tried to soothe her feverish child while his insistent cries faded to a fitful whimper. The unaccustomed stillness could only serve to emphasise her loss and her ears would ring with the crying of her baby son for months to come.

As was customary – and necessary – Little Fraser was buried on the day he died. He had not yet been christened into the Church of England, so presumably was buried in the Armenian cemetery. The small white coffin was fitted with 'best Europe ornaments' and a *chunam* vault was raised over his tomb. A bill from Lewis Collett gives the details of the infant's speedy burial. Will Ogilvie forwards it to Theodore and comments: 'I directed everything connected with the poor Dear Child's Funeral, to be furnished most respectably – You yourself, will however judge whether his [Collett's] charges are reasonable or not. He has certainly got the character of a perfect Jew on that point.'

Lewis Collett immediately offered Eliza one of his own properties at a much-reduced rent. Collett was a well-known 'Mr Fixit' in Surat. He had served in the Bombay Grenadiers for 20 years and retired in 1812 as Garrison Sergeant-Major in Surat. He married his second wife Ragina there in the same year and retired from the service soon after. Subsequently he earned a good living as a general entrepreneur and businessman. He had evidently been trading even before he left the army; Theodore bought a sword and a pair of pistols from him as early as 1810. The following year one of William's friends had written to him about auctioning a horse in Surat:

Theodore Forbes Esqr. ------ — — — — Dr

To one Small coffin Covered with Silk and one Set of

  Europe Ornaments --- — — — --- -- 30 „ .

To Building a Channam Vault and a foundation „ --- ·

  for a Tomb. — — — · — 18 ...

To Planks for Ditto. — · ' — 3 „—·

To funeral fees — — —9—·

To Carpenters Work. — · — 2 ...

                    Rupees 64 —·

                        € €

Surat 24th   *Lewis A Collett*

September 1817

Lewis Collett's Bill for Fraser Forbes's funeral on September 24th 1817
Enhanced photocopy from the original in *Ms. 2740*,
King's College Library, Aberdeen

© Susan Harvard

This bill was rendered again in July 1818 and
inscribed by Theodore on the outside:

'L.A.Collett, Surat 9th July 1818; Received 17 DD. Answer unnecessary, having
written to Lieut. Ogilvie on the subject, my letter of the 20th August 1818.'

'You may see what Whitey will fetch at an outcry at Colletts as I wish to part with him. Your brother [Theodore] seems inclined to purchase him at about Rs. 200 tell him however that at present none shall have him under the Rs. 400 which I think so fine a horse ought to fetch at Surat when the same cash was given for him at Broach.'

As soon as she could, Eliza moved from the Deriah Mahal, and tells Theodore: 'The first instant [October] I left the former house and dwelling into another house belonging to Mr Collett. The same house rent was before 30 or 35 Rupees per month,' ... 'but Mr Collett told for the sake of Mr Forbes he will receive 20 Rupees per month because Mr Forbes did a good favor on him so he did.' She ends by reproaching him for not answering her letters: 'I am very sorry to say about a month past could not obtain from you the few lines of your regardful letter which makes me also uneasy and afflecting, therefore my good and beloved Sir, may do so merciful to call me from hence.' As usual, the letter is signed 'Your very affectionate Mrs Forbes'.

At this time, amongst others, Eliza's maternal great-aunt, Mariam Khatchatoor, writes to Theodore to offer her condolences. She pleads with him: 'My dear Eliza have been not a day being happy and in good State of Health & not sleep well at Night since your Absolute Separation... I do beseech you may Please to Call her with Children to Bombay as soon as Possible, then She will be happy.' But despite what her aunt said, Eliza had managed to stay as strong as she could for Kitty and Aleck and recovered her composure sufficiently to move house within a week of little Fraser's funeral and to write to Theodore on 4th October to let him know that Dr Ogilvy was just setting out for Bombay and would tell him 'all the particular circumstance for me and our beloved child'.

How Theodore was affected by Ogilvy's description of his baby son's illness and death can only be guessed at. But when Aratoon heard the details of how the baby's gums had been lanced, he must have congratulated himself on not having surrendered to Ogilvy's lancet a year previously when the doctor had wanted to open an abscess on his belly. At the time Ogilvy had written to Theodore in Bombay: 'Your Armenian protégé... had a large abscess forming on the pot of his stomach... All my rhetoric could not prevail upon him or his friends to allow me to open it for him... he chose rather to submit to the pain, which was considerable, than to the touch of a lancet.'

Two weeks after the doctor's departure for Bombay, Aratoon wrote to Theodore and explained why he had not written sooner to offer his condolences: 'During the month of September I was dangerously ill in such maner,' he writes, 'that I never expected to leave [live] in this world' [but] 'I am goodell [good deal] better since this few days past... We beg you to accept our condolence for the death of your dear little child,' adding, 'Surely we did feel much for him.'

The very next day, more than three long and miserable weeks after the death of little Fraser, Will Ogilvie put into Eliza's trembling hand the letter she had been longing for; the first letter from Theodore for several months. Clearly relieved, she replied immediately: 'Your kindest favour dated the 15th [October] which came in hand the 20th instant... I fully conceived your sorrowness for our beloved late child little Fraser, & you have mentioned several lines to guide me to be not undergo long afflicting which will be no good for myself, you say it are very true, & in the meantime I take myself to be confortable but could not [but] suffer when I recollect of losing our beloved late child, who was like a Diamond.' His letter is dated three weeks after baby Fraser's death, but he tells her he shares her sorrow and it gives her some comfort. She is desperate for an opportunity to talk freely about their situation, to tell him how she longs for the family to be reunited, but she no longer trusts the discretion even of her Parsee scribe – and so she encloses in hers 'a letter in Persian language, which I hope [you will] to read it well, and if you cannot read well, be pleased to make him read by any trusty person to understand the content fully and do mercy to write me soon it answer.'

Charlotte Wrangham did not hear the news of the baby's death until she saw Theodore in town. She was still living with her friends, at Tannah. On the 20th October, not yet a month after the sad event, she wrote to Theodore asking him to book a palanquin for her and Miss Borchards for their visit to Bombay. A brief mention of baby Fraser's death is squeezed into the letter. The best she can manage is:

'I did not indeed know the loss you had experienced, until you mentioned it, believe me I am most sincerely sorry that your feelings have been so severely tried on such a melancholy occasion. I trust however that your remaining children will live long, to be a comfort to you.' There is no mention of Eliza's 'feelings'. Her condolences are sandwiched between her travel arrangements and a rather arch paragraph of gossip about the marriage market: 'I had nearly forgotten to tell you that I expect to be congratulated by you on my marriage with Mr Hockley. I was told that it was all settled for me in Bombay and that the day was even fixed.' ... 'How kind the people are to save the parties concerned so much trouble! – Well it is an easy way, at all events, to be married,' she comments ironically. More gossip concludes her letter: 'We hear that Mr Stephenson is positively to be Miss W's husband, and Mr Wederbourn Miss C Wade's.' She seems keen to let Theodore know that she has several suitors – but is still available – just: '– I suppose there is as much truth in this as there is in the reports about me, for there are more than one,' she concludes.

Less than a month had passed since baby Fraser's death but Mrs Fraser was already keen to move forward with Theodore's plans for his children. An indirect approach would enable her to pursue 'the subject of Kitty's future' with him without seeming too interfering. So, on the 22nd October, she wrote on the subject to Will Ogilvie. She intended that Ogilvie should forward it to Theodore with his own. Ogilvie obediently wrote immediately, enclosing Mrs Fraser's letter and lending his approval to her suggestions:

'I had a letter this morning from our worthy friend Mrs Fraser, in which she desires her best love to you, & writes in the most affectionate terms of the dear children to whom she continues most sincerely attached & in every respect interested in their welfare and happiness. – She has often expressed to me her anxious desire, to get charge of Kitty, on losing little Tom Barnard & I am certain I only anticipate your sentiments in observing that nothing could be more desirable than placing the sweet girl under such excellent & I may add Maternal care. – The only point of consideration is (& it is certainly the principal one) will the Mother, do you think, be inclined to yield to our Friends wishes, in parting with Kitty & retaining little Aleck – For my own part, I really do think [she] would accede – for had she not calculated that the children would be sooner or later separated from her, for their education, she would not in my opinion have been so anxious that they should be brought up members of our church.'

This is the first hint that it may not be considered appropriate or desirable for Aleck to be sent to England with Kitty. It is also the first attempt by Mrs Fraser to assume responsibility for the arrangements for Kitty's departure, and to remove her from Eliza's care and influence.

'My dear Sir I lose no time in replying to your letter of the 20th – which I had the pleasure of receiving last night. I have not slept since it arrived, so much interested have I been about that part of its contents which relates to our dear little Kate, upon mature consideration therefore I do not hesitate to say that the plan of sending her immediately to England, is much preferable to consigning her to my charge; and for this reason. Did her Mother know she was gone home, there would be an end at once to all communication, whereas if she were with me, the natural feelings of a parent would induce her to be constantly sending to, or wishing to see the child – and thus make herself and Kate miserable – if they are to be separated, the sooner and more effectively it is done the better. You will however I fear have very great difficulty in persuading the mother to this measure and if you think that she will ultimately be more reconciled to parting with her child, if she remains with me for a short time, pray do not hesitate proposing it to her – although I myself am of opinion that so good an opportunity of sending her to England ought not to be allowed to escape. Let us however wait till an answer from Theodore arrives if he approves of letting the little girl be with me, you may assure him & the Mother that I shall love and treat her as my own.

'Barnard will write to Forbes about securing a passage for Tom in the *Huddart.*' She concludes, '– He must go – for his health is very bad – and should Kate be his fellow passenger, one cabin, and one servant would answer for both. – Pray let me know when you think of moving that I may think of sending my little charge to Surat, I need not, I am sure recommend him to your care, your own kind heart will induce you to be good to a little helpless boy without a friend in the world but myself... we are at present at the Durbar our own house not being yet ready for our reception.'

When Mrs Fraser arrived from Broach at the end of October, she found that Eliza and the children had moved out of the Deriah Mahal, nearly a month previously. They had not gone very far; the new lodgings Collett had made available to her were on the street between the

Armenian Church and the Castle, where Will Ogilvie worked. According to Collett's will, published in Bombay many years later, he had 'three houses... situated at the Mogul Sorry Street at Surat'. It was presumably into one of these that the family had moved.

Almost as soon the family moved in, Ogilvie had called in at their new lodgings to tell Eliza that her 'Cotton chelloes' had arrived safely in Bombay. This was the news she had been waiting for. Theodore would be pleased that her dealings on their joint behalf had turned out well, and surely he would soon send for her and the children? Now she began to dream again of moving house – this time to Bombay – to Bycullah to be reunited with Theodore in his fine 'Garden House'. But the first child to enjoy the airy surroundings of Theodore's luxurious new lodgings would not be Kitty or Aleck, but young Tom Barnard.

Chapter 15

Home and Away, 1817

15

Bombay and Surat, November 1817

Only a few days after Theodore received Mrs Fraser's letter from Ogilvie, with its suggestion about sending Kitty to England with young Tom, Thomas Fraser decided to write directly to Theodore about the boy because, he says: 'Barnard is so abominably lazy that neither Mrs Fraser or self can get him to pen a few lines to you... in consequence, he [Barnard] has deputed me to write now. I shall feel extremely obliged by your letting me know... when you think it will be best to send the little fellow to the Presidency, as I shall take the liberty of asking you to receive him for the few days he will be in Bombay.' Fraser continues with some light-hearted banter about Theodore's reasons for taking on the house in Bycullah: 'There are rumours here that you are going to make a Cove [married man] of yourself, is there any truth in it?' he teases, 'That large house in the country looks something like it.'

Either incessant nagging by the Frasers had its effect on Barnard or he was not as 'abominably lazy' as Fraser had branded him, because only two days later, on October 27th he wrote to Theodore himself from Jewarra: 'I and mine, or rather I for mine, are going to be troublesome to you – Such part of the business as relates to sending young Tom home – I mean to England – I must leave to Mrs Fraser to arrange, both because I know nothing about it, and because it is allowable all the world over for Batchelors to get trouble of this sort off their hands as much as they can. I have only to say about those arrangements that you will oblige me more than Mrs F by anything you do at her request. The business of providing for him after he is in England I must settle with you – and all that is immediately requisite is to remit the sum necessary for his expences to Fraser's mother, to whose care he is to be confided. Mrs F, who is now at Broach (and to whom I shall send this letter open that there shall be no Game at Cross Purposes in our Communications) will acquaint you with particulars.'

Barnard's casual attitude and assertion that 'it is allowable all the world over for Batchelors to get trouble of this sort off their hands', might suggest that he had little feeling for his Anglo-Indian son. But he is writing to a close friend who would shortly have to make similar arrangements for his own 'natural' children and, 'man to man', he would not want to seem too sentimental. The passage to England would cost him 1,000 rupees and he would have to pay for school fees or a tutor, as well as upkeep for the boy once in England. Of course he loved his son, just as Theodore clearly loved Kitty and Aleck.

Mrs Fraser was due to visit the city again, with her husband, at the end of the month 'for the baptism of Morison's little boy'. She had already arranged that she would bring young Tom with her so that he too could be baptised. Afterwards Ogilvie was to take him to Theodore in Bombay. She was delighted to have an opportunity to visit the city where she had been so happy, and she was looking forward to staying with her good friends the Morisons. Meanwhile, Theodore was to make all the necessary financial arrangements for Tom through Forbes & Co., both in Bombay and England. Before long, young Tom's passage home had been booked aboard the *Huddart*, Captain Weller, bound for London. On arrival in England, he would be lodged with Thomas Fraser's widowed mother at Ashling House, 'sixteen miles from Portsmouth, within four miles of Chichester'.

Theodore had already invited Captain Weller of the *Huddart* to stay with him at Bycullah while the ship was in port. So, young Tom would have an opportunity to meet the man into whose care he was to be entrusted for the long voyage to England. The detailed arrangements being made for little Tom Barnard's voyage must have been an unwelcome reminder to Theodore that, though the event had been put off for the moment, he would shortly to have to send his own darling daughter 'home' to his parents in Aberdeenshire. This is another subject that he cannot bring himself to raise directly with Eliza. Instead he leaves it to Mrs Fraser and Will Ogilvie and throws himself with abandon onto the social merry-go-round of Bombay. He is clearly enjoying the ride and has been entertaining in a lavish manner. As one of the most eligible, and possibly desirable, men in the Presidency, his love life continues to be much talked about and it seems that none of his friends could or would pass up the opportunity of quizzing him about his plans for marriage. Only a fortnight after Ogilvie reported the rumours circulating in Surat about Theodore another letter arrived from Thomas Fraser: 'Are you married yet?' he asks, 'send plenty of cake up here.'

Fraser's letter has another more serious purpose; to finalise the details of Tom's passage to England and the arrangements for his arrival: 'It will be necessary,' he advises Theodore, 'that Tom should have someone to look after him on board – be so good as to enquire in Bombay if there is any person going home who would answer as a servant, as we must, if none are to be had in Bombay, endeavour to get one here, as Tom is too sickly to rough it.'

He continues: 'If the little Fellow could be landed at Portsmouth it would be sparing him as well as other people a great deal of trouble & inconvenience… If Captain Weller would be so good as to put him in a post chaise, bag & baggage, the little fellow would not be long before he got to his journeys end… Having so many Brothers in the Navy, & being in the habits of travelling backwards and forwards to Ashling there can be little doubt of the Post-Boys knowing the road & House – But if the little fellow is to go to London it will be very inconvenient, both with respect to where he is to stay and to the safety of his travelling so long a distance alone. Not having the pleasure of being acquainted with Captain Weller it would be too great a liberty on my part to think of asking him to take charge of the little fellow, till he had ascertained when the Chichester Coach leaves Charing Cross, which I believe is every other day… where the Boy would be very well taken care of by the Coachman (Kirby) who knew my father extremely well – when once at Chichester he would put him in a Post-chaise & be sent on to Ashling.' He concludes with the request, 'Forbes, may I take the liberty of asking you to mention this to Captain Weller?'

When young Tom arrived in Surat for his christening, Eliza was still labouring under the devastating blow of the death of her baby son. At eight months old little Fraser had been on the cusp of the transition from baby to little boy – just trying to shape a few words and beginning to develop his own personality. Before he died Eliza had been trying to keep the children's baptism on course. Will Ogilvie had assured her that he would make sure that the arrangements for the christening of all three Forbes children would not be forgotten. Now there were only two.

She was tormented by the knowledge that little Fraser died without being received into the Church of England and having his English name affirmed. The baptism of the remaining two children now became doubly important to her.

Eliza was stunned by Mrs Fraser's proposal that Kitty might go to England at the same time as Tom – in little more than a month's time – Theodore too seemed to have been taken aback by the speed of events. They both baulked at the idea of parting with Kitty so soon and, from Surat and Bombay, presented a united front against this insensitive proposal. Theodore was quick to rebuff Mrs Fraser's opinion that 'so good an opportunity of sending her [Kitty] to England ought not to be allowed to escape'. To his credit he declared that Kitty should certainly not be sent to England until Eliza was ready and willing to part with her. This challenge, at least, brought the couple some sort of rapprochement even if it was not the physical reunion so desperately desired by Eliza.

When it is made clear to Mrs Fraser that neither Theodore nor Eliza will agree to Kitty sailing in the *Huddart* with Tom, she revives her suggestion to Ogilvie that the little girl might come to live in Broach with her. Tom's baptism was fast approaching and the *Huddart* was due to sail before the end of the month, but still she had not entirely given up the idea of sending Kitty and Tom to England together. The christening of the Forbes children had still to be arranged. Eliza realised the strength of her position; suddenly Kitty's christening had become a bargaining tool:

'– On my arrival in town this forenoon,' writes Ogilvie to Theodore, 'I immediately called on your friend, finding her both in very good health & in tolerably good spirits, I took the opportunity of mentioning the subject to her – fully stating the particular advantages which now presented themselves of sending Kitty to England under the most comfortable and agreeable circumstances – & that I myself would take charge of the dear little girl to Bombay – I explained to her, at the same time that altho' you were desirous of availing yourself of so favourable opportunity, you by no means wished to press the matter against her inclinations.

'Her answer was what I certainly in a great measure expected – She did not object to parting ultimately with Kitty – but the idea of losing her so soon gave her most acute uneasiness, & she told me that that she could not bring herself to accede to such an arrangement, at present – but that she would two years hence – willingly resign the sweet child to what she was fully convinced was for her material advantage.

'I then mentioned to her the arrangement of allowing Kitty to reside with Mrs Fraser. Of Mrs F's kindness to herself & the children, she expressed herself in the most grateful & feeling terms – but that she could not think of parting with her little Darling till she finally leaves for Europe.'

Eliza was anxious to have both the children baptised, but she was not going to allow Mrs Fraser, Will Ogilvie or anyone else to push her into agreeing either to send the child to England aboard The *Huddart* with young Tom, or to give her into the care of Mrs Fraser. Ogilvie persisted: 'I delicately hinted to her,' he tells Theodore, 'my apprehension that Mrs Morison could not stand as one of the sponsors unless Kitty was either sent to Europe or placed under Mrs Fraser's care.' The hurtful implication was that Eliza was not socially acceptable.

Eliza's reply to Ogilvie's so-called 'delicate hint' was that 'altho' she was most anxious that the children should in the first instance be made members of our Church – she could have them now baptised by an Armenian Priest, & that they might afterwards be admitted to our communion.' Ogilvie was clearly irked by Eliza's uncooperative attitude and by his friend's refusal to overrule her. In his view, he tells Theodore, the opportunity of sending Kitty back aboard the *Huddart* with Tom 'ought to have been snatched at with eagerness'. 'But,' he warns, 'as you have determined to do nothing contrary to your friend's wishes, I would fondly hope that an equally favourable opening may offer for sending little Kate to Britain at the period which her Mother has specified & that the delay will be attended with no disadvantageous consequences to the Dear Child.' His last 'fond hope' is viciously barbed. It sounds like a deliberate reminder of the recent death of baby Fraser. Even if Ogilvie had not intended it as such, it was tactless; if he had, it was very unkind. But he continues: 'The Children are in high health & spirits – Little Kate who overheard part of her Mother's conversation with me – was a little depressed at hearing of her leaving Surat – but when I again called this afternoon I found her romping & laughing as usual.'

While Ogilvie and Mrs Fraser clearly believed they had Kitty's best interests at heart, it seems that they felt little warmth towards Eliza or any real concern for her feelings. In all the correspondence, neither of them ever refers to her by name. She is invariably called either 'your friend' or 'the mother'. She must have sensed, if not animosity on their part, at least their indifference to her feelings. There is no evidence that she knew that they and others were encouraging Theodore to find a British wife, but she was acutely aware that local rumours abounded about their split. Eliza had already complained that Dinshaw and Munchershaw… 'not giving their attention to our house as well as before' and she had reproached him:

'I might hear that you may write sometime to Lieut Ogilvie to desire Deenshaw & Munchershaw agreeable your mention [carry out your orders], but My beloved Sir, what are so private case as you not let me know to tell them? I am surprize and shameful before them, if should be any occasion [previously] you has been write me to tell them, but now you can write Ogilvie to tell them any circumstance and I think they thought as less regard by you on me and not like before affection.'

When the Frasers arrived from Broach with young Tom, Mrs Fraser began buying appropriate clothing and equipment to last him for the voyage and for his arrival in England. For reasons of economy she wanted to buy as much as she could in Surat, with funds advanced by Dinshaw for Theodore to debit to Barnard's account with Forbes & Co., Bombay. As far as she was concerned, the question of whether Kitty was to join Tom on his voyage had yet to be settled. But Eliza was adamant; she was not going to part with her little girl sooner than she would like, just so that she could travel with Tom. Neither of the children was yet five-years old – in two years time, Fazagool could go with Kitty on the voyage and see her safely to Scotland. She suggested that she might even agree to send Aleck at the same time.

Mrs Fraser was staying with the Morisons, in Nan Poora – only a stone's throw away from the house in which she and her husband had spent many happy years. When she heard of Theodore's decision she wrote to him immediately and concluded: 'I regret extremely that our charming little Kate is neither going home nor is likely to be intrusted to my protection. Believe me, my dear Mr Forbes, that she should have been in every way treated as my own – and it would have been my pride and pleasure to have supplied the loss she would at first have felt on leaving her Mother… I have not yet seen your dear little ones, but intend sending for them this evening – and hope to find them, in good health and spirits.' In the same letter she makes no secret of her loathing of her husband's new station at Broach: 'I am as miserable there as I was happy here,' she declares.

To Eliza, the arrival of Mrs Fraser with young Tom and the knowledge that he is shortly to be taken to Bombay to stay in Goodwin's 'Fine garden House', serves as a bitter reminder of how long it has been since Theodore has seen his own children. She writes impatiently to him, the day before Tom's christening: 'Now I am hourly expect the answer of my letters in English and Persian Language' … 'My Dear your Honor are my Eternal Protector and Crown of head, which desire you to understand the mean of my Intreating such utmost request in Persian letter, which I am sure you are more sensible than the other Gentlemen and will [have] improved [in] the Persian Language.'

She admonishes him: 'I am very astonish that between us was so affectionate, which you had never drink a drop of water without ask me, and now do not know what is the reason passed absolute separation, being 7 months ago we were heartly love each another – was not to love of Jewels money, riches etc but was only heartly affection which you now entirely forget.'

Theodore read this heartfelt reproach five days later, folded the letter and labelled it 'E. Kewurk, Surat, 29th October 1817, Received 3rd November'. And again he writes firmly 'Answer Unnecessary'. The following day Eliza was dispatching more provisions to him by 'a Pattamar boat belonging to Jugjeevundass Kuranee Furdonjee'. She lists 'A bag of fine Camod rice, 120 Seers of Surat, a jar of Toorinj [t'orange] Preserve for your own use and a pot of sweetmeat for Antoon.'

On Friday 31st October 1817, in the garrison chapel at Surat Castle, four-year-old Tom was baptised by the name Thomas George Barnard by the Reverend Thomas Carr, a young chaplain to the garrison. The boy's date of birth as written in the register is 'said to be November 2nd 1812'. So on the Sunday following his christening it would be Toms' fifth birthday. He is listed as 'natural son of Thomas Barnard, Broach, Judge and magistrate'. Tom's journey from Surat to Bombay was now the only thing remaining to be fixed. He had stayed with the Forbes children before and he still had a little time left to spend with them. Will Ogilvie had suddenly been called away on duty due to 'serious commotions at

Poona' and sent his regrets that he was now unable to take the boy to Bombay himself. 'The poor little fellow, I am happy to think, will still be in good hands,' he assures Theodore, 'Ogilvy has a most excellent Attentive Parsee, who goes with him, and I am certain that as soon as he reaches your House, he is in every way safe and comfortable.'

Diwali fell on the following Saturday; the whole city was celebrating the triumph of light over darkness and good over evil, and for the children's sake Eliza abandoned herself to celebrating the festival with them. Her mother was half-Indian and the significance of the celebrations was part of her background; Diwali would bring her new hope. You didn't have to be Hindu to enjoy the festival and she wanted her own children to share in the excitement she had felt as a child. There would be fireworks, feasting, gifts and goodwill for five days, and on the second day, there would be little Tom's birthday to celebrate too.

In Bombay, on the 8th November, Theodore received another letter from Aunt Mariam begging him to call Eliza and the children to Bombay as soon as possible, On the outside Theodore wrote simply: 'Mukhanee Khalah, Surat 1st November 1817. Rec'd 8 do do. Answer Unnecessary. T.F.'

Kitty and Aleck must have known that their young friend was shortly going to be staying with their father, but there was still no word from Bombay for Eliza; Theodore had not even replied to her private message in 'Persian language'. With a degree of optimism she did not truly feel, Eliza reassured the children that it would not be long now before they too would see their Papa – and they would all be able to stay in his fine new home and play in his wonderful garden.

On November 15th 1817 Mrs Fraser said a final farewell to young Tom Barnard and he set off on his great adventure with Ogilvy's trusted servant, two peons and a mass of baggage. After three days at sea, the oddly-assorted party – the frail little Anglo-Indian boy, two bearers and a dignified Parsee – arrived in Bombay, and made their way to Bycullah. Mrs Fraser had paid the servants in advance and told them that they were not to return to Surat until the *Huddart* had sailed. Until then they would all stay with Theodore who, having been a guest of Tom's father in Broach less than six months previously, would not be a complete stranger to the little boy. Old Antoon, who had attended Theodore there, was another familiar face. He had always been a great favourite with the

Forbes children and, according to Eliza, Kitty often asked for him, so he would certainly be kind to young Tom.

Two days after Tom left Surat, Eliza sent Diwali presents to Theodore – rustic cheeses in their own straw baskets, stem ginger and orange marmalade in pottery jars. Diwali was a happy time and, happily, she still had both her children. If Theodore had not backed her up in her refusal to part with Kitty, she might even now be mourning the absence of another child. She appreciated his unwavering support and now sent him:

'A basket of sweetmeat called Deevalee Khaylonahs of child, which it Khaylonahs forwarded by our beloved Ketty & Alexander, who says let send first sweetmeat Khaylonah to our beloved Papa who will keep it carefully and by thank God the meantime we can go to Bombay to embrace to the Papa, then we will eat it there on the table with Mama & Papa in fine new garden house.' It is a transparent ploy and a shameless attempt, while young Tom is staying with him, to make Theodore feel guilty for abandoning his own children.

As December approaches, Eliza is still waiting to hear from him. Angry at his neglect of Kitty and Aleck, whose birthdays are approaching, she writes: 'Now I am very surprizing and disappoint, as you do not write me the answer of my 3 or 4 letters before this, which makes me very uneasy and several suspect, therefore My beloved Sir, I do beseech your merciful Honor may please to write me the answer of your intention, to let me know as soon as possible, then I will let you know my best wish to see you at Bombay, in short time, because you were mentioned in your former letters as at Present only our absolute separation for short time, instead now being long period & appears me the fraudulent and changed your mind... Ketty and Alexr birthday are very near as they hopes to enjoy the pleasure on that day with our beloved Papa at Bombay or Surat.'

Chapter 16

Friends and Family, 1817 – 1818

MR. BABER'S HOUSE, AT TELLICHERRY.

European House, Tellicherry on the Malabar Coast c. 1820.

16

Bombay and Surat, November 1817 – January 1818

As soon as Theodore was told of Tom's arrival in the house, he sent for the boy. The frail five-year old was led before the sahib and proudly handed him a letter from Mrs Fraser: 'This will be delivered to you by my poor little Protégé Tom, I have… intrusted him to the charge of the Doctor's servant, who is a most careful, trustworthy man, and will, I am sure do everything for him you may direct. I enclose a list of his Clothes, and a memorandum of the few articles which were not procurable here, and will trouble you purchase them for him. He is a fine tempered boy and will give little or no trouble. A standing Bedplace fixed in the cabin will be requisite, and with a high side, for fear he should fall out. – Pray write me a few lines announcing Tom's arrival in Bombay, for I shall be very anxious about him. Any thing that he may want, and may have escaped my memory, pray procure for him. Barnard is able and willing to pay anything and everything for him. I fear I am giving you a great deal of trouble, but indeed I am much interested about this little fellow, and am most anxious that he should have everything comfortable.'

Opposite page:

Mrs Fraser's list of Tom Barnard's clothes bought for his voyage aboard the *Huddart*, 1817.

Photocopy of document in *Ms. 2740*, King's College Library, Aberdeen.

Reproduced by kind permission of the Brose family of Boyndlie.

~~Masters~~

List of ~~The~~ Barnard's Clothes

8½. dozen pr. of Pantaloons, of Size

1½. —" — Jackets.

6. dozen, and 3. Shirts.

18. night Shirts.

20. Flannel Banyans.

16. - Ditto - Drawers.

5. ditto - night Caps

1. Flannel Caps.

21. muslin night Caps

18 - muslin Banyans.

34. muslin dresses, to be worn as night dresses or when the weather is hot. —

16. Pillow Cases.

23. Sheets

2. Palamposes.

2. quilts.

1. Flannel Dressing Gown.

1. Great Coat

4. Cloth Suits,

1. Camlet

1. dozen pr. of Shoes

100. Tannah Towels

4. dozen pr. of Stockings

2. Hatts

2. Blankets

1. Europe Trunk

1. Pewter Guglet & Bason

1. Cot complete

6. pr. of Europe Soap

    Brushes & Combs.

1. Shawl Handkerchief

Close on the heels of the new arrivals in Bycullah, comes a letter from Charlotte Wrangham. She writes that she is on the point of leaving Tannah to return to Broach, but first she is going to Surat. When arrives there, she writes again: 'I hope little Barnard is well, I did not know he was with you until yesterday evening... Miss Borchards and I arrived here on Tuesday, and were kindly received by the Morisons... I have not heard anything of your little ones, I have just sent Sapoorjee to enquire after them.'

She is able to close her letter with the news that Sapoorjee has since reported back to her that Kitty and Aleck both look 'very well indeed' and had 'made a thousand enquiries' about him. It seems that Miss Borchards and Miss Wrangham are going to spend Christmas together at Broach with the Frasers. She writes again when they are about to leave Surat for 'that lively place, Baroach' – 'I cannot say I go with pleasure,' Charlotte tells him, 'though I am very anxious to see my dear sister.' Theodore has been invited to join the party.

December 1st dawned; it was Kitty's fifth birthday and there was still no word for her from her Papa. She was old enough to have remembered last year and the excitement of his return from Bombay. She was, in Eliza's words, 'all in dishope'. In eight days' time it would be Aleck's third birthday, December 9th; despite Eliza's recent reminder it seems he still had not written, or sent anything for the children's birthdays. Tom had been with him for at least a week. Surely this must have made him reflect on his own children – his five-year-old daughter, all too soon to be sent to England herself and his little boy, about to turn three? Apparently not.

At last, on December 7th, the time came for little Barnard to embark aboard the *Huddart*. Theodore took the child down to the Fort Stairs and put him and his luggage aboard the ship, and left him under the kindly eye of Captain Weller. The present of rice and preserves from Eliza arrived at his house in Bycullah three days later; Eliza's note enclosed with her gift is signed as usual 'Your very affectionate Mrs Forbes' and marked 'The freight I have paid here'. It is not enough to change Theodore's mind. Once again, his only response is to write 'Answer Unnecessary'.

Poor Eliza was desperate. He had written only one letter to her since baby Fraser died in September. She had tried everything. Her anguished pleading; the wellbeing of the children; her own health; her scolding; the sanctity of their marriage; their cotton commissions; Kitty and Aleck's birthdays and even her gifts – none of them, it seemed, could soften Theodore's heart. Now another disappointment was on its way: he had made other plans for his Christmas holiday. He would be spending it in Broach. He had accepted Mrs Fraser's invitation.

Weller and his young charge were to sail from Bombay on December 7th with the 'land wind' which 'set in around eleven o'clock in the evening'. Theodore had made it his business to entertain the captain well while the *Huddart* was in port, and so he was confident that little Tom would be well looked after. The captain had promised to send Theodore news of the boy whenever possible during the long voyage. The *Asiatic Journal and Monthly Miscellany, Volume 6* records the bare facts: 'Bombay Departures Dec. 7th. HC's extra ship *Huddart*, Captain C Weller to London. Passengers: Lieut Col. Smith his lady and two children, Major Mackanochie, Surgeon ffoyes, Capt. Pierce, Lieut Rybot, Miss Llewellyn, Master Barnard.' Unlike most young British and Anglo-Indian children leaving the land of their birth, Tom had no father or mother on the quayside to cling to. He did not have to endure a tearful farewell and watch from the poop deck as his parents receded into the distance, waving until his arm ached. At barely five-years old he was expected to evince the manly British quality of emotional restraint. Colonel Smith's children had both parents with them and it is to be hoped that Tom and Miss Llewellyn soon made friends with them and were treated as part of their family.

Not long before midnight, the *Huddart* got under way. Into the darkness they sailed. Soon, Old Lady Island and the Colaba lighthouse had been left far behind. The lighthouse continued to wink and flicker in their wake for hours as Captain Weller set their course by the stars above. He was taking them south along the Malabar Coast to the old port of Tellicherry, known today as Thalassery, where he hoped to pick up more young passengers. Next morning Tom would wake to find that they were sailing on the open sea with only an occasional glimpse of land to their port side. It would be ten days before they made their next landfall – plenty of time for him to get his 'sea legs'.

The *Huddart* dropped anchor off the little port of Tellicherry on December 17th. It was a Company garrison town and their arrival was signalled by the boom of the Fort cannon. The familiar Union Flag fluttered above the Fort just as it did above his home in Broach and from the Castle at Surat. The dwellings and warehouses of the town were also reminiscent of Broach – but Tom's home town was perched on an outcrop above the tidal banks of the River Nerbudda rather than overlooking the sea shore. The British bungalows gleamed brightly through the stands of nodding coconut palms. Wheeling gulls greeted their arrival loudly and the bright colours of the clear ocean waters cheered everyone on board as they were rowed ashore. The boom of their cannon had signalled their arrival and a welcoming party awaited them. All on board could now look forward to spending time on dry land, and to joining in the celebrations of the British community at Christmas time. Theodore had carried out his responsibilities well; Captain Weller was true to his word and wrote to him from Tellicherry to let him know that the ship had arrived safely, and that Tom was 'quite well and happy'. He went on to thank Theodore for his hospitality while in Bombay. When he wrote, it was only three days before Christmas, and the lad was, he told him, at that very moment 'on shore with me at Mr Fell's'.

Mr Fell was the 'Forest Conservator'. His title did not carry the same implications it might today. Though he lived in a fine bungalow on the coast and checked the inventory of timber as it was hauled down from the vastness of the Malabar forests, his position had been created solely to enforce the Company's recently imposed timber monopoly; much to the dismay and the financial detriment of the timber merchants who had been carrying on their trade there for many years. The aptly named Mr Fell had nothing to do with conservation; in fact, he was said never to have visited the forest at all.

Just as he had hoped, Captain Weller picked up three more children in Tellicherry, and he predicted that 'something more will turn up before we sail'. The three children he had already booked for the passage to England were: 'The daughter of Mr Wilson, who has been particularly kind [to young Tom] … the daughter of Mr Sheffield, and a son of the Clergyman.' The kindly Mr Wilson, according to Francis Buchanan ten years earlier, was the collector for the area. He lived in an impressive stone house, 'reckoned a superb building' by the locals – 'It is in the form of a square surrounding a court in which there is a well and a small tank… The building is two stories high.' This may be the same as that occupied by the Collector T. H. Baber in which the future Duke of Wellington lodged in 1800.

The second mentioned of Captain Weller's new charges was the daughter of William Sheffield, a magistrate in the Hon. Company's Civil Service. The Bombay section of the *Asiatic Journal and Monthly Miscellany, Volume 6* for July 1818 reveals that a tragedy had occurred the previous November, shortly before the *Huddart* sailed from Bombay. An announcement of a birth under the name Sheffield, and dated 12th November 1817 reads: 'At Tellicherry, the Lady of Wm. Sheffield Esq. of the HC Civil Service of a son.' In the next column, the death is announced of the new mother on December 3rd. So, when the *Huddart* dropped anchor, poor little Miss Sheffield, who was to be Tom's shipmate, had suffered the loss of her mother a mere fortnight earlier.

The clergyman Weller refers to, whose son was also to join them on the voyage, was the Rev. Francis Spring, a chaplain appointed to Tellicherry when the Church Missionary Society established their mission to Malabar in the previous year. According to Charles Williams in his *Military Gazetteer*, the Rev. Mr. Spring had translated the church catechism and liturgy into Malayalam and also established a school 'of 50 scholars'. The original school buildings still exist in modern day Thalassery and the school has grown and prospered over the centuries.

While Tom and Captain Weller were being entertained in Tellicherry, in Surat Eliza was trying to hide her anxiety. She must make Christmas special for the children. Last year it had been full of joy when Theodore was there with them. She was still hoping, against all signs to the contrary, that he might arrive as he did then, with an armful of presents for the children. How crestfallen she would have been had she known that his Christmas plans did not include them or her. On December 22nd he had not yet left Bombay, when a letter from Barnard reached him there, concerning the 1,000 Rupees he owed Forbes & Co. for Tom's passage. Barnard cannot resist teasing Theodore about yet another potential wife: 'It is not long ago that the news-mongers informed me you were going to advance upon Miss Pitcairn, and assigned in proof that you had taken the large house lately occupied by Goodwin.' However, whether or not Miss Pitcairn was the object of his desire, he was on the point of embarking for Broach to stay with the Frasers and he did not write to Eliza before he left.

Two days later, on Christmas Eve, she had to content herself with sending a brief note to Theodore: 'I am expect of your Honors letter being long ago, and also I myself, Ketty and Alexander often ask to our Excellent friend Captain Ogilvie as any letter from Papa, then he speak to us – "when I will receive the letter from Papa I shall bring immediately" – therefore my beloved Sir, I beg you to write 6 or 7 lines for God sake, which will be comfort us to hear your health and happiness.' She seals the letter and gives it to Ogilvie to send to him in Bombay, as usual. But Theodore had already arrived in Broach and Ogilvie forwarded the note to him there with a covering letter:

'From the address of the enclosed you will perceive that your Friend here is, as yet unacquainted with your journey in this direction – I have thought it most advisable to say nothing on the subject to her, and conceal the circumstance as long as possible, as it would only cause unnecessary anxiety, & perhaps raise hopes & expectations which cannot be realized. – Should she become acquainted with your having left B'bay – I shall then mention what you desire in your last – To guard as much as possible against discovery on her part, I shall send this under cover to Barnard, as the Parsee who writes your Friend's Letters is, at present, employed in the Post Office Department, during the sickness of Byramjee and he would, I am disposed to think, immediately inform her, of your present residence. – I am truly happy to add, that both she and the Children are in excellent health – Kitty continues the same fine promising girl she ever was – & Aleck is a truly delightful chubby fellow – & can now talk pretty well.'

For the moment Theodore was secure in the knowledge that Eliza knew nothing of his whereabouts. However, on the very last day of 1817, New Year's Eve, Ogilvie wrote again to Theodore at Broach: 'Some days since, in calling on your Friend, I found that she had heard both of your having left Bombay, and your arrival in Broach, and enquired of me if the report was true – I was under the necessity of feigning ignorance of your movements – but assured her that as soon as I heard any correct information – I should immediately acquaint her with it. Next morning your note of the 25th reached me – which afforded me a very favourable opportunity of giving her the desired intelligence, without exciting any suspicions – by attributing your supposed previous silence regarding your movements, to a press and hurry of business – The enclosed, no doubt, most urgently solicits your presence here – I mentioned to her – what you formerly wrote me on that point – and when the time of your proceeding farther North arrives – everything can be again placed to the score of business, which I informed your Friend, in general prevented both Merchants and Soldiers, from being their own masters.'

It is not hard to imagine how hurt and troubled Eliza must have been when she discovered that Theodore had chosen to spend Christmas with the Frasers and their guests rather than with his own family. The confirmation of his present location was all that she was to receive – and it came only indirectly through Will Ogilvie. It seems that he was becoming as adept as his friend at scheming and had entered wholeheartedly into the spirit of Theodore's game – 'feigning ignorance' and not 'exciting any suspicions'.

While Theodore was enjoying his Christmas break with the Frasers, a letter arrived for him from Bombay. It was from John Allan MacPherson, one of his colleagues at Messrs Forbes & Co. He was evidently a close friend – in less than three years' time Theodore would leave him a generous legacy of one thousand Rupees. MacPherson writes: 'The Grove since you left us makes but a sombre appearance – a proof that some sadness reigns within – No 1 & 2 are often abroad – but poor No 3 remains at home – this looks well! – so pray return as soon as possible.' It seems possible that he had found an Indian mistress in Bombay. If 'poor No. 3' mentioned by MacPherson is Theodore's *bibi* she will prove to be no match for the mother of his children. Though Eliza is feeling betrayed and neglected, she has not given up all hope of winning him back.

In Tellicherry, Little Tom Barnard's health had been greatly improved by the mild weather and refreshing sea air of the voyage. The *Huddart* was to remain at anchor off Tellicherry over the whole of Christmas and the New Year. Visitors were a rare treat in such isolated outposts, so Captain Weller and the *Huddart*'s passengers were sure to have been included in any feasts or parties going on in Mr Wilson's splendid house, and probably in other expatriate homes too. It was very likely the first time Tom had experienced a Christmas with so many other children around. On Saturday January 3rd, Captain Weller wrote again to Theodore telling him how Tom had already become a great favourite with everyone because of his 'quiet and good disposition'. This augured well for the rest of the voyage.

Weller took the opportunity of the *Admiral Davy* being in port on January 4th to send his letter back to Bombay. 'We will sail,' he tells Theodore, 'tonight, with the land wind.' And so, around an hour before midnight, the children in their cots heard the captain's voice booming out the orders to haul in the anchor and hoist the sails and the ship's repose was rudely brought to an end. To the newest young passengers, the groaning of the windlass, the creaking of the timbers and the shouts of the sailors as they hauled the sails aloft and brought the ship about, were strange and disturbing noises, but as she left her safe anchorage to face the waves of the Arabian Sea, it seemed that she lightened. Her sails filled and like a spirited horse put out to grass, she leaped boldly forward into the darkness. The pitch and roll might have been unsettling to the new children on board – 'land-lubbers all' – but young Tom was by now an 'old hand' and he would sleep soundly in his cot.

1817 had petered out dismally for Eliza, with no word from Theodore. Ogilvie's confirmation that he had gone to Broach, and the suspicion growing ever stronger in her mind convinced her that all his promises had been 'fraudulent'. The arrival of the New Year was celebrated across the city by the British while the old Mughal Serail slept. Collett's house was within earshot of the rise and fall of distant laughter from the garrison, reverberating along the darkened streets; the cheery voices and noisy carousal carried across the city on the cool night air; muffled sounds of revelry from the nearby British Factory echoed off the city walls and the masculine cheers and shouts from noisy mess games resounded from the direction of the Castle to make Eliza acutely aware of her loneliness. Even the strains of far-off dance music shimmying on the tide from the distant bungalows of Nan Poora seemed to mock her. They were a poignant reminder of happier times; of Theodore stumbling home in the early hours, merry from Hogmanay and first-footing; clumsy, loud and loving. She could picture him now, celebrating with Barnard and the Frasers in Broach, glass in hand and a smile on his face, and the stark reality of their separation became ever more hurtful.

The bittersweet sight of Kitty and Alexander's blithe enjoyment of the traditional Armenian festivities with their big cousins on January 6th was a painful reminder that one day she would have to part with them too. It was already more than a month since little Tom had left Surat. If he had been hers she would have found the long wait for news intolerable. But he was already sailing west aboard the *Huddart*, across the wide expanse of the Indian Ocean, bound for the African coast and the Cape of Good Hope and Captain Weller's letter, containing the encouraging news that the boy was well and happy, was safe aboard the *Admiral Davy* northbound up the Malabar Coast, on its way to bring reassurance and comfort to all who loved and missed him.

While young Tom was settling once again into the routine of life on board ship, in Surat, Eliza was becoming increasingly unsettled. As the Eastern orthodox celebration of Christ's nativity and baptism approached she was worried. Theodore still did not write and once again her health began to suffer. On the eve of the Armenian celebrations, Will Ogilvie wrote to him that she had been unwell for the last two or three days: 'Your poor Friend here has, I am sorry to say, felt indisposed, during the last few days. She first complained on Friday – and on Saturday morning – I carried Sharp the Capt. Surgeon of the 5th to see her – She complains of stomatick pains and mentions that she was troubled with similar ones whilst at Mocha – Last night she felt particularly uneasy – But Sharp gave her a composing draught – and she feels much better today, and I trust will be soon quite well. Alex and Kitty are, I am happy to say, in high health and spirits.'

It seems that Eliza had not been well enough even to enjoy the feasts on the 6th, and by the 8th her condition had worsened. Ogilvie, was seeing her 'twice a day, in passing to and from the Castle,' and reported that 'she passed a restless night – with a slight return of the pain in her chest.' He continues: 'This I immediately communicated to the Dr, who has sent her a draught to be taken at night and will see her either this evening, or tomorrow morning.' He goes on to comment that 'Sharp is certainly not an Ogilvy in abilities or anything else – but I must do him the justice to say that he has evinced much feeling attention to your poor Friend – during her present illness – and seems to understand her complaint – The sweet children are I am happy to say in high health and spirits.'

Ogilvie suggested to Theodore that they might be able to arrange a meeting at Khim Chokee, a marketplace conveniently situated mid-way between Broach and Surat. So, the two friends agreed to meet there at the caravanserai, the travellers' rest house, on the weekend of 10th –11th

January. As they were keen to keep their rendezvous secret, Ogilvie first made discreet enquiries about the travel plans of any acquaintances who might have been going that way and was able to reassure Theodore that their meeting would not be interrupted by anyone from the Surat establishment who might recognise them.

While the two friends were enjoying their relaxed Sunday morning 'tête a tête at the Khim', with no thought of work, in Bombay, trouble was brewing at Forbes & Co. Theodore's clerk, Jaggananth Wissvananth, at that very moment was writing him an urgent missive. Michie Forbes had just called in unexpectedly at his house: 'Asking for the office books,' he tells Theodore, 'which are locked up by you and taken the key with you.' Apparently Michie was not pleased to have to leave with only the letter book for 1809/10, which Jaggananth had been copying from. 'The other letter book in which I am copying the letters,' writes Jaggananth, 'I did not shew him,' adding, '– everything is in good order.' It seems that the austere Michie had already formed a poor opinion of Theodore, and hoped to catch him out in some way. Jaggananth, aware of the growing friction between the two men, was doing his best to protect his master.

Ogilvie's prediction proved to be correct; their meeting at the Khim was not interrupted by any of their acquaintances. But if he thought that Eliza could not find out about their conspiracy in any other way, then he was mistaken. Next morning he called in, as usual, at her lodgings on his way to the Castle. No sooner had the servant admitted him than he was confronted by a very agitated Eliza. The previous day, at the very moment of the friends' clandestine rendezvous, she had apparently felt rather unwell, and had sent Markar to General Laurence's with a note. Finding that Ogilvie was absent he asked where he might find him. Ogilvie had not advised the general and his servants of the need for secrecy, and they told Markar about the meeting at the Khim Chokee. Markar returned to Collett's house to give Eliza the devastating news that Ogilvie had gone to meet Theodore. 'She had thereby discovered my absence and where I had gone,' wrote Ogilvie to Theodore, commenting, 'This had naturally produced considerable anxiety and uneasiness.'

Poor Ogilvie was totally unprepared for the situation and, unsurprisingly, he baulked at the prospect of telling the truth about Theodore's final determination to a near-hysterical Eliza. His first instinct when he was confronted by her had been to make up a story that 'would have the greatest effect in quieting her mind'. So, he assured her that Theodore still intended, if possible, to pay a visit to Surat before he left Broach, but that the 'press of business' during his stay there meant that he could not say when that would be. According to him, Eliza 'then made little reply'. Relieved that he did not have to deal with a further emotional outburst, he left quickly, saying that he would call in again on his way home from the Castle.

He returned that evening. When he knocked at Eliza's door for the second time that day, he did so hoping that she might have regained her composure. However, she had not been taken in by his assurances. Suspicious that she had not been told the whole truth, 'she most earnestly entreated me to let her know,' he tells Theodore, 'what your real intentions were – telling me at the same time, that she entertained great apprehensions – that they were not according to her wishes – I immediately conceived that her request on this point afforded me a favourable opportunity of hinting to her your final and determined resolution – I therefore mentioned to her that it was my real opinion that the change and seperation which had taken place must ever continue.'

It was not what Eliza wanted to hear; her worst fears had now been confirmed. It was already almost a year since Theodore had left her in Surat – and suddenly she understood that, for the whole of that time, he had been lying to her. She remembered his affectionate love making after Chotabhoy was born, his pride in Kitty and Aleck, his easy familiarity with Aratoon and her wider family. She could not believe that he had stopped loving her, that he no longer cared about their children, or that he had forgotten how happy they had been together in Mocha and how her family had welcomed him on their return. For a moment or two she was stunned into silence.

'At first,' Ogilvie tells him, 'she appeared in some degree prepared to hear that your union was not to be renewed.' But she was not silent for long. Searching desperately for any hope to cling to, she begged him to persuade Theodore, at least to grant her 'a parting interview'. Ogilvie tried without success to convince her that such a meeting would only serve to upset them both. His words fell on deaf ears; they 'seemed to make little impression' and she 'continued to entreat that she might hear... in person' that they were never to meet again.

'I used every argument to convince her that what she proposed and wished would be productive of the most acute anguish to you both,' he tells Theodore. As kindly as possible, he had insisted that, 'As a friend to both,' he was 'most decidedly' opposed to it. Eventually Ogilvie assured her that he would not fail to pass on her request to Theodore. He ends his letter with the hope that she would 'in the course of a short time, reflect and consider more maturely on what I mentioned and be convinced of the propriety of implicitly acceding to your wishes.'

The phrase 'more maturely' and 'propriety' in describing his hopes for her future conduct subtly imply the substance of her initial reaction to his message. A vision of tears and tantrums is conjured up by Ogilvie's description of her desperate entreaties. The upset had an immediate effect on her health; once again she sought refuge from her worries by calling in the *hakim*, and finding a house in a more salubrious area. Ogilvie's dramatic account of her reaction to his resolution seems at last to have touched Theodore. As soon as he read it, he dashed off, according to Eliza, a 'very affectionate letter from Broach'. It reached her on January 18th. Although she was gratified by the warm tone of the letter, the anniversary of Fraser's birth was only a week away and she needed to move out of the Mughal Serail. By the end of January, she had moved, she told him, to the 'Mumdeas garden near Dutch Bunder by the permission of Hurgovind Nathoo, for few days without rent only to recover health.'

While Ogilvie said that he had merely 'hinted' that a permanent separation was Theodore's 'final and determined resolution', he also said that he had left Eliza in no doubt that in his own view the separation 'must ever continue'. However, Theodore's letter seems to have reassured her that he still cared for her and the children. His apparent concern for her health rekindled the hope that, given the right circumstances, she might be able to win him back. She still hoped that when Theodore left he Broach might return to Bombay by way of Surat. Her belief that he would not be able to resist her, if they could meet again 'eyes to eyes', remained unshaken. She did not reply immediately.

Chapter 17

Seaside and Ship to Shore, 1818

From ship to shore – Portsmouth. c.1820. Engraving after J M W Turner RA.

17

Surat & Portsmouth, February – June 1818

With her move to the house in the 'Mumdeas Garden' complete and the children settled, on February 18th, after due reflection, Eliza sent for her scribe and began to dictate her reply: 'My dear Sir, your kind favour and very affectionate letter from Broach dated the 17th [January] reached me safe on the 18th ultimo… My dear Sir, you said to be not vex myself, as to mind my health it is very true, but you ought to consider how could be easy myself and children without seeing your prosperous face with your merciful eyes… Your Honour are known as I have no father mother and no other supporter, but except Almighty God and your honour are of my protector in every respect, which the whole world knows that only you are of my crown of head and adorn till my life… I did not anything so as you can displease with me, really say I do not know on what account you have attached in your heart so hard with me and children… Since a year past I am unwell on account considering the absolute Separation between us, and most part about two months ago my former complaint attached me in my breast.

'P.S. Ketty and Alexander often ask after you to see their beloved Papa, and I let you know they are in good health… pray let us hear soon of your Health and safe arrival at Bombay, and send answer of this letter.' She must have written the post script with a heavy heart, knowing that he was not returning by way of Surat.

As usual she gave the letter to Ogilvie to forward but, whether deliberately or accidentally, he delayed sending it on until he was able to put it under the same cover as his own. It was another six days before he wrote again to Theodore: 'Your Friend's health has improved much of late, particularly since she removed to a House belonging to Hurgovindass, (on the River near the Dutch Bunder) of which she has got the loan, as it is at present untenanted. – The enclosed was sent to me, a few days ago… the Children are in the highest health and spirits –

and their Mother as I have already mentioned, is regaining her strength daily.'

As usual, before sending it, he first called on Eliza so that he could give his friend up-to-date news about the family. But he had evidently not admitted to her that he had not yet sent her letter. Just as he was leaving, Eliza handed him another and he sent both letters under the same cover. The tone of Eliza's second note had changed from pathetic to persecuted: 'Many days ago I have not find a letter from your goodness, I beg you the favour to let us hear soon of your health... you made me in such high degree, upon which many enemies came jealous in their heart and they hopes to see me in poor distress situation, therefore I pray you will not do so as the enemies wishes but pray you must keep the same regard and affection till my life because you are good sensible and I am under your protection about 8 or 9 years ago with respect and affection and at present I think your affection being little less upon which I pray to God better is to take soon my life, and also my temper and affection are continue the same, but the temper being now a little slow then before by observing and considering of the worlds business.'

Eliza is beginning to worry that as Theodore's affection for her has cooled she is losing not only her husband, but the respect of the traders and merchants of the city, who seem to have realised that her hold on his purse strings has begun to slacken. As for Theodore, he had already returned to work in Bombay, refreshed and carefree enough to write letters to all his family in Scotland, but not to Eliza. He was still actively engaged in courting any eligible and attractive young ladies in the British community, as well as consorting with the girls of the Lal Bazaar, only a short distance from the Bycullah Road.

A letter from his friend Wilkins, Collector and Magistrate in Jumbooseer was waiting for him when he arrived back from Broach, and gives a hint of his activities at this time: 'I now have to request that you will do me the favour to order, the moment you get this,' writes Wilkins, 'one of your Kumatee Hummals to call my Kumatee Nursoo, well known as a famous Pimp of a late and well known old Goat whose bones are now in the church not a mile from your office – I gave him leave to go to Bombay some time ago and now beg you will do me the favour to tell him that I am coming down immediately and he must not on any account come back to Jumbooseer as I shall want him in Bombay. He will be of great service to both of us.'

Two years later Poor Wilkins's own bones were laid to rest in the English Cemetery in Surat, a mere two months after Theodore's burial at sea. A fine monument was inscribed: 'Erected out of Regard, To the Memory of Mr Wilkins By a Few of his Brother Servants.' The rest of the long inscription reveals that Wilkins shared other passions with Theodore besides those of the flesh:

'As an Oriental scholar generally The deceased was highly distinguished Having in early life acquired a taste For the languages and literature of The East under the tuition of his Uncle, the celebrated Orientalist Charles Wilkins T.L.D. His knowledge of the Sanscrit and Persian languages was not excelled By any of the Bombay establishment.'

This friend and near-contemporary who 'Departed this life on the 30th November 1820 Aged about 29 years', was also a fellow member of the Bombay Literary Society. By 1818, when he wrote to Theodore anticipating their shared use of the services of his pimp, the proceedings of that august society record that Wilkins had already translated the entire *Mahabharata* from the Sanskrit.

While Theodore was putting his health to the test with his rackety lifestyle, the weather was still balmy enough in Surat to bring a refreshing salt breeze from the tidal reaches of the river and Eliza's health was improving with the change of air. The Dutch Bunder near her new lodgings, was the long-established VOC (Dutch East India Company) Factory and wharf a short distance to the south of the Castle, where the 'Dutch Gardens' still provide a splash of green for the citizens of modern Surat. It was a much more open and airy part of the city – right beside the river and not far from the spacious residences of Nan Poora. As Eliza's health began to improve, Ogilvie's suggestion that she and the children should go to the seaside at Domus for a break was shelved. 'Our excellent friend Captain Ogilvie desire me to go to Domus for change air, but I think there is too far and will be great deal a expence,' she writes.

Whether, at the beginning of March, a paying tenant was taking over the house in the Mumdeas Garden; whether Eliza felt her health had been sufficiently improved by the change of air; or whether she just missed being near her church and family, she decided to move the family back into the Mughal Serail. On 12th March she found an excuse to contact Theodore again. She wrote to him to beg a favour for Mr Chatoor who, she says, 'is poor, honest and large family man'. He is their friend Stephen's [Estaphanoos] brother-in-law. He had apparently advanced money to an army officer who had recently died. As the estate is in the hands of Forbes & Co. Eliza asks Theodore to reclaim Mr Chatoor's money from the officer's son.

Her letter must have crossed with his. When Ogilvie called to deliver it he found Eliza in the midst of all the bustle of unpacking and settling the children into yet another house belonging to Lewis Collett. She was still ordering the new household when he put the long-awaited letter from Bombay into her eager hand. It was not, as she had hoped, an affectionate letter nor did it summon her to Bombay: instead it contained Theodore's strict instructions that she really must not exceed her monthly allowance of two-hundred and ten rupees, to be drawn on his account with Dinshaw.

Knowing the contents, Ogilvie left her to read it in private, and on March 15th wrote again to Theodore: 'I have since seen your family twice and I am happy to say that they are all in good health – They have again moved into the Mogul Seroy – and I trust that your Friend will experience no return of her illness – She has not entered upon the subject of your letter – but I shall take advantage of the first convenient opportunity – and again mention and point out to her, the necessity of the strictest economy and not to allow herself to be imposed upon by a set of self-interested people of her countrymen, both clergy and laity.'

The criticism was somewhat unfair; the rapidly dwindling Armenian population in Surat was suffering real financial hardship. She was a devout churchgoer and a staunch supporter of her community. Mesroub Jacob Seth describes her as 'Mrs Elizabeth Farbessian', the 'only one of any means'. Although the government still subsidised the church and *vartaped* – and would continue to do so for some years to come – fewer and fewer opportunities for profitable trade were open to the handful of Armenian merchants who remained in the city. Year on year, younger men and whole families were moving to the fast growing commercial centres of the three Presidencies: Bombay, Madras and Calcutta. Always generous with Theodore's money, and despite Ogilvie's clear disapproval, Eliza was doing her best to support her church and help the aged and impoverished members of her community.

Though Kitty and Aleck were being brought up within the Armenian Eastern Orthodox communion, Eliza desperately wanted them baptised into the Church of England so that they could be registered as British subjects. The Rev. Thomas Carr had performed the ceremony for little Tom Barnard less than five months ago, but Eliza's aspirations rested not on the goodwill of the padre but on the sponsors. Mrs Fraser had been the key to a successful outcome for young Tom. She had taken charge of every detail of his baptism, and Theodore had played his part admirably in arranging a passage in the *Huddart* for the boy and putting him up in his own house until the time came for him to go aboard. Eliza could not understand why he was being so dilatory over the baptism of his own children. To Theodore, it was the next step that mattered; once they had been baptised they could be sent to England on a Company ship. But perhaps he wanted to hear of Tom's safe arrival in England before he committed his darling Kitty to such a long sea voyage.

Meanwhile, half a world away, far, far to the west; across the emptiness of the Indian Ocean; beyond the jungles and mountains, the deserts and savannahs of the whole continent of Africa; little Tom was now off the Atlantic seaboard of West Africa, making steady headway towards a new life in England. The New Year had seen Captain Weller's ship make good progress. Just two months after leaving Tellicherry, the ship had already crossed the Equator, rounded The Cape of Good Hope, and arrived at the Island of St. Helena in the South Atlantic. The twin-peaked volcanic outcrop was an impressive sight, with great men-o'-war anchored offshore and numbers of both Company and Regular Army soldiers garrisoned under canvas amongst gleaming new fortifications. All this recent activity on the island had been centred on securing the imprisonment of Napoleon Bonaparte, self-proclaimed Emperor of France, self-styled King of Italy and now the world's most famous prisoner of war. The British had learned their lesson from the laxity of the guard during his exile on the Mediterranean island of Elba. This time they were taking no chances.

While the *Huddart* was being re-provisioned, Tom and his fellow passengers had an opportunity to go ashore to stretch their legs. Some even hoped to catch a glimpse of the diminutive 'Terror of all Europe'. But according to Buckingham's *Oriental Herald*: 'The passengers of the *Huddart*, who went on shore with an expectation of seeing Bonaparte, stated that he still continues sulky, and will not allow himself to be seen by any English visitors. He rises, at this season of the year, about three o'clock in the morning, and after walking in his garden for an hour, retires to his house, where he remains the whole of the day.' The *Huddart* stayed off St. Helena for a week and on March 21st 1818 she sailed from the prison island on the final leg of her voyage.

In Surat, while the streets grew hotter and hotter, Eliza was still waiting for another letter from Theodore: 'Since long ago I expect to hear your Health and happiness,' she had written on March 12th, 'and makes me very uneasy of not receiving the answer of my last three letters which I hope you will be so kind to write me soon.'

On April 12th a letter arrived from him at last, and she opened it eagerly. It was not an invitation to come to Bombay, nor was there any word of the children's christening. Instead, in reply to her request for funds to settle the account of the *hakim* or native doctor, and other bills, she was disappointed to receive yet another lecture on the necessity of curbing her extravagance. Theodore claimed that in the last year she had drawn no less than four thousand rupees on his account with Dinshaw. This was an enormous sum, nearly double the whole of her annual allowance.

At the time, Ogilvie was based in Bhimpore, a seaside village where some of the garrison were encamped for the hot season. It was very near Domus [Dumas], where he had suggested Eliza and the children should take a short break. Availing himself, Ogilvie said of a 'quiet time and place' he now sat down to write to Theodore 'to perform what ought to have been done long ago'. The result was a long and informative letter written over the course of several days:

'Both Kitty and Aleck,' he says of his last visit to the family, 'were I am happy to say quite well and enjoying their usual flow of spirits – Their Mother's health, as I have at different times stated, has been for the last 12 months, very unsettled: but this, as far as I can pretend to offer an opinion, is to be attributed more to the situation and air of the Mogul Seroy than to the general climate of this part of the country – This great and apparent inconvenience attending their present abode, I have been long endeavouring to remedy – and I now entertain hopes of soon procuring a house situated in a more open and healthy part of the town – and also on more reasonable terms – which is certainly another most desirable consideration.'

After receiving Theodore's last letter, with its reprimand about her extravagance, Eliza had found the family somewhere cheaper to live. Only a little over a week later they had already moved. Their new lodgings were not far from their old home in the Deriah Mahal and much closer to the Armenian Church. Although it was still in the Moghul Serail and only a short distance away from Collett's house, it was larger and lighter and, most importantly, cheaper. He continues: 'I propose going up to Surat again either tomorrow or next day, when I shall strongly urge your friend to come down and pass a few weeks in the Serjeant's house at Domus – as I am convinced that the sea Breeze will have a wonderful effect not only in re-establishing her constitution for the present, but also in fortifying it against future attacks of indisposition.'

The beach resort is now known as Dumas and was described by Dr Buist in his *Notes on a Journey* c.1850, published by the Bombay Geographical Society, as 'a very considerable fishing village with fine groves of trees'. There were 'a number of handsome residences close by, the favourite hot weather retreats of the wealthier European and Native residents of Surat.'

Ogilvie tells Theodore that he intends once again raising the subject of sending Kitty to England and continues, 'I shall therefore, not close this, till I have ascertained her wishes on what I mean to propose'. Before signing off he adds a note: '– I have just seen your Family and have the pleasure to add that they are all in good health – they moved the day before yesterday into a house opposite the Racket

Court – which your Friend had discovered to be untenanted – It is large and airy and the rent 15 Rs – She has consented to go down to Domus in the course of a few days – and I shall, on my return to that quarter make preparations for their reception.'

So Eliza had at last agreed to take the children for a short holiday at the seaside, where they could escape from the heat of the city, and she, from the over-zealous attention of her creditors. She still owed the Parsee merchant, Cowasjee Jewajee, for shoes and the other items she had listed almost a year ago in July 1817. Hormajee's bill for the silk stockings, light blue satin for her dress and the green sprig-muslin for the baby's cot, was also outstanding from a year ago. Theodore himself had still not settled Collett's bill for baby Fraser's funeral.

On April 30th she wrote to let Theodore know their whereabouts and also to remind him of his duty to share with his family: 'My dear Sir, I having been applied you for the money which was very need, and... obliged to give some money to the native doctor, who daily attend... two or three times, therefore I was request your Honor, but you should not mind my needful request, upon which you have wrote me so large and heavey displeasing lines which my God knows how I am very disappointed for the money... I let you know that now you are made so hard heart upon us since a year past, do not send any kind of Piece Cloth to me, nor to Children... it is very surprising to me, and I did request for the Tea and Sugar Candy, but I have only received the tea, which I thank you, and for the Sugar Candy you desire as can get cheap at Surat than Bombay it is very true, if should be get cheap here that no consequence, but... if you would send for our use which you ought to rec[k]on as you use yourself. My dear Sir if you have kind regard on me... you would be to send here without my applying.'

She ends her letter on the subject that was of most interest to Theodore – the children:

'Ketty is in health, but Alexander having been unwell about 7 days ago, I was supply the medecine by Native Doctor, but now 4 days ago Doctor Sharp arrive here, and our friend Captain Ogilvie was attend with him and have begin to supply the medecine by Doctor Sharp. – I now give you much joy that our beloved Ketty are taking very care for the pice [cotton piece-goods] etc. She purchase the soap... to wash the romall or handkerchief and after the same soap she immediately shut in her small scrutor [escritoire]. If any servant privately take out from her scrutor she same time came to complaint with great angry and noise before me, then immediately I obliged to find to get her soap – Ketty beg the favour Papa you may send for me some Mangoes and Liche[e]s fruits of Bombay... Your affectionate Mrs Forbes.'

Despite her earlier complaint that Theodore had put off doing anything about getting the children christened, the initiative to proceed with the business of arranging Kitty's homeward passage now seems to be coming from Theodore himself. Ogilvie professes to 'perfectly coincide' with him 'in opinion, that it is most urgently necessary that Kitty should leave this country at the end of the present year, at the latest,' and having underlined the last phrase three times for extra emphasis, he continues:

'There will, I am well aware, be on the part [of] her Mother, strong and urgent entreaties to retain the sweet child – but, (as I think) I mentioned to you, when we last met, I have every reason to imagine that if the point was gently yet resolutely persevered in, she will yield – and under this impression, I shall from time to time, if you approve the measures, mention Kitty's departure for Britain, as an event which must soon take place, and as our good Friend Mr Fraser formerly wrote to me, the sooner it is accomplished, the better both for the dear child and her Mother, and more particularly for the future comfort of the latter – for every day which they remain together must render their separation more trying to her maternal feelings.'

It was now five months since the frail four-year-old Tom was taken away from his Indian mother in Broach, Theodore and Ogilvie and, certainly, Mrs Fraser, must often have wondered, as they planned Kitty's voyage, what had become of him. They may not have been very optimistic about the safe arrival of a small child described as 'too sickly to rough it'. On June 2nd, just two-and-a-half months out of St. Helena, the *Huddart* arrived off the south Devon port of Plymouth. From there she was scheduled to sail along the south coast into the Strait of Dover and safe anchorage off the little port of Deal, where the East Indiamen clustered while they made ready to sail east once more. After passing the treacherous Goodwin Sands, site of countless wrecks, her passage would take her round the headland of North Foreland and into the mouth of the Thames to Gravesend, from where it was but a short voyage up the Thames to the Port of London. Worryingly, neither *The Asiatic Journal* nor *The Oriental Herald* gives the names of the passengers who disembarked from the vessel at Gravesend or even whether 'sickly' little Tom survived the voyage. The whole voyage From Bombay to Gravesend had taken two days short of six months.

However, all fears for the boy's survival are dispelled by reference to the ship's journal in the India Office Library. Captain Weller records that Master Barnard was safely disembarked on June 5th 1818 at Portsmouth, just as Thomas Fraser had requested. Portsmouth was not a scheduled stop for the ship. Captain Weller's log states that when the ship arrived off the Isle of Wight, 'she was in urgent want of provisions'. Accordingly, he sent a message to that effect to Messrs. Lindegren in Portsmouth, Agents to the East India Company. A boat was speedily dispatched from their extensive wharf with the necessary supplies. Less than three days out from Plymouth and so close to the end of their voyage, was this urgent request to re-supply perhaps a ruse on the part of the kindly captain, to ensure that his little protégé was safely landed at the nearest point to his destination, exactly as Thomas Fraser had suggested? When Messrs. Lindegren's boat arrived alongside, it would have been a simple matter, once the necessary, or perhaps unnecessary, supplies had been taken on board, to a small child into the vessel and give the master a tip to see the little lad safe onto the Chichester post-chaise.

In Sussex, the gentle landscape of the south coast in early June is dressed to impress. The fields Tom saw along the way were well-greened and populated by sheep far fleecier and cows far fatter than any he had ever seen in India. The walls of private parks, houses, barns and cottages gleamed with hard grey and white flints – a world away from the buildings of Gujarat. The soft reds of the brick-capped walls and tile-hung upper storeys of yeoman farms lent their warmth to the stony harshness of the flint. Here and there the sight of a smithy open to the road, with the clank of the smith at work; a shepherd boy whistling his dog; an old man in smock and gaiters tending his humble plot; or just a row of washing flapping by a low weather-boarded cottage were a present reminder that this had been a working landscape for centuries past.

What a fine way for a boy to end his journey; to arrive in a canary yellow coach with a postilion astride the lead horse, and the blast of a post horn to announce his arrival. When the post-chaise rattled to a halt and little Barnard, 'bag and baggage', was set down at Ashling House, a warm welcome from Fraser's mother awaited, and the long days of a mild English summer stretched out before him.

Chapter 18

Baptism in Surat, 1818

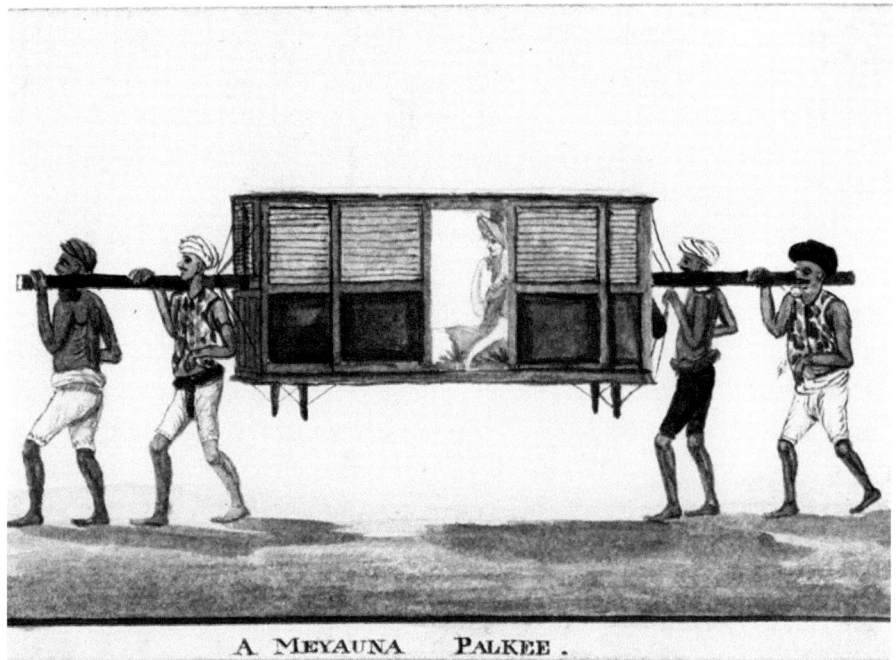

A MEYAUNA   PALKEE.

Contemporary sketch of a British lady in a palanquin of the type Mrs Fraser
would have taken from the Morisons' house in Nan Poora to visit Eliza in the
Mughal Serail.

18

Surat & Bombay, April – November 1818

On April 21ˢᵗ, just as Eliza and the children were moving to their new lodgings opposite the Nawab's racket court, Theodore was reading a letter from Eliza Fraser: 'It is at present our intention to take a trip to Surat shortly,' she writes, 'which place I shall certainly not leave without having your little ones christened – it ought really to be done now – Kate is getting quite old.' It seems that Mrs Fraser was finding life in Broach ever more tedious. 'The girls have been in Surat upwards of a month,' she tells him, 'paying a visit to Mrs Bell – this place is so dull that I could not find in my heart to retain them here when they had an opportunity of going elsewhere.'

Mrs Fraser yearns for the parties they used to give in Surat: 'Your really a little unconscional I think in expecting me to write you long letters from this dullest of all dull places, while you, who are in Bombay, giving Balls, concerts &c and must have so many interesting anecdotes to communicate, content yourself with writing a few hasty lines on the envelope of a Europe letter. Your note to Fraser was 14 days on its passage up – it amused us much – as a woman you know – I am allowed to be a little contradictory – and cannot help thinking (merely from your anxiety to convince us to the contrary) that there is some foundation in the report of your going to be married to Miss Greaves! – Well – time will show! Sincerely as I hope and trust that whenever you do become a Benedict you will be as happy as you deserve to be. I need say no more. – But now do tell us if my suspicions are correct, all these parties too; you really ought to have a wife to preside at your table, it would save you a world of trouble.'

Barnard had left Broach for Bombay and life was very 'dull'. But she was about to find that even Surat was not quite so much fun now that her closest friends had gone; her former next-door neighbour in Nan Poora, Dr George Ogilvy, had recently left to take up a new appointment in the Presidency. This was torture for a socialite such as Eliza Fraser. She had been the star of the sparkling Surat social scene and she was used to being surrounded by a crowd of attentive men, described by Will Ogilvie as her 'satellites'. She missed her old friends and resorted to the favourite occupations of bored women in British India – gossip, meddling and matchmaking – she adds a note to her letter to Theodore on the subject of his rumoured marriage: 'P.S. [on outer sheet] Pray remember us most kindly to Ogilvy when you see him. And above all things dont forget to send me some bride cake. I am not entitled to it, but you may as well give me a little for old acquaintance sake. E. F.'

She seems equally concerned about the likelihood of finding a wife for Barnard, currently in Bombay on court business: 'You of course frequently see Mr Barnard – is there any likelihood of his bringing up a wife? – I heartily wish he would. The Durbar sadly wants a mistress to keep its master and everything else in order – it is now undergoing some slight repair and will in consequence be ready for the reception of the lady.'

Mrs Fraser's husband, Thomas, writing to Theodore at the same time, teases him: 'Now for a little prattle about your ladies party: I am free to think it looks somewhat like a change in the deportment of your life; on account of your having refrained so long from anything of that kind, and nothing now, old Theodore, will thoroughly convince me that you are not (as old Sturt of the marine says) "bucking up" to some fine lass or other: I shall be happy to hear of it coming to truth, as I am convinced a man of your experience & judgement will chose your intended as an ornament to most of the wives of the present day, hem!... Let me hear how your party got on & who, if I am not presuming, did you hand to table. Do not blush! you are [a] cunning chap we all know.'

Cunning or not, Theodore certainly seems to have been 'playing the field' as far as the ladies of Bombay were concerned. In the year after he abandoned Eliza and the children in Surat, his frequent attendance in the drawing rooms of polite society had marked him out as a charmer, notwithstanding a by-no-means-unattractive suspicion of rakishness which hung about him. His familiarity with the amenities of the Lal Bazaar was well known to his male compatriots. The brothels of this notorious quarter could provide girls of seemingly limitless variety, to suit all tastes, and were widely patronised by all classes of the British in

Bombay. Theodore seems to have regarded a visit to the Lal Bazaar or the procuring of a girl for his guests as part of his duties as a host. When Captain Weller wrote from Tellicherry to give him news of young Tom and to thank him for his hospitality he had asked Theodore to 'make my best respects to Mr & Mrs [Michie] Forbes, Mr & Mrs Ashburner' and added cryptically 'not forgetting the ladies of Nesbitt Lane!' Were these perhaps the numbered girls of 'The Grove', referred to by MacPherson?

By May it seems that the presents Eliza had sent him, the messages from the children, the cooler, more reproachful tone which has crept into her letters are beginning to garner results. On the 22nd Theodore sends her 4 small baskets of onions, a dozen ducks and a pair of geese, accompanied by a letter which Eliza again describes as 'affectionate'. 'Ketty and Alexander are very much please and very happy to play with those animals,' she tells him in her reply. Aratoon had already told her that Caitan said Theodore would be angry to be asked for 'trifling' things. She tells him that if it is true, she will not ask him for anything again 'for the childrens use' but adds: 'I am very surprizing myself how you can eat the fruit etc. without the share of children and family.' In his letter Theodore had asked her to send some of his personal belongings to him in Bombay including a watch and a tortoiseshell snuff box. Perhaps he had hoped that his present of ducks and geese might trigger the speedy dispatch of his valuables. But Eliza did not hurry to reply.

In early June, while young Tom Barnard was watching the fleecy white clouds of summer borne in on the gentle breezes of the south coast of England, his friends on the west coast of India watched as towering black storm clouds gathered. Surat was soon being buffeted by gale-force winds and driving rain, restricting trade and preventing any boats from leaving the city, while in the English countryside it was a time of awakening, and a time of refreshment. It was a time for cricket too, and in Sussex, where village cricket had been established for the past two hundred years, in a household which had been home to so many boys before him, surely young Tom cannot have been denied the challenges and pleasure afforded by the game. His health improved by the day; he would grow up strong and healthy and one day he would return to the land of his birth.

Once again, Eliza was stuck in Surat as the heat was rising and the monsoon clouds rolled in, just as she had been a year ago. But at least this time the children's christening was looking likely. At the beginning of June, Mr and Mrs Fraser arrived from Broach and, on the 18th, Thomas took the opportunity to write to Theodore in Bombay on the subject of sending Kitty to England:

'This morning I called in the city and saw your dear little children who I am truly happy to say are quite well. Kitty retains her good looks but, my friend, the sooner you give the <u>order</u> to Bob about her departure to England, the better, as her complexion will spoil in this detestable climate, it does not so much matter with the boy, he has grown very much.'

As they were staying with the Morisons, rather than sending for Kitty and Aleck, Mrs Fraser summoned up their palanquin. Having donned her bonnet and gloves, picked up her parasol and eased herself into the shuttered conveyance, she was soon being borne in style among the buildings and houses of the mainly Parsee area, and along the shady tree-lined avenue that ran right past her old home. Soon the gardens and glades of Nan Poora gave way to narrow streets and crowded thoroughfares where all religions and races mingled their domestic and mercantile lives just outside the Mecca Gate. The survey of a year earlier had reported the Mecca Tower to be 'in ruins' and the inner side of the Sheherpanah to be 'much decayed and the parapet nearly all fallen down'.

The old point of departure for Muslim pilgrims was served by a bridge which crossed over a narrow arm of the Tapti. Mrs Fraser was carried across and through the crumbling old gate, into the inner city and stronghold of Surat. She was borne past the impenetrable wall of the vast square court of the Nawab's Serail and the elephantine bulwark of the castle along the crowded main road and into the Old Mughal Serail; to the upper limit of the Moolna Chukla, where at last her porters set the English memsahib down outside the old house opposite the racquet court.

There is no record of what was said at the meeting and Eliza does not elaborate when she mentions the visit in her letter to Theodore. Mrs Fraser may have simply wanted to ensure that the children would be suitably dressed for their christening or to let 'the Mother' know if and when her presence was required; but one thing is certain – when the English memsahib arrived at Eliza's door, it was not a social visit. In

November 1817, when she was arranging Tom's christening, she had expressed her regret that 'our charming little Kate is neither going home or is likely to be intrusted to my protection'. It would not be surprising if the boredom of life in Broach after the loss of her little protégé, Tom, and the absence of her own daughters, had prompted her to have a last attempt at persuading Eliza to let her have charge of Kitty until she sailed for England.

On 28th June, a whole month after she had received Theodore's letter, Eliza decided that at last, it was time that she should reply. The rains had arrived, and she was now unable to send Theodore his watch and the tortoiseshell snuff box he had asked for. She began to dictate: 'I am very happy to send you these things – but now in the rainy season no any boat can leave from hence.' She appeals to him to forgive the delay: 'My beloved sir, you must not displease that I now write after many days the answer of your letter.' She had not replied sooner, she explains, because she knows how his 'affection and mind changed' over her and she does not want to give him the trouble of reading her letters; it might be a burden to him if she were to write too often.

Now she returns to the familiar subject raised by Theodore – her extravagance. She insists that the outstanding bills he mentions are all household bills dating from before her monthly allowance was fixed: 'You have mention the particular account of Money received from Deenshaw, are right but you sure from those Money, before of my Allowance were fixed, all was made the House expence, and not a Rupee from those sum I had kept in my Pocket, which I solemn declare, and have forward you the Particular account Books Copy accompanying Caitan.'

Having dismissed this delicate subject, she laments, 'I did not thought the world are so treacherous,' and continues, 'I communicate to your good honor that some persons has new friends and acquaintance those they have so good luck and became intitled to sit with you to talk flattering words, which they can get something by your favour according to their wish... since long ago... I get no reward, but instead of that I now remain very far from you, so as I cannot see [you] to talk between us the cause of my misfortune.'

On June 29th, as he forwarded Eliza's letter to Bombay in his own, Will Ogilvie was able to write to Theodore that, after the protracted negotiations, he now had 'the heartfelt pleasure of mentioning that I have at last obtained the full consent of your Friend to Kitty's being sent home at the end of the present year [1818].'

Eliza had always known that Theodore wanted to send Kitty to his parents at Boyndlie. If the little girl was to leave India on a Company ship in the current year she needed to be baptised into the Church of England as soon as possible; but by the end of June the baptism had still not taken place. In a post script to her letter, Eliza had told Theodore: 'You ought to send Fazagool with Ketty.' Her suggestion that Fazagool should go with Kitty had delighted Ogilvie because, he says, he feels that the arrangement 'evinces her firm determination to abide by what she has acceded to' and he went round to the Morisons' house in Nan Poora to tell Mrs Fraser:

'...I lost no time in communicating it to our excellent friend Mrs Fraser, who most fully concurred in my opinion, of the great advantages which will result to the sweet child's comfort, both on board ship and on her first arrival in Britain – and also to the poor Mother's peace of mind, in knowing that her little darling is attended by one who has ever shown the most warm attachment to the family – and is herself particularly desirous of accompanying her charge to the North of Scotland... The only seeming drawbacks to the plan in question – are that the poor woman is wholly unacquainted with our language – and that the longer Kitty and she remain together, their attachment will become stronger, and their final separation thereby rendered more difficult to be accomplished – The first of these supposed objections may, however, be answered by observing that the Ayah will be able during the passage to pick up sufficient English to assist her during her short stay in Britain, and with regard to her parting with Kitty – the latter will, I am confident, soon render herself such a favourite with her excellent grand-mother and all around her – (and with none more than honest old Susy, if still alive) as to be perfectly reconciled to a change of attendants... Having now, as I trust, satisfactorily settled a most important point in the sweet child's future prospects – and happiness – I shall proceed to the circumstance of her's and Aleck's intended Baptism, and I am requested by Mrs Fraser to mention to you, with her kindest regards, that the ceremony may take place during the present week.'

Eliza writes: 'Our excellent friend Captain Ogilvie desire me that having appointed to make baptism of Ketty and Alexander after 4 or 5 days... In the month of November next, he shall proceed to Bombay... he will carray our beloved Ketty with him, and Alexander would be remain with me till two years which I am very glad to hear, and I told him very well do as think Proper Agreeable to my Master's wish... but I think better is to send Europe to both children together accompanying Fazagool, or if you have no please to send Alexander with Ketty then you ought to send Fazagool with Ketty because she not stay separate a moment without her daydee.'

It is unlikely that Eliza and Fazagool would attend Kitty and Aleck's christening unless in the guise of servants. A mere eight months earlier, in the same chapel, the Rev. Thomas Carr had baptised young Tom Barnard under Mrs Fraser's sponsorship – another child of mixed race; another christening without either parent being present or taking part in the service. As well-bred English women, Mrs Morison and Mrs Fraser would not allow themselves to be seen in company with 'the Mother', not even as Kitty's 'sponsors', even though in private they might develop a friendship of sorts. This attitude was becoming commonplace in British India.

Ogilvie continues: 'In one of the many conversations which we have lately had regarding the family, she [Mrs Fraser] mentioned to me the propriety of making a present to Mr Carr – on the occasion – and on this point I took upon myself to assure her, that I felt confident that I would be only anticipating your wishes in presenting Mr C – in your name, with whatsoever we might ultimately agree upon – Mrs F tells me that 100 Rs were given when little Tom Barnard was baptised – I therefore think that 150 or 200 Rs will be amply sufficient on the approaching occasion – however we will finally settle that point previous to the Ceremony taking place.

'P.S. – Your former letters mentioned that our Friends the Frasers, Mrs Morison, the Doctor, and your humble servant, should be the sponsors for your little ones. – This will be duly attended to – but the particular distribution (farther than that Mrs F and Mrs M are to stand for Kitty) – have not yet been made.'

The Forbes children were duly baptised in the Castle chapel. The service was conducted by the young chaplain to the Surat Garrison, the Rev. Thomas Carr. Described later as 'charismatic', he was clearly destined for higher things; in a few years' time he would leave Surat for Bombay to be made Archdeacon, and in 1836, when St. Thomas's church was re-consecrated as the Cathedral Church of St. Thomas, Bombay, he was appointed as the first bishop of the new diocese. On his return to England he was made Rector of Bath in Somerset and held the living there until his death in 1859. The impressive sculpted marble monument to him can still be seen in St. Thomas's Cathedral Mumbai. When he baptised Kitty and Aleck in July 1818, he was almost exactly the same age as Theodore; a family man, whose own youngest child was only five-months old. Like Theodore's friends and most of the other Company Servants, he lived in Nan Poora, but at the edge farthest from the river, where the less luxurious bungalows were situated.

As soon as the service was over and she had reclaimed her children, Eliza knew that a sweet victory was hers – she had defeated Mrs Fraser's attempt to take Kitty to live in Broach with her, yet despite Will Ogilvie's 'apprehensions', Mrs Morison had still agreed to stand as 'sponsor' for the girl; the charismatic young chaplain had still christened the children in the Castle chapel; they would be written into the baptismal register of the Bombay Presidency; they would have the baptismal certificates to testify to their British nationality and, most importantly, they would be acknowledged there as Theodore's. She was thrilled, moreover, that she might now be able to contrive a meeting with their father.

After being separated from him for more than eighteen months, Eliza was naturally impatient to get to Bombay, and her impatience is evident in the last letter to Theodore that is known to exist from her. She would have had no hesitation in starting out immediately but for the sudden squalls and torrential rains of the capricious monsoon. She would not put the safety of her two surviving children at risk. She knew that she needed to wait for fine weather and quiet seas. Ogilvie had intended taking Kitty to Theodore's house in Bombay himself. The date had even been set for the beginning of November. But though the beginning of November was an excellent time to sail to Bombay, she would go before that if she could. In the closing sentences of her last letter to Theodore she tells him: 'My good sir, I pray you must let me know, by your leave I will bring my child to give in your hand myself, and after Ketty dispatching to Europe, then I can stay in Bombay or come back to Surat according to your wish – and when you will call me to Bombay then you must write to captain Ogilvie as you are call me to Bombay by your leave.'

The 'fine garden house' is almost within her reach; her beloved will call her to Bombay. She is excited at the thought of seeing him again 'eyes to eyes'; he will not resist her. How can he send her back to Surat with Kitty looking on? She sees herself in charge of the grand country house that was home, when she was last in Bombay, to 'Mr Goodveen', one of the most senior and distinguished Company Servants in the Presidency. Richard Goodwin was Theodore's old boss, the head of the Secret and Political Department. Could it be that she and the children would at last live openly with Theodore, as a family, in his 'fine garden house' in Byculla? She saw herself being received through the main entrance with the children and pictured them with space to play safely in the gated garden, attended by an army of servants. Caitan and the other servants would have to acknowledge her authority once more, when she was re-instated as the 'same Mrs Forbes'. She relished the prospect.

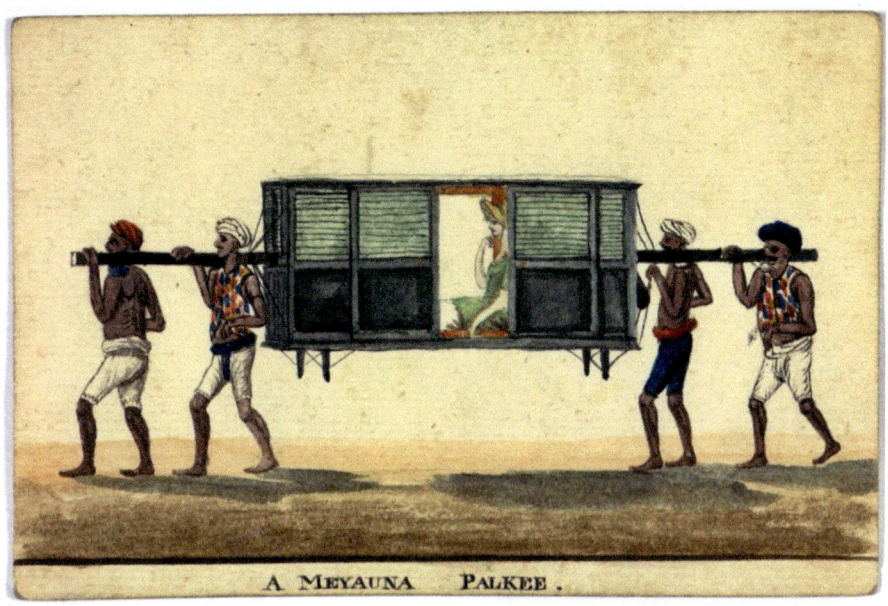

Palanquin such as Mrs Fraser might have used to cross the city, from Nanpoora to the Deriah Mahal, when she visited Theodore's children and 'the mother'.

© British Library Board

Theodore enjoyed smoking the Hookah, as James Silk Buckingham later recalled. In his will, he left his pipe and smoking apparatus to his friend John Cameron.

© British Library Board

The Garden of Randal Lodge, on the lower south side of Malabar Hill.

© British Library Board

Bombay c.1820. Note the prosperous Parsee merchant centre right.

Aquatint after Captain Robert Melville Grindlay

Dwelling of Charles Forbes. Note the two figures in Bobbery Hunt dress and the Indian Syce leading a horse.

© British Library Board

Entertainment given to Charles Forbes before his return to England. Four days later the Bobbery Hunt gave him a dinner under canvas on the Esplanade.

© British Library Board

Inside of the Grand Illuminated Temporary Building, on the Esplanade Bombay, at Night 20ᵗʰ of May 1811.

Front of the Grand Illuminated Temporary Building, on the Esplanade BOMBAY, at Night 20ᵗʰ of May 1811.

The extravagant entertainments of Bombay Society 1811.

Views of a grand temporary building, from a contemporary album

© British Library Board

PART IV

SACRED AND PROFANE

Chapter 19

Return to Bycullah, 1818

A small coastal *pattamar*, from a 19th century engraving.

19

Bombay, 1818

In Gujarat, when the clouds burst and discharge their heavy burden onto the baking cities and the parched land below, the River Tapti swiftly becomes a torrent racing towards the maelstrom of the Gulf of Cambay. In 1818 the rains came early and the streets of Surat were pock-marked with pools of muddy water. Along with the wet conditions, came the *cholera morbus*. The epidemic was less widespread than expected 'but although the cholera was not carrying off its thousands,' wrote Dr Kennedy of the 1818 outbreak, 'still the epidemic fever which always prevails towards the termination of the rains in Guzuratte was singularly destructive.' Although the numbers affected were no more than usual, he concluded: 'The mortality was unprecedented, every disorder seeming to assume from the first a tendency to a fatal termination.' As the winds changed direction and the humidity dropped so did the progress of the epidemic. By October the wind had dwindled to a refreshing breeze, the humidity dropped to bearable levels, and the cases of cholera were reduced to single figures. At the return of temperate conditions and a tranquil sea, the coastal waters of Gujarat were open once again to the passage of sailing boats. Eliza began to pack up the household and get the family ready for their trip to Bombay.

The exact date of their departure is not recorded, nor is their arrival in Bombay, but after the christening in July, Theodore received no more reports about Eliza and the children from Ogilvie or Aratoon; there are no more discussions about the Surat household expenses; no more bills from Dinshaw; no teasing letters from the Frasers and, tellingly, no more letters from Eliza pleading with Theodore to call her to Bombay. She must have left the city as soon as she could after the rains.

In the halcyon days of November1818, when it was originally

planned that Ogilvie should bring Kitty to Bombay, the voyage down the coast would have been 'plain sailing'. Never far from land, at whatever time they sailed, Eliza and the children probably had the comforting presence of Aratoon on board; he was almost as keen as Eliza to see her reunited with the man he regarded not only as his brother-in-law but also as his friend and benefactor. He and Guyane had welcomed the children into their family and into their hearts. For more than a year Theodore had prevaricated – determined to leave his family, but too cowardly to admit it to Eliza's face. He had never let it be known to Aratoon, or to the Surat tradesmen that the separation was to be permanent, though they certainly suspected it. Ogilvie had encouraged his friend to persevere in his intention to divorce himself from Eliza and been his sole messenger and confidant. If she ever suspected that 'our excellent friend Captain Ogilvie' was not necessarily her excellent friend, she never showed it.

Aratoon had earlier described how 'she get herself very sulkey with me & she answered that was nothing to me in anything concerning her, you must consider that she submit every thing & every councel she listen of Dossaboy Parsee & others that made me little distant from her.' Though Eliza had refused all advice from him, she was nonetheless his wife's little sister, and their differences were not serious. The children were still his niece and nephew. He was considerably in Theodore's debt and could not have refused a request to take them to Bombay in his *pattamar*.

It must have raised Eliza's spirits to note the familiar landmarks so speedily left in their wake, and to know that she was on her way to reclaim her husband at last. Past Bhimpur they sailed, where last year the British garrison had been encamped to escape the heat of Surat; past Domus where she had recovered her health and sanity; out of the Tapti Estuary, that had kept her in Surat for far too long; out into the freedom of the open sea. Their swift coastal *pattamar* sped past sandy strands and rocky shores, mangrove swamps and palm-fringed beaches and Eliza was elated by the knowledge that soon she would be reunited with her beloved husband and he with his children. They would be a united family again, together once more in his large country house. She would be his queen and he her king, just as they had vowed to be when they exchanged their blessed marriage crowns, only seven years ago, and they would rule their domestic domain together until the end of their days.

The flapping of the boat's sails carried a poignant echo of the couple's happy voyage less than three years earlier. They had left Surat for Bombay after a joyous reunion with Eliza's extended family, both of them secure in their love and full of optimism for their future. They had no inkling of the cruel stricture that Forbes & Co. were about to impose. For five months they had lived in the Fort as a family; Chotabhoy had been conceived there in a close and loving relationship; she had left Bombay in the second trimester of her pregnancy with no hint of a separation in view. She could only guess at what influences or pressures had subsequently prompted Theodore to devise his elaborate plan of deception. Her best guess had to be his change of employment.

The coastal strip unfurling to the landward side signalled a second chance and the salt sea spray on her face tasted of victory. As they sailed past the off-shore islets of Salsette, the choppy waters whispered of her nearness to her journey's end. The Christian Koli fishermen, going about their time-honoured work, gave the devout Eliza the reassurance of an age-old continuity, a mark of God's watchful presence, of her obedience to His holy law. The slender palms seemed to nod their approval from the golden sands dotted along the rocky shore; God willing, soon she would be with her beloved husband.

On coming ashore at the small harbour of Mahim, Eliza lost no time in engaging *palkee burdars* and palanquins for their little party. Once clear of the Mahim woods and past the grounds of Government House at Parel, the route to Bycullah was relatively level and straight. She was eager to get to her journey's end and impatient to be with Theodore again. She knew the property from the time, when they arrived from Mocha and she had lodged in the area with Khumburzeefuh; when Theodore was staying not far away at Mazagaon, where so many of the prosperous and cultivated members of the British community, known as 'The Mazagaon Set' chose to live.

Since the building of Bellasis Road in 1793 Bycullah had seen rapid development. The house Theodore had taken was ideal for a wealthy bachelor with relatively easy access both to the seat of government at Parel and to the commercial centre of the Fort. It also occupied an enviable position between the fashionable enclaves of Mazagaon and Malabar with their exclusive villas, which were so often the venues for lavish parties and balls. To the south were the native settlements of the 'black' town and the red-light district of Lal Bazaar, now known as Kamathipura. To the north was the seat of government at Parel. Eliza's route from Mahim included a considerable stretch of the Bellasis Road. But the structure and condition of the 'Road' did not live up to its reputation as a vital thoroughfare. From the date of its construction the surface had begun to deteriorate. Just thirty years after Eliza bumped along its winding length it had still not been improved and was described as 'a small straggling uneven and silting pathway'. Though the way ahead of her was laden with dangers and discomfort, these things meant little to her in comparison to the knowledge that at the end of the road lay all she 'loved and had been dreaming of'.

Perhaps 'Agah Aratoon' agreed to accompany them, as far as Goodwin's house and pay a social visit to Khumburzeefuh, to talk about the marriage of his eldest daughter Johanna to her son 'Agah Zdr'; or to pay interest to Theodore on his loan; or maybe in a spirit of brotherly love he would simply feel that he should go with his young sister-in-law and her children to protect them from the 'dacoits' and footpads who still roamed the less populated stretches of the Bellasis Road.

Having lived in Bycullah for four months when they arrived from Mocha, Eliza knew the exact location and size of the house Theodore had rented – at least by repute, even if not personally, as a guest of 'Mr Goodveen'. Nevertheless, having only just moved from the stuffy Mughal quarter of Surat she would in all likelihood have been stunned by the rapid development of the new suburb and the spaciousness of the generous gardens surrounding the new mansions now rented out to the higher échelons of the Company and merchant communities. The extent of their grounds could easily be measured by the length of the many new *chunam* boundary walls, with their lodges, wrought-iron entrance gates and gravelled carriage drives. Inside each enclave of what had so recently been wilderness, populated only by the native birds and beasts, were newly-cultivated lawns, borders and shrubberies, now tended by busy gardeners. There were lodges manned by ever watchful *chowkidars* and stable yards with *syces*, or grooms, and coachmen. The sounds of birdsong had been superseded by the lively chatter of a multitude of servants and their families.

When Theodore took on the lease of his large 'garden house' in October 1817 it may well have been, as Thomas Fraser had teased him, because he intended 'bucking up to some fine lass or other', keen to follow the advice of so many of his friends to find himself a British wife. He had moved to the house only a matter of days after Chotabhoy's death and less than a month after he had given him the name Fraser. In Surat both Eliza and Aratoon had heard of the move within a week of the lease being signed and separately both had sent him their congratulations. The spinsters of Bombay regarded the news as evidence of his wealth and eligibility; his friends had repeatedly suggested that it was a sure sign of his intention of taking a British wife. With or without conviction, Eliza had always given him the impression that she truly believed that he had taken on such a large house and garden to accommodate her with the children.

Twenty long months had passed since Theodore left Surat for the northward – twenty months of worry and upset for Eliza. It had been a strain on her health but she had not given in to despair or lost her faith in God. She had held the family together and kept the presence of their Papa a reality for the children. But for Theodore, absent in Bombay, those twenty months had been a time of unfettered licence. Though Eliza had now contrived to bring Kitty and Aleck to see their Papa, and there was no doubt he would be pleased to see them, it still remained to be seen whether or not he would welcome her into his bed again. The familiar haunts along the way must have awakened memories of happier times. But to Kitty and Aleck it was all new.

Much had happened since Eliza and Theodore lived together in the Fort. The growing fashion for country houses and a continuous influx of free merchants meant that in the two years that had passed, Bycullah, Malabar and Mazagaon had all undergone substantial development. Although only a few miles from Bombay, 'the country' was still an apt description of Bycullah. The ease of commuting from there to the Fort was the main reason for its popularity, but it was also noted for the opportunities it provided for popular country sports. The flat central area to the north was a natural choice for horse racing, and before long would be the site of an elegant grandstand in European neo-classical style. Areas of jungle, marsh and wasteland – undeveloped as yet – gave shelter to hyenas, jackals and wolves, making it a favoured area for the Bobbery Hunt. Every evening the sunset sky was speckled with chattering wildfowl drawn in by the rich resources of the marshes, and day and night the air vibrated to the boom of the bittern and echoed to the harsh cry of the heron.

The new villas were noted for their luxuriant gardens and Goodwin's house was no exception. The British community of Bombay would have referred to any of the fine detached villas beyond the 'black town' as a 'country house', given the ample space around them and, of course, the fact that they were beyond most people's concept of walking distance. The growing suburb of Bycullah was favoured by members of the highest echelons of Bombay society. These were men at the top of their professions, legal, administrative, military and naval, many of whom intended to retire there. One such was Commodore William Manwaring of the Honourable Company's marine who was described as Theodore's 'neighbour', and was still living in his house at Bycullah at the time of his death, aged 68, in 1827.

Like Parel to the north, Mazagaon was originally one of the seven islands that would be gradually subsumed into what is now the great metropolis of Mumbai. The rocky and well-wooded island of Theodore's day is now scarcely recognisable. Gone are the elegant toddy palms which used to cast their shade onto the bright fields below, gone are the thatched native huts dotted throughout the dappled clearings and gone are the cries of the colourful birds as they flew from tree to tree. Even the rocky hillocks were being quarried away bit by bit for building and reclamation projects. Most of the country houses owned or leased by Europeans were bungalows but there were some more substantial 'upper-roomed' mansions, such as the renowned neo-classical house in Mazagaon, called Tarala. Theodore's house may not have been quite as grand as Tarala, but would have had many architectural features in common, such as a shallow-pitch roof, broad verandah and windows shaded by shutters or blinds. These were all dictated by a need to keep the interiors as shady and cool as possible. These 'garden houses' were valued as much for their shady walks and arbours as for their architectural features.

Tarala was built in 1788 by Pestonjee Wadia, of the famous Parsee ship-building family. He chose a spectacular site; high up on a lightly-wooded hillside above the coastal village and harbour of Mazagaon, overlooking his family ship-building yards. The numerous established trees of the hillside around it lent themselves to Pestonjee's grandiose landscaping schemes, but he never lived there. He and his family took up residence in another mansion he had built near Parel called the Lal Baug. It was from here that he hosted lavish parties and entertained the élite of Bombay. The names Pestonjee gave to his two mansions give the impression that the surroundings of his houses were as important to him as the buildings themselves – for Tarala translates from Sanskrit as 'Palm Green' and the Lal Baug as 'The Red Garden'. Though to his friends it was simply a large country house, to Eliza, Theodore's new house was defined by its fine garden, just as Tarala was to Pestonjee Wadia.

For most of its early years Tarala was let to officials high up in the Bombay Government. In particular, from 1808 to 1811, when Theodore was a griffin, or newcomer, it was the home of Sir James Mackintosh, Recorder of Bombay, author of *A History of England* and co-founder with Charles Forbes of the Literary Society of Bombay to which Theodore and most of his close friends belonged. In *Journal of a Residence in India*, published in 1812, Maria Graham has left a description of Tarala, which paints a vivid picture of what Theodore's house and garden might have looked like. Maria Graham stayed for six months at Tarala, as a guest of Sir James and Lady Mackintosh. Sir James was then the Recorder (Chief Justice) of Bombay, and during his term of office he created a new post of Executive Head of the Bombay Police. The man he chose was Richard Goodwin, former tenant of the house to which Eliza was now hurrying so excitedly. Though Tarala was not the country house mentioned by Thomas Fraser, Maria Graham's glowing description of the garden and its native plants might equally apply to the surroundings of Theodore's new home:

'The walks are... covered with small sea-shells from the beach of Back Bay, instead of gravel... On each side of the walks are ledges of brick, chunamed over, to prevent them being destroyed by the monsoon rains. We are always sheltered from the sun by the fanlike heads of the palmyras, whose tall columnar stems... support an innumerable variety of parasitic and creeping plants... At the lowest part of the garden is a long broad walk, on each side of which grow vines, pamplemousses, figs and other fruits... At one end of this walk are chunam seats, under some fine spreading trees, with the fruit walk to the right hand, and to the left flower-beds filled with jasmine, roses, and tuberoses, while the plumbago rosea, the red and white ixoras, with the scarlet wild mulberry, and the oleander, mingle their gay colours with the delicate white of the moon-flower and the mogree.'

The stucco-bordered shell-walks and *chunam* seats described by Maria Graham were part of the vernacular garden design, led by the availability of local materials. No doubt Goodwin's garden boasted similar adornments and the native flowers and fruit that filled the borders would have been common to both. Perhaps Theodore was searching for an Indian Haddo: he may have found it in Bycullah.

When the Forbes children left the Mughal Serail with their mother and Fazagool it was understood that at least two of the party would not be returning to Surat. Kitty and Fazagool were definitely to travel on to England as soon as a suitable passage could be arranged, but Aleck's future had yet to be decided. It is a curious coincidence that at the time that Eliza was taking Kitty to Bombay, the very ship that was destined to carry the little girl on the next leg of her momentous journey was being prepared for launch from the Kentish dock yard of Northfleet. *The Asiatic Journal and Monthly Miscellany* for 1818 reports that:

'On Oct 31 was launched at Messrs Pitcher's yard Northfleet a beautiful ship built for Messrs Chapman expressly for the East India trade. At a quarter before two the lady of Chas Forbes Esq. MP and family went on the platform and the ship was then christened by the daughter of that gentleman by the name of the *Katherine Stewart Forbes* and soon after the ship glided off the stocks into her natural element in a very fine style to the admiration of all the spectators.'

On her return voyage from the east, in August of the following year, it was this elegant ship, *Katherine Stewart Forbes*, that would take little Katherine Scott Forbes away from her parents for ever.

Eliza had offered to let Aleck, not yet four-years old, go with Kitty and Fazagool to Scotland, hoping to seduce Theodore into allowing her to stay on in Bombay. What she did not know was that Theodore saw his little boy, literally, in a different light to his fair-complexioned daughter. Though he was described as 'fine' and 'high spirited', Aleck was a 'chubby', dark-skinned little fellow; Thomas Fraser had expressed the opinion that it was not as important for 'the boy' to be sent back to England as it was for Kitty. Perhaps Theodore too realised how difficult it might be for Aleck to succeed in life against the bar of racial prejudice that British society was beginning to raise against mixed-race children from the East and West Indies. He had therefore determined that his son should stay in India – indefinitely.

Chapter 20

Heartly Love and Family Ties, 1818 – 1819

Bombay Green, c.1820. Aquatint after Robert Melville Grindlay.

20

Bombay, November 1818

When Eliza and the children arrived in Bombay in 1818, the dreaded *cholera morbus* was the talk of the town. The epidemic had started in Bengal and spread across the subcontinent; in August, only two months later it had reached Surat. It left fearful numbers dead in its wake – and the fearful living trembled in its path. Even though this outbreak did not seem to be quite as infectious as some had been, it gave rise to more than usual concern, because according to Dr Kennedy's testimony it had a much higher incidence of mortality. This may have had a bearing on Eliza's failure to return to Surat with Aleck after leaving Kitty and Fazagool with Theodore. Theodore would not have wanted to risk sending them back to Surat. They would be returning to the unhealthy atmosphere of the Mughal Serail where a disease such as cholera might even now be spreading rapidly among the densely packed houses. He knew from their own bitter experience how dangerous the crowded quarter could be for young children, and he would not want to risk the life of another of his children. Eliza could not bear to lose another child, and would have begged him to let her remain until Kitty and Fazagool sailed.

Even if Theodore did not want her to stay in Bombay, Eliza was determined enough to refuse an order to go away and confident enough in her attractiveness to assume that he would soon relent. She would prefer not to have to bid Kitty farewell until the moment 'her darling' sailed for England and Kitty, who had not seen her father for a year and a half, would have clung to her mother if there was any talk of her leaving. Eliza had Fazagool to help her, and Kitty and Aleck should be together for as long as possible. It was the best solution for their children, and for her, though maybe in the opinion of her errant husband not the best for him. He was still under instructions from his senior partners to conduct himself 'with due propriety', and he was enjoying his busy social life.

When Eliza and the children turned up, it seems that Theodore was still openly courting any eligible lady who crossed his path. Only in August, one of his military friends, stationed in 'the Northward', had written to him: 'Allow me to wish you joy of your approaching nuptials... The widow is undoubtedly a fascinating woman, but I am rather puzzled to account for her having so completely supplanted the Russian lady in your affections.' The identity of the Russian lady is not disclosed but the widow in question was probably Hester Petronella Ellis, a widow whose husband had been a Lieutenant in the 1st Royal Scots Regiment of Foot, stationed at Aurangabad. She sent Theodore her 'pension papers' each month to pay in to Forbes and Co. A regular correspondence had begun, which lasted from around January until October 1818. Mrs Ellis confided in Theodore that she was worried about her 'darling little boy'. She had left him in Bombay under the charge of the Reverend Padre Lewis, while she and her young daughter went back to Aurangabad to arrange her affairs. Theodore seems to have been involved in keeping an eye on the boy after Mrs Ellis heard to her consternation that he had been allowed to run around 'barefoot in the street and play with the native children'. She was due to set out for Bombay at the beginning of October 1818. It is not clear if the romance was a serious 'match' or whether it was just another of his dalliances. What is clear is that after Eliza arrived in Bombay, the correspondence between Theodore and Hester Petronella Ellis appears to have come to an abrupt end. Perhaps Eliza's arrival had persuaded Theodore that marriage with 'the widow' was not what he wanted after all.

At Boyndlie his parents must have had quite a shock when a letter arrived from Theodore, telling them about the little granddaughter who was shortly to be landed on their doorstep along with her nurse – and it may not have been very convenient for them. By now, Theodore had been away more than ten years and his parents were not as fit as he remembered them. John Forbes suffered from gout, a painful inflammatory disorder, and as a result was often grumpy. They had been heavily involved in the upbringing of his illegitimate son Frederick for the last six years. Although they had now moved into the new family home at Boyndlie and Frederick was boarding at Inverkeithny School near Haddo, they may not have been best pleased at the prospect of another mouth to feed, and the cost of a governess or tutor for the new granddaughter. John Forbes was already paying for Frederick's board and school fees.

As the year 1818 came to an end, a widespread failure of the crop in the northern cotton-producing areas of Gujarat had seriously damaged the Bombay cotton trade. Raw cotton, the locally produced cloth and the piece goods made from it were already being gradually superseded as the commodity of choice, by the more profitable business of trading in Indian opium, grown in the adjacent province of Malwa. The drug was smuggled into China with the encouragement of the British Government and against an express edict issued by the Qing Emperor. The glory days of huge profits from cotton for Bombay merchants were coming to an end. There was still a buoyant two-way trade with the Far East in other commodities. But the vast fortunes made in India by the *nabobs* of old such as 'Bombay Jock' Forbes and his nephew Charles were rapidly becoming a thing of the past.

At this time Theodore's relationship with Michie Forbes, already under stress, appears to have taken a sudden turn for the worse. It is unlikely that the adverse trading conditions would have been factors in the complete breakdown that seems to have occurred. There were no issues concerned with his younger brother, James, who was in Michie's employment back home in Scotland; but Eliza's arrival in Bombay with the children does appear to have coincided with the start of Michie's personal animosity towards Theodore. Just a week after Ogilvie's letter to Theodore arrived with the news that Kitty and Aleck had been christened in Surat, Michie too had become a father. The birth was later announced in the *Oriental Gazette*: 'On July 11th 1818, At Bombay to the Lady of Michie Forbes Esq. of Crimond Aberdeenshire a son and heir.'

But becoming a father for the first time, which today might be seen as an opportunity for the men to find common ground, did nothing to prevent the rift between them from becoming even wider. In line with the accepted conventions of the day, the disparate social status of their children meant that they would never have had an opportunity to mix socially, or even informally, to provide a platform on which their fathers might develop a lasting friendship.

The 'Lady' who had borne Michie's son and heir was his step-niece, Mary Ashburner, the very same young girl whose kidnap and rescue had been the cause of so much worry for her mother and her step-father, Charles, less than a decade earlier. Mary was nineteen now – only half Michie's age. He had courted and won her while he was in London in 1816, married her there and brought her back to Bombay, where the newlyweds quickly settled into Charles Forbes's well-appointed house in the Fort. The couple had arrived from England back in April 1817 while Theodore was on his travels to the northward, and he had written a 'boot-licking' but nonetheless warm letter of welcome from Broach, so there had certainly been no rancour on his part at that time:

'When I last heard from you at Mocha there certainly was not the most distant prospect of our being ever so closely connected as we are destined to be, altho' I can assure you the arrangements that have led to that connection so far from being the less pleasing to me on that account are on the contrary a source of additional satisfaction as by being associated with you in the firm of Forbes & Co I flatter myself I shall Possess a firm and sincere friend whose advice and ample experience cannot fail to be of the utmost benefit to so complete a novice as I am in all matters of business... I came up to the Northward some time ago both with a view of obtaining some little insight into the Cotton Trade, as well as for other reasons which I will explain when I have the pleasure of seeing you as communicated by letter... I leave this in a few days for Bhownaggheer & Dollerah by way of Jumbozeer & Baroda. Whenever you are at leisure I shall beg to receive a letter from you addressed to the care of my friend Mr Barnard the judge here. You are I trust by this time comfortably settled in your brother's house, which Ashburner has no doubt had in perfect readiness for you as well as servants & I regret much not being on the Fort myself to give you what little assistance I might have been able in that or any other way.'

The Ashburner referred to was Mary's older brother and Charles's step-son, William Page Ashburner, already a partner in Forbes & Co., and a future Mayor of Bombay. In the course of the four years following the birth of Michie's 'son and heir', Mary Forbes gave birth to another three sons. The couple were to produce seven children in all, before returning to England and living out their days together in comfortable retirement in an opulent mansion in the very English surroundings of Silwood Park, Sunninghill, close by Royal Ascot racecourse.

It seems that around the time that Eliza brought the children to Bycullah, it was not only the partners of Forbes & Co. who were beginning to find Theodore's behaviour tiresome. His closest friend John Wedderburn wrote to him on 11th November 1818: 'My dear Forbes, I have been exceedingly pained indeed to hear such an account of your conduct last night to a young lady, for whom I entertain the highest respect and esteem, as to make your friends quite ashamed for you. I have long been perfectly aware of what had passed between you before, and must say that the story was very little to your credit, but I made allowances for irritation of feeling at the moment and as you said nothing to me I forebore to touch on the subject. To proceed however after such an interval deliberately to insult a young lady, of the most amiable disposition and gentle manners, before a large company, shews such a want of correct feeling as I am more shocked at than I can express, and which can only reflect disgrace on yourself. This may seem strong language but without candour there can be no friendship, and I have only to add that unless you make such an apology for your conduct, as such conduct requires, it is impossible for us to continue on the same footing of intimacy as we have done for the last ten years. Believe me however in the meantime to be your very sincere friend.'

It is a strong rebuke and Wedderburn does not say what the 'insulting behaviour' was, or name the 'young lady'. Could it have been Theodore's first reaction when Eliza turned up at his house while he was entertaining guests? Did he rebuff her in a cruel manner? Surely not; Eliza, would not have presented herself 'before a large company'. On the other hand, the servants knew her as 'Mrs Forbes', and as their mistress; she would have had little or no trouble in persuading them to let her into her own husband's house. Wedderburn would certainly have been well-acquainted with her from her last two sojourns in Bombay. But he would be unlikely to have taken the matter up with Theodore and demand that he apologise. Theodore was a man much-talked-about in the match-making markets and Wedderburn admits that the matter was only hearsay. It is more likely that the 'young lady, of the most amiable disposition and gentle manners' would have been a young English woman, one of those named in his friends' teasing letters; or perhaps one such as Charlotte Wrangham, encouraged by her sister to 'set her cap' at him, flirted with and callously cast aside; or the 'fascinating' widow Hester Petronella Ellis, recently arrived from Aurangabad. It seems that she was attractive enough to have supplanted the 'Russian Lady' in his affections; was she perhaps the 'young lady' in question? There do not appear to be any further letters to Theodore from her after this date.

Theodore was handed Wedderburn's letter at half past eight on the evening after the incident, just as he 'was leaving the Fort'. When he arrived back at his house in Bycullah later that night, he attempted to draft a reply. He writes that he is 'perfectly ready to explain to any person who has any right to demand such an explanation in respect of my conduct.' It is faintly written in pencil and the only legible snatches include tantalising phrases such as 'you appear to have heard only one statement of the business' and 'my cutting'… 'Cambay' and 'certainly not as you say'. The rest is largely illegible with numerous crossings out and was presumably never sent. Instead he called on Wedderburn the following day and marked the letter 'Answered 13 dd. Verbally'.

On the 19th Wedderburn sent him another letter: 'Not having heard anything from you since we met, I conclude that you have made your mind up not to apologise – in which case I have only to say that I am very sorry for it, as it shews how essentially we differ in opinion on some points – but that is no reason we should do so on all and I have no wish therefore to push the matter further and to let it drop.'

This might seem to be conciliatory but Theodore could not have failed to notice that Wedderburn now signs off as his 'well wisher' rather than, as he had done previously, his 'very sincere friend'.

The incident in question could have been connected with any of the many amorous adventures his friends had encouraged him to engage in during his separation from Eliza. But equally, having at last decided on keeping his family in Bombay with him, could it be that he had become defensive and sensitive about any hint of the racial prejudice that had begun to pervade British India and had forced his separation from the woman he loved? Might the young lady in question have made some insulting allusion to Eliza's colour or to Kitty and Aleck? Petronella Ellis was certainly disdainful of the 'native children'. The reason for the 'quarrel', as Theodore himself terms it, will probably never be known or any further light thrown on the identity of 'the young lady'. Unless a description of the incident turns up in the correspondence of a third party, we may never know the truth of the matter.

In June 1819 Theodore received a letter from home. It was from his father's spinster sister Helen Forbes. She had penned the long and newsy letter on January 19th in a neat and legible hand, from the Forbes's family town house in the Guestrow, Aberdeen, where she was hourly expecting her brother and sister-in-law's arrival from the chilly Aberdeenshire countryside. She makes no direct reference to Kitty's impending voyage. Aunt Helen may not yet have heard from Boyndlie the news that little Kitty, who would have been presumed to be yet another of Theodore's illegitimate offspring, was about to be sent to them from India, but she takes it upon herself to issue a mild reproof to him, about his firstborn son:

'It is now a long time since we mentioned poor little Frederick... his board you may believe, is regularly paid by your Father, but as he has during the late bad seasons had more demand for money than usual – I think you should remitt a small thing for defraying his expenses, it is very moderate, from 30 to 40 £ a year will serve for board, cloaths, & education.'

Apart from the nudge to give his father some financial assistance with Frederick's school fees, the letter was full of news about the rest of the family. Back in Aberdeen there had been a family wedding to celebrate. In the late summer of 1818 Theodore's younger sister Jane was married to Lieut. Will Ogilvie's older brother, Dr John Charles Ogilvie. The marriage ceremony was celebrated in St. Nicholas Kirk, Aberdeen, where Theodore's parents had themselves been married thirty-five years earlier. The two friends had been delighted to hear of the engagement of their siblings. Theodore had evidently speculated that by the time his letter of approval and congratulation arrived he might have become an uncle for the first time. Aunt Helen replies:

'I never doubted its having your intense approbation, as having so justly, a great regard for all the amiable Family. The Dr is in every respect a worthy good young man & so very fond & kind to Jane, I fear he will spoil her. She is I think, in a fair way to bring a young connection but not so soon as you expected – as they were only married the 22nd of August last – they did not hurry as Jane wished to take part of summer at Boyndlie.'

This union was the foundation of the Ogilvie-Forbes family of Boyndlie, under whose guardianship Theodore's extensive correspondence has been preserved, and ultimately deposited in the library of King's College Aberdeen. The twenty-five-year old bride was destined to be the only one of John and Katherine Forbes's eight children who survived to produce a legitimate heir to the titles and estates of the Lairds of Boyndlie. After her older sister and all her brothers had died and she herself was a widow, she became Laird of Boyndlie and suffixed her maiden name of Forbes to her married name Ogilvie.

Aunt Helen's letter also gives Theodore the news that his younger brother James, the last of the Forbes children to leave home, has been working for both the senior partners of Forbes & Co.: 'His line of business [surveying and factoring] seems rather at a stand, except some little jobs about new Piers at Fraserburgh, and Roseharty, also a little employment in managing Mr C. Forbes's Estate of Auchmedden, and Mr M. Forbes's of Crimond, both [of] which he is most anxious to turn to the best acct & will I'm sure serve them both most concientiously & properly.' She confides to Theodore that she is 'at present more anxious about a Wife to Alex'r who stands much in need of a good help mate, but he seems very Slow & difficult to fix, and as you say, they would need to have a little Money, as well as beauty.' In fact, he was so 'slow and difficult to fix' that it was not until 1853 that he married – at the age of sixty-six.

Aunt Helen's long letter bears out her reputation as an inveterate gossip. As long ago as 1811 Theodore's childless elder sister Catherine Scott had confided to him that she and her husband, Dr Scott, had intended to foster little Frederick:

'As to your son, Scott and I meant to have taken care of him as soon as he was able to run about. I would have taken him,' she says. But it seems that some of 'Aunt Helen's Gossops' found out about the plan. Considering that Frederick was illegitimate, this might have been considered inappropriate to Dr Scott's status in strait-laced Aberdeen. 'Of course she could not keep such a mighty secret,' continues Catherine, 'for though she means well and would do anything to serve any of us, I would as soon cry a thing at the church as tell her, if I did not wish it to be known.' But Jane reassures Theodore, 'It has turned out well for Mr Frederick. Our mother, Jane and Susan are all quite delighted with him [and] think he is a prodigy of cleverness and Beauty, and although I see nothing about him nor any resemblance to yourself the child is very well – & I hope shall turn out good, he is an amusement to them – but Father does not much approve of the plan & indeed I cannot say that I think it a proper precedent.' Consequently, young Frederick, aged three when Catherine wrote, and whose mother lived in nearby Inverkeithny, had continued to be a frequent visitor at Haddo until the family moved to Boyndlie in 1814.

In the same letter, written shortly before his appointment to the Mocha Residency, Catherine had raised the subject of Theodore's health. In a premonitory homily she had written that: 'We were for some time very uneasy about you, as William mentioned that you had been threatened with that liver complaint, but were happy to find by his next letter you were free of the pain in your side, for you never mentioned it yourself which was not right of you to conceal anything that was the matter with your health... I hope the warning you have had shall make you very careful of your health.'

Catherine instructed him that should he have any more problems with his health he must not hide it from them but return home. The 'liver complaint' she mentions in 1811 was perhaps an early symptom of the condition which made him susceptible to his fatal bilious attack on board the *Blenden Hall* nine years later.

Theodore was not so efficient in making the travel arrangements for his own daughter as he had been for young Tom Barnard. By the end of 1818 he had done nothing about finding a berth for Kitty on a homeward-bound ship. It was to be many months after she arrived in the Presidency before he finally booked two passages 'home' on the *Katherine Stewart Forbes* – one for Kitty and another for Fazagool. The little girl and her nurse did not embark until August 1819. What could be the reason for a ten-month-long delay? It may be that he was waiting for a sailing that included passengers, known to him personally, who might look kindly on his little girl; it may be that he wanted to enjoy family life again for a while and see more of Kitty before she left for England; but it may also have been because when he and Eliza met, 'eyes to eyes' again, he felt once more that 'heartly affection' for her that she had spoken of in her letters. The circumstances of her staying there can only be guessed at. A romantic might imagine that after eighteen months apart Theodore could not resist his 'dear Betsey', and asked her to stay – or perhaps she found that his health was not good and he needed her. Whatever the case, it was not until August 8th 1819 that Kitty and Fazagool set sail at last for England aboard the *Katherine Stewart Forbes.* In the meantime, correspondence from Ogilvie, Mrs Fraser and even from his good friend Thomas Fraser seems to have dried up completely, and there is no written evidence that Eliza returned with Aleck to Surat until their presence there is mentioned in Theodore's will, made on board the *Blenden Hall* a year later.

Chapter 21

Sweet Sorrow, 1819

Landing at Gravesend c.1810, where Fazagool and Kitty
disembarked in December 1819.

'Many a mother trusted her darling child to the waves, nay much more to
the care of strangers, in the conviction that depriving herself of the delight
of watching over it was to secure its permanent advantage.'

Maria Graham, *Journal of a Residence in India*, 1813.

21

Bombay, August 1819 – Aberdeen, January 1820

Children embarking on a long sea voyage need an enormous number of clothes; Tom Barnard must have needed several large trunks to accommodate everything listed by Mrs Forbes. Eliza's first task on reaching Bombay was to beg Theodore for funds to kit out their little girl in readiness for her voyage, and to buy the requisite furniture for her berth. Though he was not keen to loosen his purse strings for Eliza, he could not find it in his heart to deny Kitty anything that might make her journey more bearable. He knew from experience how Eliza enjoyed spending his money in the bazaars and shops of Bombay. Though he had helped to buy all that was needed for little Tom's voyage, a complete wardrobe for a little girl might be another matter; for this he needed Eliza. His daughter should want for nothing. He could be certain that he would get everything at the best possible price: Eliza would not fail to haggle her way to an excellent bargain.

Theodore would be sure to be enchanted all over again by Eliza as she arrived home fresh from the bazaar, flushed with pleasure and impatient to show him some new bolt of cloth for Kitty's wardrobe or some pretty trifle for the child that she did not need but just had to be bought at such a bargain price. Eliza could not have concealed her delight in her purchases or her affection for her husband. It was a combination Theodore would find difficult to resist and, if the past was anything to go by, he would not have tried very hard. He had missed his 'Betsey' for eighteen long months; he had looked for consolation in the Lal Bazaar, but found none; he had flirted with scores of empty-headed women and failed to discover 'a permanent partner for life' as desirable. How easy it would be for him to slip into their old intimacy once more.

After all her waiting and worrying in Surat; the loss of her baby boy; her ill health and constant changes of accommodation; the protracted negotiations for the children's baptism; the long-awaited reunion and reconciliation; after all the many and various preparations for Kitty's long sea voyage were over, the day came at last when Eliza had to say goodbye to her oldest child – and Theodore to his darling Kitty. He had secured the little girl's passage to England aboard one of the newest and finest ships to sail out of Bombay harbour that year – the *Katherine Stewart Forbes*, named after Charles and Michie Forbes's mother, and returning to London after her maiden voyage to India. The ship was as up-to-date and well fitted out as any parent might wish, and by 1819 they had the reassurance of knowing that the ship would carry a qualified 'ship's surgeon' on board for the duration of the voyage. 'The provision of ship's doctors has become common on the passenger services between India and England,' noted the *Asiatic Journal*, 'but,' it cautions, 'is unavailable for coasting and other Asian voyages.'

Theodore would have been especially gratified that Lady Grant-Keir was also on the passenger list. Maj. Gen. William Grant-Keir, her husband, was shortly to set out at the head of the punitive expedition against the pirates of Ras-al-Khaimah, who had continued to harass merchant shipping after Theodore resigned from the Mocha Residency. Lady Grant-Keir was given a grand leaving party, hosted by the Parsee shipping magnate Hormajee Bomanjee Wadia:

'On Friday, July 30, the friends of Lady Grant-Keir gave her ladyship a farewell ball and supper at Lowjee Castle, the hospitable owner of which afforded to the stewards all the accommodation in his power. Under their superintendence the avenue was lighted up and the house tastefully illuminated. On the passage to the ball room a transparency of the *Katherine Stewart Forbes* under sail met the eye of the visitors.'

The Grant-Keirs's only child, their young daughter Isabella, was on the passenger list as well as nine-year-old Master George Malcolm, whose father, Brig. General John Malcolm, was later to serve as Governor of Bombay. Both these Scottish military families would have been known to Theodore. Kitty might be considered to be a more suitable playfellow for their children on the long voyage, now that the apron strings tying her to Eliza had been cut.

The *Katherine Stewart Forbes* was due to leave India on August 8th. On arrival in England at some time between December and March, Kitty and Fazagool would have to contend with the English weather and then the freezing Scottish winter. Their wardrobes needed to include good warm clothes. All Kitty's dresses would have to be made with tucks and double seams to enable them to be let out. A six-year-old grows fast, even with the lack of exercise and restricted diet on board ship. Before they embarked they would lay in a stock of extra rations to take with them. Perhaps Eliza and Fazagool would have set to, busying themselves in making special treats for Kitty: halvas and spicy biscuits; little nutty cakes and fruit jellies; mangoes wrapped in waxed paper; lychees in their spiky brown jackets; fragrant oranges and lemons wrapped in tissue and stowed in little wooden crates; all lovingly prepared and carefully packed for the voyage. It seemed highly likely that, shortly before they reached their destination, Kitty would celebrate her seventh birthday on board. The little luxuries might not last for the whole voyage, but they would see them through the first stage and there would an opportunity to re-supply at Cape Town, where they would lie-off for a few days for passengers from India to disembark and others bound for England to come aboard and take over their recently vacated berths.

The *Katherine Stewart Forbes* sailed from Bombay, as planned, on August 8th. Though everyone wished her 'God speed' as they waved her off, they knew that the voyage could take anything from four to six months. The great ship would sail across the Arabian Sea to the islands of Mauritius and Réunion, won from the French only nine years earlier; on past Madagascar and along the Mozambique Channel, where the Indian Ocean's deep waters were destined, in a year's time, to swallow up Theodore's canvas-shrouded corpse; then around the Cape of Good Hope, where the southern tip of Africa divides the Indian Ocean from the Atlantic. After visiting Cape Town, Captain Lamb would set his course by the stars to take them north, up the Atlantic coast of Africa, its interior in 1819 still largely unexplored by Europeans, apart from intrepid explorers such as Mungo Park whose fate Theodore was ordered to investigate when he went to Mocha in 1812, but who had died on the Niger seven years earlier. They would visit the Atlantic outpost of the East India Company, St. Helena, where Boney was still living in glum exile. Leaving the coast of North Africa in their wake they would pass by the Strait of Gibraltar, where the Rock, bastion of the Royal Navy stands guard at the mouth of the Mediterranean; then up the coast of Portugal as far as La Coruña, the Dunkirk of the Peninsular War, where, almost ten years earlier, the retreating British Army had buried their general on the ramparts, as the last remnants of his army crowded aboard the ships of the Royal Navy to slip the grasp of the pursuing French. Next the captain must see his ship safely across the turbulent Bay of Biscay and past the Channel Isles, before arriving home at last off the south coast of England.

Though played out to a set regime, life on board ship during the voyage would not be one of unremitting boredom; there were other children on board, just as there had been on the *Huddart* when Tom Barnard sailed to England, and the adults would do their best to keep them all entertained. Their route would take them twice across the Equator. As they approached this important marker on the navigational chart for the first time, all the children making their first crossings would be hoodwinked with tricks such as being invited to look through a telescope with a hair cunningly placed across the lens to appear like a line – a visible equator – the sailors would make a great show of sharpening their hatchets, preparing to cut through the Equator and let the ship sail unhindered into the next hemisphere. Weather permitting, they might be honoured by a visit from Old Father Neptune and his entourage of sea nymphs – all sailors in drag, draped in dripping dreadlocks of kelp or wrack. Any younger sailors or other youths on their first equatorial crossing were captured by Neptune's lusty helpers, lathered up and shaved – to the great amusement of all around.

After braving the violence of the seas, where the continental landmass of Africa tapers to a point, forcing the currents of the South Atlantic and Indian Oceans together, the voyage from the Cape up the Atlantic coast of Africa would have been a time of relative tedium, except when they crossed the line for the second time off the Gulf of Guinea, when there might be an opportunity to play the same tricks on any first-timers who had embarked at Cape Town. Those already initiated, like Kitty, could join in the fun and feel quite superior.

As a sailing ship enters the Northern Hemisphere in October, the change in the climate becomes very obvious. The sails too often hang limply under almost constant cloud cover, listlessly flapping in the absence of strong winds to push it along. These are the notorious 'Doldrums' where progress can be frustratingly slow. It is still hot in October, but it is hot and humid. Sailors sweat and mop their weather-worn brows as they work the sails. Passengers welcome the intermittent breezes that, more often than not, bring gentle rain to refresh them and perhaps clear the sky for a while and fill the sails again. The captain taps his barometer and the passengers watch their weather glasses wearily for signs of rising pressure.

With the thunder that so often grumbled and rolled around the ship day and night, Kitty was fortunate to have Fazagool to hold on to. A flash of lightning on the horizon might warn of an approaching storm but then pass them by – miles away. Just as often they might have a day of sunny spells and freshening winds when the ship seemed to fly as fast as the scudding clouds, until a spume-capped shadow on the surface of the sea is spotted racing towards them and a sudden squall whips the sea up all around to take them by surprise and spur the sailors into frantic action, lowering the sails and battening down the hatches.

Day after day, the ship made steady progress, and by the time Kitty's seventh birthday dawned on December 1st, the *Katherine Stewart Forbes* must have been somewhere off the Iberian coast, scene of the recent Peninsular Wars. So far from home, Fazagool must have wanted to make the day as special as she could for the little girl. So, when Kitty opened her eyes in the morning, she would see her 'daydee' at her bedside waiting to kiss her and wish her a happy birthday, then get her up and dress her to go to the ship's cuddy for breakfast. Presents from her Mama and Papa would appear as if by magic and nobody seeming to know how they got there. Later she would have been the centre of attention, the toast of the whole company, and treated by everyone like a little princess.

Passengers in a sailing barque crossing the Bay of Biscay in December are unlikely to enjoy a smooth passage, but Kitty had her sea legs by then and may even have been able to giggle as Fazagool tried to keep her balance on the tilting boards of floor or deck. Passing between Portsmouth and the Isle of Wight, where young Tom had been landed from the *Huddart*, they were soon within sight of the white cliffs of the Kent coast, and into the Straight of Dover or, as the French call it, the Pas-de-Calais.

The *Katherine Stewart Forbes* arrived off Deal three days before Christmas. She dropped anchor off the Kent port among a fine collection of ships of all kinds. As well as being home to a busy fishing fleet and a hub of activity of the Royal Navy, Deal was a meeting place for merchant ships both outward-bound, and incoming from the East Indies. East Indiamen were constantly arriving from loading at Gravesend and lying-to with just the last few passengers to collect from Deal before their departure for the east. Among them, as Kitty watched the chalky ribbon of the Kent coast unfurl ahead of her, she would have seen a three-masted barque, riding low on the waves, a little smaller than the vessel she now stood upon, not quite as new but just as handsomely fitted out, with a figurehead of a highland chief proudly breasting the waves. Perhaps the elegant vessel might even have held her attention as they manoeuvred past each other port to port: it was the *Blenden Hall*, Captain Greig, bound for Bombay.

Before this handsome vessel returned from the east, her father's corpse would have been borne across its well-scrubbed deck to be tipped into the Indian Ocean and sink to his eternal rest. By chance, the two ships were navigating the waters between Gravesend and Deal at exactly the same time but in opposite directions. They may have been close, as they rode at anchor off Deal; they may have passed near to each other off the shoulder of Kent at Broadstairs; they may even have been within hailing distance off the Isle of Sheppey, or at the neck of the Thames. It is even possible that they 'spoke' and a packet of letters from passengers on the incoming *Katherine Stewart Forbes*, telling their loved ones in Bombay of their safe arrival in England, could have been passed to the outgoing *Blenden Hall*. These are things that history does not relate, but one thing is certain, that the one docked at Gravesend and the other departed Deal on the very same day: December 29th 1819.

After their ship slid into her berth at Gravesend and dropped anchor, Kitty's trunks and other luggage were, with Captain Lamb's assistance, marked to be sent up to Aberdeen. The pair had to stay and await the departure of one of the Aberdeen smacks, which sailed up the east coast from Gravesend. Three or four passenger smacks plied direct between Aberdeen and London and carried nine passengers each. Then there were additional services sailing into ports such as Leith (the port for Edinburgh), Dundee, and Montrose from where ongoing vessels connected with Aberdeen and sailed on as far north as Inverness. Though these small passenger vessels were considered by the author of an article in the *Quarterly Journal* to be 'the finest sea boats in the world and fitted up with every attention to comfort and elegance', they were essentially just single-masted vessels, built along the same lines as a fishing boat, but fitted out below decks for between nine and twelve passengers. It was a bleak time of year for such a voyage. But there was still a good chance that if the weather was fine, they would not have to wait in Gravesend for very long before they were able to embark for Aberdeen.

Arrivals.

Dec. 28 Portsmouth, Jan. 4 Deal, 9 Gravesend, Brampton, Green, from Bombay.

28 Falmouth, Jan. 5 Portsmouth, 17 Deal, 24 Gravesend, Triumph, Street, from Bengal — July, Cape of Good Hope 29 Oct., and St. Helena 12 Nov.

29 Gravesend, Katherine Stewart Forbes, Lamb, from Bombay and the Cape of Good Hope.

31 Portsmouth, Jan. 5 Deal, 9 Gravesend, Heroine, Garrick, from Bengal 28 June, Madras 1 Aug., Cape 27 Oct., and St. Helena 9 Nov.

Jan. 22 Portsmouth, Caledonia, Roberts, from Bengal and the Cape of Good Hope.

Departures.

Dec. 29 Portsmouth, Jan. 1 Torbay, Thomas Coutts, Marjoribanks, for Bombay and China.

— Portsmouth, Bulmer, Barclay, for Bengal.

— Deal, Blenden Hall, Greig, for Bombay.

31 Gravesend, Jan. 3 Deal, George Home, Telfer, for Madras.

Jan. 3 Portsmouth, 7 Cowes, Ophelia, Dawson, for China.

10 Gravesend, 14 Deal, Castle Huntly, Drummond, for Bengal and China.

— Gravesend, 14 Deal, Astell, Cresswell, for Bengal and China.

— Gravesend, 22 Deal, Asia, Balderston, for Bengal and China.

14 Cork, William Neilson, Pearson, for Bombay.

23 Gravesend, Ajax, Clark, for Madras and Bengal.

Aberdeen was a truly maritime city: shipbuilding, freighting for the Baltic trade, whaling, fishing of all sorts and the associated service industries accounted for the majority of its trade. The sailing smack was not an elegant vessel, but it was rugged and manoeuvrable. When Fazagool and Kitty reached Aberdeen, their vessel had to jink its way past whalers, schooners and sloops in the waters outside the harbour mouth before manoeuvring between the smaller fishing smacks and nudging its way into the harbour.

At last the mooring rope was tied fast and Fazagool and Kitty stepped onto the hard grey granite of the pier. Kitty must have shuddered, and not just at the cold – was this dour place really to be her home? She already looked out of place; this pale child just turned seven, clutching the hand of her black African nurse and clinging to her side for fear of being lost in the strange grey city. If Fazagool shared her fears, she knew not to show it. The place was alien to them both. And yet a hint of all the places Kitty had ever known in her short life: Mocha, Surat and Bombay hung about the northern port. The air was heavy with the smell of fish scales and salt seawater. The quarrelsome gulls circling in the wake of each new arrival seemed to share a common language with those well-remembered seabirds so familiar to her throughout her childhood and her recent voyage. Their insistent pibroch echoed off the hard stone walls, doubling and redoubling their mournful lament. They, at least, gave utterance to a *lingua franca* of all gulls, but the shouts of the fishermen, sailors and porters seemed to be in a strange language that Kitty could not understand. Poor Fazagool's command of spoken English had not been good when they set out from Surat. Ogilvie had expressed the hope that it might improve on the voyage; she had done her best, but this broad Scottish with Scandinavian overtones was a tough introduction to the 'English language' in the country where she was destined to stay for the next year or more.

Their letters of introduction from Theodore directed the weary travellers to Kitty's Aunt Jane and Uncle John Ogilvie. It was not hard to find a porter for their luggage and a boy to run to Dr Ogilvie's house in Union Street and announce their arrival. It was right in the centre of town, and not far from the docks. They were certain of a warm welcome from the young couple. Kitty had been entrusted with presents for all the family from her Papa and from Lieutenant Ogilvie, who had magically, so it seemed, become her 'Uncle Will' when the news of Aunt Jane and Uncle John's marriage reached India. She had also brought a letter from her Papa in reply to Aunt Helen's, which he had received in Bombay in May of the previous year. It was dated August 8th 1819, the very day the *Katherine Stewart Forbes* left Bombay. He had written it just before they left for the harbour and given it to Kitty when he said goodbye. It would be a good 'ice-breaker' for the little girl to hand it to her great-aunt Helen herself at the Forbes' family townhouse in the Guestrow.

The Guestrow, where Aunt Helen lived when she was not staying with her brother at Boyndlie, was a narrow cobbled wynd. It ran close to Provost Skene's house and the ancient St. Nicholas Kirkyard. Originally spelled Ghaistrow, it was said to be named from the ghosts of the long dead denizens of the tombs in the old graveyard, who were rumoured to haunt the area. Theodore's parents were in the habit of spending a week or two in Aberdeen in the days following Hogmanay. With luck they would have been there to greet their little granddaughter and take her back to Boyndlie with them, though Aunt Jane would most probably have had the sense to beg a brief respite from travelling for the child.

When she arrived at her uncle's house in Union Street, Kitty discovered that she now had a little cousin; her namesake, another Katherine, Aunt Jane's firstborn, a baby about six-months old. Aunt Helen had mentioned the forthcoming event in her letter to Theodore, dated April 1819:

'The Dr and Jane are really a very happy couple as can be, and there is a prospect of a Young one about the month of June, I think.' Kitty's baby cousin would have been just a month or so younger than little Fraser was when he died. As she leaned over the cradle, only Fazagool could have known what it meant to her. Whether or not one of them told the family the reason for Kitty's tenderness towards her little cousin, it cannot have failed to impress the baby's parents.

In January 1820 Dr and Mrs Ogilvie were still enjoying the first flush of parenthood. Their eldest son George (later, Ogilvie-Forbes of Boyndlie) was not born until the September after Kitty and Fazagool arrived. The doctor was later to offer to be Kitty's guardian, and she would come into Aberdeen to live with his growing family, but for the moment her destination was still her grandparents' house at Boyndlie.

Chapter 22

Journey to Boyndlie, 1820

The tower of King's College, Aberdeen. From an old engraving.

22

Aberdeenshire, 1820

On the day arranged for their departure, Kitty and the grandparents must have set off in their carriage from the house in Union Street, and travelled north along the long straight thoroughfare of King Street. As they bumped along the granite cobbles, Kitty must have caught sight of the dome of King's College, intermittently visible on high, between the newer housing developments along the way. The stone dome with its flying buttresses and keystone finial hewn into a giant crown was reminiscent of the grand domed tombs she was nused to seeing in the English and Dutch Cemeteries of Surat.

As their carriage gained the higher lands and wooded knolls above King's College, they passed the High Kirk of St. Machar, a place of Christian worship since the sixth century. Next, the 'Brig o' Balgownie' would take them over the deep pool, where the rocky banks of the River Don are close enough together for its 13th century builder to have constructed an elegant single-span bridge, of one high-pointed Gothic arch. As the carriage rattled them across the antique bridge and away from the security of the city, there was much to distract Kitty from any conversation. The little girl from Gujarat would have wondered at the strangeness of the cold winter woodland and the sparkling waters below. The skeletal broad-leaved trees and jagged Scots pines of Donside were so very different in form and colour from the toddy palms and palmyras of Bombay and the peepuls and banyans of Surat. Along the way, the Scots briars, stiff with cold, armed with cruel thorns and dripping with blood-red hips, gave a hint of ancient savagery, and all the while the crisp white snow lingered in the violet shadows. She must have marvelled to watch her own breath curl on the frosty morning air; to see the leafless trees outlined in silver, their slender branches crusted with rime; to glimpse the glassy icicles hanging from the eaves of cottages they passed along the way; to hear the carriage horses' cloudy snortings and see how their flanks steamed as they clattered on and left the city far behind. Yet Kitty was bred from this unfamiliar soil and the blood spilt on it by kin and clan was the self-same blood that ran in her veins. The child was a stranger in her own land.

Once they reached the coastal margins of the county, the wildness of unspoiled nature that characterised Aberdeenshire in those far-off days and the harshness of the climate that still persists would provide subjects for Kitty's curiosity no less than reasons for her discomfort. Her grandparents were fortunate to have plenty of opportunities to break the journey if needed. John Forbes's half-sister Christina, his junior by eleven years, was married to Sir Alexander Innes of Pittmedden, and his estate was close to their route home. Katherine and John Forbes of Boyndlie were well-known and well-connected throughout the county, and if any of their own families were not at home, other Aberdeen landed gentry would be happy to give hospitality to unexpected visitors from their own social circle. A little further on, near Ellon, her grandfather might have pointed out the walled parkland of Haddo House; not the Haddo Kitty's father might have talked about – his childhood home near Huntly – but the stately seat of the disconsolate widower and future British Prime Minister, Lord Aberdeen.

Having crossed the narrow upper reach of the River Ythan at Methlick they were more than halfway to their destination. And now, mile by mile, the wintry landscape became colder and bleaker. With only a scattering of low granite steadings and the stunted trees around them to break the monotony of the wide expanse of withered grass and cowering whin, they persevered through the windswept coastal farmland. By the time they passed by Strichen, home to more family connexions, with the landmark of Captain Fraser's white horse gleaming out from the shallow turf of Mormond Hill, only seven more miles remained of their journey. At last their carriage turned off the public road at a low octagonal lodge and Kitty's grandparents announced that they were now 'home'. The horses knew it, pricked up their ears and picked up their pace. It was not more than a few hundred yards from the lodge gates to the house, but it must have seemed a long way to a tired seven-year old.

Kitty had always lived in an urban environment. Here at Boyndlie, when she woke next morning, she found herself in the strange surroundings of an isolated country house and, although near to the coast, she was not within sight or sound of the sea. But again the gulls seemed to have followed her, and in the days to come she would be able to take a little comfort from hearing them quite often; from seeing large flocks hunkered down on a sheltered expanse of turf when the violence of the waves had driven them inland; or from flurries of them wheeling overhead as they regrouped to return to their rocky seaside roosts. When spring came they were there again, glinting silver in the early sun, behind the ploughman and his patient horse as they drew dark furrows across the stubble fields, turning the newly brightened land from ochre to dark umber and pale brown.

Fazagool was at her side when she woke on that first day in her grandparents' house. But it had been agreed that she was to return to India as soon as Kitty was comfortably settled in at Boyndlie House. Old Susie Cruikshank, who had looked after Theodore and all his brothers and sisters, and who was still with the family, would care for Kitty when Fazagool left. Ogilvie had predicted that Kitty would soon become a great favourite with everyone and especially her father's old nurse. Nevertheless, to be parted from her own 'daydee' would inevitably be an upsetting separation. And so it had been agreed that Fazagool should not return to Surat as long as the child needed her. She was still in Scotland a year later.

Everything at Boyndlie was so different to the life Kitty had known in India. True, there were servants at Boyndlie; but very few by comparison with Theodore's house in Bycullah. In Surat she had Uncle Aratoon as well as aunts and cousins always close at hand; but her Uncle Alexander was a bachelor, and was now farming at Haddo, Uncle James was also working away, and the grandparents were elderly. There were no other children to play with. She had been told that she had an older brother, Frederick, here in Scotland, but she was puzzled to find that he was not at home. When she asked about him, they said he was at school. She did not really know what school was; Eliza and Fazagool had taught her everything she knew. It seemed odd to her that her brother was always 'at school'. She probably began to miss little Aleck – younger brothers can sometimes be a nuisance but, in the absence of any other children, he would have been a welcome companion. When she did meet Frederick, they formed an instant bond that was to last a lifetime.

Frederick could only come to visit Boyndlie out of term time; Inverkeithny was too far away for a casual visit. Everyone seemed to like the boy. Even their grandfather, who was sometimes said to be rather tetchy on account of his gout, spoke highly of him. Uncle Alexander suffered with his rheumatism, but when he came over from Haddo he too had nothing but praise for the boy. Frederick was four years older than Kitty, and was said to be very, very clever. He had been acknowledged and welcomed into the family and he too was allowed to carry the name of Forbes. In a letter dated January 1819, a year before Kitty's arrival in Scotland, Aunt Helen describes him to Theodore as: 'Poor little Frederick, who is grown a fine creature & a good scholar, he has now been above three years boarded with Mr Morison (sic) Inverkeithny. As yet he is but little of his age,' she continues, 'but as like you in face, temper & disposition, as its possible to be.' Her description here infers that Theodore was of taller than average stature.

Frederick's school in Inverkeithny had a far-reaching reputation for excellence, largely due to the 'Dominie', Peter Morrison. Besides Frederick, there were other boarders whose parents were abroad in the East or West Indies. Frederick and his fellow pupils were entrusted, so Aunt Helen writes, to 'the care of Mrs Morrison, as to health and behaviour'. At the time the fees alone were £25 per year for boarders, a considerable sum in 1819.

In the same letter Aunt Helen tells Theodore that 'Old Susie is still alive & pretty well – she is much interested about you.' There is no record of how old 'Old Susie' was when Kitty arrived early in the following year, or when she died. She was evidently well-known to family friends – Will Ogilvie had mentioned her by name and one of the resolutions William had listed on his way out to India in 1808 was to keep in touch with 'my old nurse, Susan Cruikshank' and 'send her a little money from time to time'.

Back in India, after nearly a year of anxious waiting, Eliza heard the welcome news that Kitty and Fazagool had reached Scotland, and she thanked God for their safe arrival. It is not clear if she had remained in Bombay with Theodore after the *Katherine Stewart Forbes* sailed; Theodore's correspondence places him in the city, but amongst the incoming letters there are none from Eliza telling him how Aleck is progressing; nothing from Aratoon; and no bills from the Dinshaw brothers. It seems likely that Theodore did allow her to stay on for a while; if not in his own house, perhaps nearby in Bycullah with

Khumburzeefuh. It is difficult to imagine Eliza wanting to endure a further separation from the man she loved and still regarded as her lawful husband. In any case, it would have been a humiliating prospect to return to the old familiar haunts of Surat as a rejected woman. The circumstantial evidence points to her having stayed in Bombay at least until he booked his passage aboard the *Blenden Hall*. Another possibility is that they had both returned to Surat with Aleck for the Christmas break in December 1819 and gone back together to Bombay the following February. Whatever the case, the teasing letters from the Frasers and other close friends about his forthcoming marriages seem to have all petered out in the years 1819 and 1820 and, at the same time, relations with his partners at Forbes & Co. became strained to breaking.

A serious clash of personalities had arisen between the 'peevish' Michie Forbes and the outgoing and sociable Theodore. The bad feeling between the two men seems to have grown into downright enmity. When he arrived from England in 1817, Michie had taken over as senior partner and acting-manager, and at some point a complete breakdown in his relationship with Theodore occurred. Michie carried his animosity into the workplace and even gave instructions to members of staff that Theodore was not to be given access to the books of the House. The youngest Forbes boy, James, writing to their brother Andrew in Riga in 1821, tells him that since he arrived in Bombay he had been told that Michie, 'for a long time, kept back from his knowledge the most important transactions of the House, and latterly was not on speaking terms'. Michie could not simply dismiss another partner; the benign Stewart would have resisted any such designs, but it seems probable that he may have tried to force Theodore to resign.

It was around the time that the news arrived from Aberdeen of Kitty's safe arrival that Theodore began to consider the possibility of joining her there. His health had been unsettled periodically over the years. The bills from his wine merchant for claret by the barrel and beer by the cask, and for Madeira and Port wines, tell a story of a regular and copious consumption of alcohol in the heat of Yemen and India. His liver and kidneys had taken the strain. His older sister Catherine had quizzed him about a troublesome pain in his side as long ago as 1811 and, as late as November 1819, his doctor friend, J. M. McNeill, wrote from Hon.

Company Ship *Cornwall*, part of the expeditionary force against the pirates of Ras-al-Khaimah and enquired: 'Bye the by, how are your water works?' But perhaps it was not only his health but also the advertisements for berths to England that made him think of going home. Notices on billboards appeared in the Fort, and one in particular drew his attention:

'The *Blenden Hall* (Greig), of 474 tons, will sail for England on 13th August. Passengers apply to M/s Remington Crawford & Co. A Doctor is on the crew.'

Had he been a superstitious man, the proposed sailing date might have persuaded him to postpone his passage home. But his situation in Bombay was becoming intolerable. Yes, he would go home, there was no hope of coming to any sort of accommodation with the 'peevish' Michie. Moreover, his partnership in Forbes and Co. had not produced such good returns as his partnership with Eliza. When he reached England he would call on Charles Forbes, resign his partnership and go back into the service of the Hon. Company, as both Eliza and Aratoon had urged him to do. He would be able to travel on to Boyndlie, see his parents and other family members, meet young Frederick and, of course, see his darling Kitty again. Fazagool could return to India with him.

And so Theodore went to the offices of M/s Remington Crawford & Co. and booked his fateful passage on the '*Blenden Hall*, Capt. Greig, bound for England.' Walloo was to go with him. Old Antoon and the dog Tipoo were to stay with Wedderburn in Bombay. A proclamation from Bombay Castle, four days before Theodore's ship was due to sail, must have gratified the former Political Resident. It announced the blockade of Mocha in retribution for the *Durya Beggy* incident described by Dr Aitken: the sacking of the British Factory, the desecration of the graves of his and Theodore's successors, and the imprisonment and beating of Lieutenant Dominicetti of HCS *Mercury*. An important aim of the expedition was stated by the governor to be to 'retrieve the degradations which the national character has so deeply sustained.' As Theodore prepared to embark on his final voyage, and bade his Bombay friends farewell, perhaps the news of the imminent blockade brought the unimpeachable record of his residency in the 'Arabian Gulph' once more to everyone's notice. There must have been others including many in Mocha who, like Dr Aitken, were 'well convinced' that had Mr

Theodore Forbes HEICS continued in the post, Dominicetti's troubles would have been averted and the present action rendered unnecessary.

The *Blenden Hall* weighed anchor, as advertised, on the inauspicious date, and Theodore began his final voyage. When he went on board he was, by the accounts received by his brother James from his fellow passengers, 'hale and hearty'. Though he would not be alive to hear the outcome of the expedition against Mocha he would have been gratified that it did bring about the disgrace and dismissal of the rascally Dola. In addition, a new treaty was signed with the Imam of Sana'a. It provided for lower customs duties and a burial ground for the British. Had he lived, he must have chuckled to learn that the British were henceforth to be permitted to ride horses inside the city, the very privilege denied to Dr Aitken, which had been the cause of the disagreement between Aitken and the Dola during his own Residency.

After an exceptionally speedy voyage, the *Blenden Hall* docked at Gravesend with the news of Theodore's death and burial at sea. The four months since they left Bombay had included a whole week anchored off Mauritius and two days becalmed off Cape Town and now, yet again, it was the 13th of the month. If any sailors, considering signing on for the next voyage of the *Blenden Hall*, were put off joining her crew by the repetition of the ill-omened date, their superstition would have served them well: her next voyage would be her last. She was destined to founder on the reef of Inaccessible Isle, close to Tristan da Cunha in the South Atlantic, where her passengers, captain and crew, would be marooned for six months, subsisting on a diet of sea lion and wild celery. *'Fate Of The Blenden Hall, East Indiaman: With An Account Of Her Wreck'*, the tale of the 'sufferings and privations endured by the survivors' was published twenty-six years later in New York. It was based by Captain Greig's son, Alexander M Greig, on his 'journal, kept on the islands, and written in the blood of the penguin', on scraps of paper retrieved from the wreck.

That is another story, but it does contain a description of the ill-fated ship and its owner as well as information about the members of her crew, their names and their jobs. The very men who had provided the last offices for Theodore; Robert Perry, ship's carpenter, and James McCulloch, sailmaker, were both among the crew marooned on Inaccessible Isle. In his account of the wreck Alexander states that Perry 'sustained an irreproachable character' and had been in his father's employ for fifteen years. McCulloch too was an old hand on the ship.

Captain Greig had already sent Theodore's will to Bombay from the Cape. As soon as the *Blenden Hall* reached England, he sent another copy straight to their London office. In it, Theodore had named as his sole executors 'Charles Forbes Esq. M.P. of London, and Michie Forbes Esq. of Bombay, or whoever may be the senior Resident Partner of the House of Messrs Forbes & Co. of that place'. When the *Blenden Hall* docked, James Forbes was already in London, awaiting a passage to Bombay. He described to his brother Andrew in Riga how he had been 'on the eve of setting out to join poor Theodore in India' when news of his death arrived. In Volume 11 of *The Asiatic Journal and Monthly Miscellany*, published a month or so later, a printed report of the ship's arrival appears, with a notice of Theodore's death:

'December 11 Deal, 13 Gravesend, Blendon Hall, Greig from Bombay 13th Aug., Mauritius 16th Sept., and Cape 15th Oct. Passengers Mrs Dickinson, Mrs March and Mrs Campbell, Capt. Sealy Hon Company's marine, Capt. MacIntyre, Capt Denhahine, Lieuts Harrison, Webster, Waterfield, Harris, Spencer, and Richards; Dr Shank; Mr Brown Brig. Gen; Mr Theodore Forbes died at sea.' The voyage, including their stay in Mauritius and being becalmed at the Cape, had taken exactly four months.

As soon as James heard of his brother's death, he called on Charles Forbes at his house in Fitzroy Square and, before long, William Bridgman Jr. of Forbes & Co.'s London office contacted him to arrange for the deceased's effects to be taken from the ship at Gravesend and put aboard one of the Aberdeen smacks. With the trunk was a covering letter addressed to his brother-in-law, Dr Ogilvie, in Union Street. When the news reached them, poor Jane must have realised that on September 19th last, while she had been among family and friends, happily celebrating the birth of her firstborn son, George, her dearly loved brother was lying mortally ill on board the *Blenden Hall*, alone, at sea in the Indian Ocean.

The doctor and Jane went to Boyndlie to break the distressing news in person to her parents and young niece. It was a terrible shock to everyone. Kitty's beloved Papa had been on his way home to Scotland – home to see her and to meet young Frederick, then just twelve-years old.

The news of his death affected everyone differently. It must have hurt Old Susie to hear that, while she lived on into a venerable old age, yet another of her boys had died. As James wrote to his brother Andrew, their parents immediately began to panic about his plans to go to India. They had now lost three of their boys working abroad. John Forbes instantly posted off an express letter to James in London, begging him not to proceed further.

'Our Father has born the heavy loss we have sustained with the greatest resignation,' James later wrote to Andrew, 'and our Mother with more composure than on some former occasions... The melancholy event of our dear brother's death... has thrown a sad damp over my prospects in going to India,' he continues, 'and you may believe has made our Parents very averse to my persevering in that measure, and if I had seen any chance of getting a decent livelihood at home, would have made me relinquish it at once on their account.'

Uncle Alexander undertook to break the news to Frederick when he returned to Haddo and, from then on, childless himself, he took a fatherly interest in all Theodore's children. Years later Frederick wrote of him to Kitty: 'His uniform kindness to me and to all of us, I cannot be too sensible of – he has truly supplied the place of a father.'

Fazagool felt that it was her duty to stay at Boyndlie to look after Kitty as long as she could. Though it was almost exactly a year since their own arrival, she had not yet left Boyndlie when Dr Ogilvie and Jane came up from Aberdeen to break the dreadful news of Theodore's death at sea. Before leaving Bombay, Kitty had been able to re-establish her relationship with her father. She had been able to see him frequently while she was waiting for a suitable passage to England. By the time she and Fazagool left him at the Fort Stairs with Eliza and Aleck he had become part of the family again and she must have missed him. Now, at the very moment when he should have been walking through the door to surprise her, and she would have been leaping into his arms, she had lost him again. This time it was forever. It seemed like a double loss to hear that he had died on his way home. Now that Theodore was dead, inevitably, Kitty worried that she might never see her mother and Aleck again.

Chapter 23

James Forbes, 1821 – 1830

An excavated temple on the Island of Salsette, from an aquatint by Thos. and
William Daniell c.1800.

23

Bombay, 1821

James did his best to allay his parents' fears but, ignoring their pleas, he booked his passage to Bombay. Before he sailed from London, he wrote to his brother Andrew in Riga about Theodore: 'Everything that I have heard from those who knew him has been a testimony of his worth and goodness of heart – Our Father will probably have acquainted you with the particulars of his will, in which although we must regret his having left so large a provision for his natural children, it appears his affections have been... [paper torn] set upon them, & it cannot be helped, – and in other regards he has shewn the most affectionate remembrance of us all – My going to Bombay may be of considerable use in the settlement of his affairs, for although they cannot be in better hands than those of his executors, yet as they may have so many weighty concerns to attend to, my being in the spot may be of service, though this is no doubt a minor consideration.' The comment about Theodore's natural children seems rather mean spirited, particularly since Kitty had been with his parents for more than a year by this time, and he must have known young Frederick very well.

On the eve of his departure he wrote again to Andrew in Riga: 'The Kent (Captn Cobb) is a fine new ship of 1,300 tons, and is to be quite full of passengers, upwards of sixty I believe, and among them several ladies, so that we shall have very good society – Mr Stewart takes his wife and two children with him, – I have seen very little of him as yet, but I understand he is a very excellent man, and much-liked in Bombay.' It was the maiden voyage of The Kent, a fine East Indiaman destined to be totally destroyed by fire in the Bay of Biscay only five years later, in an incident made famous by the dramatic ship-to-ship rescue of the majority of the passengers.

Writing to Andrew again, some months later, from Bombay, having had an opportunity to talk to Wedderburn and Henderson, James wonders at Theodore's 'goodness of heart' and declares himself astonished at how he could have put up with Michie Forbes's humiliating treatment for 'so long', and 'without allowing it to affect his spirits, or appear [to] at all, but to one or two of his most intimate friends.' The animosity between the two men, James says, 'was the principle cause of his desire to return to this country,' and in the same letter he describes Michie's conduct as 'most cruel and unjustifiable,' adding, 'all without assigning any reason, for none there was but some little failings and his rather too free mode of life, which was nothing compared to the way in which many live here, and little notice taken of it.'

He goes on to describe his voyage in *The Kent*: 'We left Portsmouth on the 14th of March and arrived here on the 9th of June, being an unusually quick passage of only 87 days, and I found it on the whole more agreeable than I anticipated so long a voyage to be. – The kindness and generousity of our excellent friend Mr Charles Forbes made everything easy for my admission into the house here, which took place on the 1st of August, the period when the interest of our lamented brother ceased. – Mr Stewart, whom I accompanied from England, has also been a most kind and good friend to me throughout, and I have hitherto been a resident in his family.'

Theodore's 'rather too free mode of life' may have referred to his attendance on the ladies of the Lal Bazaar, his drinking, or it might simply have been the fact of his living openly with Eliza. According to the tenets of Bombay society, she was not his 'lawful wedded wife'. In the eyes of the parvenus of Bombay, little Aleck's dark complexion would have been proof of Theodore's depravity. This is only supposition, but James's revelation in the same letter, that Theodore was returning home, 'with the intention of going back in the Company's service' lends credence to the idea – because of the Company's long-standing tolerance of 'irregular' relationships, and because this was the very course of action that Eliza had suggested during their separation:

'I have heard now having Great deal alteration the Civil Gentlemen,' she had written, 'therefore if you can think for yourself to enter again in to the Civil Service, I think it is the better for you with less trouble and will be good for your health and I also hope you will be Governor of Surat if you intend to do the same, you can easily get any fine station.'

It was fortunate that Michie's poor opinion of Theodore was not shared by all the male British expatriates, who always treated him as one of their own. He continued to attend public functions in the city, and his old friends did not waver in their loyalty. The *Quarterly Journal of Science, Literature and the Arts* reports that 'On Monday the 27th November 1819,' three months after Kitty embarked on the *Katherine Stewart Forbes*, 'the anniversary meeting of the Bombay Literary Society was attended by members who included among others Mr Erskine, Mr Babington, Mr Wedderburn, and Mr T Forbes.' These were all old friends and housemates from his bachelor days in Mazagaon. The following year, shortly before he embarked on the *Blenden Hall*, he was numbered among those called to serve on a grand jury, on which Michie Forbes was also one of the jurors.

When James arrived in Bombay he soon discovered that Michie was as widely disliked as Theodore was liked: 'Michie Forbes staid longer than was expected after our arrival,' he writes to Andrew in April 1822, 'having only left this in January. He leaves but few friends here behind him, more I believe from his peevishness and great irritability of temper than from anything really bad in his character.'

In the same letter he goes on to describe how 'poor Theodore's little boy is at Surat with his mother, but I have not seen either of them, but am daily expecting him down here to be put to school – he is not to be sent home.' On his acceptance into Forbes & Co., James had taken on the senior partners' responsibility for administering Theodore's will. Despite his reiteration of Theodore's wish that Aleck should remain in India, only two years later he would disobey his older brother's instruction and send the boy to Scotland. He does not explain his reasons for this decision. It may be that he wanted to remove his young nephew from the dangers he was exposed to by remaining in Surat; in 1822, the city had been badly damaged by flood; Dr Buist in his *Notes on a Journey*, published c.1850 describes how:

'In 1822 the Taptee swollen by a long by continuance of rain began to rise on the 15th of September and continued for three days to increase. The water advanced so rapidly that some gentlemen only saved their horses by taking them up stairs. By this time the flood had risen four or five feet higher than it had ever done before, extending to the eaves of many of the lower roomed houses. Nearly 300 yards of the outer wall of the city were washed away, two bridges were destroyed, part of the wall of the Adawlut was carried off... About thirty lives were lost and about 1400 head of cattle were swept away. 2000 houses in all were believed to have fallen of which above 600 were substantially built.'

Fires in the crowded Mughal Serail and plagues of various descriptions were also regular occurrences. Little is known of Aleck's early education, but it is possible that his command of English had been deteriorating while he remained with Eliza and his extended Armenian family. This may have been the determining factor in James's decision in 1822, first to enter him into school in Bombay and, just two years later, to book his passage to London aboard the *James Sibbald*.

Before the boy embarked, James wrote to William Bridgman Junior, at the London office of Forbes & Co., to recommend to his 'notice and friendly offices, the son of my late brother Theodore, a little fellow of about ten years of age.' Two of the Forbes partners, John Campbell and John Stewart, had health problems and were also preparing to sail home on the same ship, so the lad would have friends aboard who had known his father well. Mr and Mrs Stewart had their own young son with them, and Mrs Stewart had, according to James, 'been good enough to get Aleck provided with everything necessary for his comfort on the voyage.' He would have a playmate in Master Stewart, the services of his father's personal servant Walloo, and the supervision of Mrs Stewart. James also told Bridgman that he was certain that his old landlady, 'Miss Rose in St. Mary Axe', would 'receive and be kind' to Aleck and he asked further that he 'be good enough to take a passage for the little fellow and the servant on one of the Aberdeen smacks, and consign him to the care of Dr Ogilvie in Union Street.'

John Campbell, returning home to recover his health, died a week into the voyage, aged only 20-years old, and his body was 'committed to the deep' in Quilon Roads, off the coast of Kerala. Young Aleck then learned at first-hand how his own father's funeral would have been performed four years earlier, a funeral that Walloo would have remembered well. Apart from this early upset, the voyage seems to have passed without incident. When the *James Sibbald* dropped anchor off Plymouth on July 12th 1824, keen to be once more on dry land, the Stewarts landed there and made their way 'by easy stages' to London. The ship reached Deal on the 15th and a few days later, Aleck and Walloo disembarked at Gravesend and travelled up the Thames to London. They contacted William Bridgman at the offices of Forbes & Co. and stayed a few days with Miss Rose before sailing for Aberdeen, which they reached safely on August 3rd. The journey had taken five months in total; Walloo returned to London almost immediately, reported Bridgman, and was 'lodged with Mr Stewart to await his return passage to India, together with Mr Stewart's own native servant.'

When Aleck walked through the door of the house in Union Street with Walloo it seemed to be thronged with children, one of whom was his sister. He had been longing to see her but she was not the Kitty he remembered from five years ago. She seemed so grown up now; in only a few months' time she would be twelve years old. But it was still easy to pick her out. She was the oldest and tallest of all the children there, the others were mere babies; Kitty's namesake Katherine, the babe in arms when she first arrived was now five-years old – just half Aleck's age; his little cousin George was, as yet, the only other boy in the household, a mere four-years old next month; then there was the two-year-old toddler, Rebecca; and to crown it all, Aunt Jane was expecting another baby early in the new year. It must have been a great disappointment to him to find that, with so many other children around, there was not one near enough his age to play with him. Kitty and Aleck were by now almost strangers to each other, and though they always kept in touch, she was to remain much closer to her older half-brother Frederick.

Aleck's arrival, laden with presents and loving messages from Eliza, must have been a painful reminder to Kitty of the five long years' separation she had so far endured. She must have missed the warmth of Surat and of her Indian family. How often in her dreams had she sailed back to India and felt, for a fleeting moment, her mother's love a heartbeat away – only to wake and find herself alone in Scotland still? How often had she looked from the nursery window at the dour Scottish sky and wished for the warmth and bustle of India? How often had her heart leapt with empty hope at a familiar turn of the head, a voice, a laugh, a gesture that reminded her of the family she had loved and left behind? When she moved into Aberdeen with her uncle and aunt, just starting their own family in Union Street, her walks would sometimes take her close to the quayside, where among the fishermen from the herring fleet, and the sailors from faraway lands, from time to time she might thrill to glimpse a smile shine out from a dark face, or a pair of brown eyes looking kindly down at a child in whose face they recognised an emptiness, they themselves still felt so far from home.

August was harvest time on the estates of Boyndlie and Haddo. Jane loved Boyndlie in summer time and, five months into her fourth pregnancy, this would be the best opportunity for her to take Kitty and Aleck to visit their grandparents. For some time now, John Forbes had not been well enough to take charge of Kitty. He was frequently incapacitated by painful attacks of gout, and so it had been decided that both Kitty and Aleck should stay in the guardianship of their Uncle John Ogilvie in Aberdeen. Only a few months later, on December 6th 1824, John Forbes 5th of Boyndlie died and their Uncle Alexander became the 6th Laird.

Alexander was still unmarried and remained so until 1853, when, at the age of sixty-six he found at last in Annabella Reid 'one of the many nice girls in this country' with the store of beauty and 'a little money' that Aunt Helen had wished for him so many years before. Not long after John Forbes died, his widow Katherine moved into a house in Golden Square in the centre of Aberdeen. Of her eight children who had survived beyond infancy, only Jane and Theodore had produced grandchildren for her; the move would give her an opportunity to see them all more often. They were now all living in the city, with the exception of Frederick who, at sixteen-years old, was just finishing his education at Inverkeithny School, where, under the tutelage of the 'kind and respected teacher' Peter Morrison, he had received an education of sufficient quality to enable him to enrol at Marischal College, Aberdeen, where he would gain an MA in Medicine.

Frederick's old 'Dominie' died in his schoolroom in July 1825, 'seized with a fit of apoplexy'. William Barclay describes in his *Schools and Schoolmasters of Banffshire*, how 'The poor boys in their ignorance tried to prop him up in his chair, and consequently life had fled before his wife had time to come and help.' Perhaps hearing of, or even witnessing, this inept attempt at first-aid might have inspired young Frederick to settle on a career in medicine. Seven years after his teacher's unfortunate death, having received his degree, young Dr Forbes was accepted into the East India Company's Medical Establishment. Early in 1830, just as he was entering the final years of his medical studies, had come devastating news from Bombay – in the December just past James had been killed in a tragic accident.

When the family received the first-hand accounts of the incident, the details were puzzling. It had happened during the Christmas holidays of 1829. James and three friends were visiting the island of Salsette to explore the ancient ruins and caves there. After the four young men had enjoyed a hearty picnic, they set off for a walk. James seemed to be drawn back to a hermitage built on the top of a Hindu temple the friends had just climbed and he twice left the party to return to it alone. On the second occasion they heard a muffled thud and when he did not reply to their anxious shouts, they retraced their footsteps and found him lying on the ground, bloody and insensible, and gurgling in an alarming manner. He had fallen from the very top of the building into the courtyard of the temple. They carried him to a nearby house where he was given what first-aid they could muster, but he died the following day without regaining consciousness. Later descriptions of the unfortunate event do not mention his companions, who were witnesses to it, but they do describe the ruin. It seems that it was an excavated Buddhist cave temple. According to Gerson da Cunha, Mr Vaupell visited the site in 1838 and stated that James had 'imprudently climbed the wall at a corner with his boots on, where the roots of a peepul tree served as a ladder... after sitting for a while admiring the prospect, in the act of rising, it is supposed, part of the crumbling wall giving way under his feet, he slipped and was precipitated into the court of the temple below, a height of between sixty and seventy feet.'

Alexander had been styled 'Forbes of Boyndlie' since their father's death. Now, as head of the family, he had to deal with the death of yet another brother. His own foray into foreign travel and spell of imprisonment in Denmark had convinced him of the wisdom of staying at home, and it seems that he was right. His only surviving brother, Andrew, returned home from Riga when his employers, Messrs Helmsing & Drachenhaur had dissolved their partnership and filed for bankruptcy. He was not well, and died aged 37 in September 1831. He was buried beside his father in the family vault in the little churchyard at Tyrie. His mother only survived him by three months. In the space of three years Alexander had lost his last two remaining brothers and his mother. He was still unmarried, and on his death the lairdship would pass to his sister Jane Ogilvie.

Alexander Forbes, 6th of Boyndlie, now turned his attention to Theodore's estate, and more particularly to the children's legacies, still not paid after ten years. He wrote to Sir Charles Forbes to press for a final settlement of the accounts. It was obviously of vital importance to young Frederick, who was about to qualify as a doctor and wanted to join the East India Company's Medical Establishment. Alexander questioned the lack of funds in James's estate. The reply was not what he expected. From Sir Charles Forbes's reply it seems that James had been living beyond his means. Unlike Theodore, he had brought no capital with him into the partnership. During the eight years he was in Bombay he had lived much of the time rent-free, first with the Stewarts and afterwards with other junior partners in Charles Forbes's own house, close to the office, as he had explained in a letter to his brother Andrew not long after his arrival:

'There is little chance nowadays of a fortune being made here, as a share in the firm of F & Co. was sure to produce formerly, – but with its extensive connections and well-established agency business, there will always be an independent competency to those connected with it. Mr C. Forbes, with his usual liberality advanced my share of the Capital, as I had none of my own that could be yet made available, and I fear it will take the savings of several years to pay off this large debt to him.'

James's arrival in India in June 1821 had given Eliza an unexpected but welcome link with Theodore. On August 1st of the same year, Forbes & Co. had issued the following notice: 'Our partner Theodore Forbes died and his interest in the firm ceased w.e.f. 31st July 1821. We have admitted his brother James Forbes as a partner from today.' As he was now a partner in Forbes & Co., just as he had supposed, he was tasked with the executorship of his brother's estate. He made several immediate disbursements to various beneficiaries, and he soon discovered that Eliza was to receive an allowance of only 100 rupees per month under the terms of Theodore's will, rather than the 210 that she had been receiving prior to his death. Even 100 rupees per month was considered at the time to be an adequate sum on which to live very comfortably in Surat. Eliza though, was a woman of some quality – she was accustomed to more than just an adequate competency – she needed to buy shoes, imported Chinese silks and ribbons; to have funds to pay her dressmaker and her servants, and to help the dwindling Armenian community. She styled herself 'Sahiba' – the Sahib's Lady – Mrs Forbes. When she was widowed she was still in her mid-twenties – a fashionable young woman whose pride obliged her to keep up appearances. The reduction in her income was a bitter disappointment to her. But worse was to follow.

Chapter 24

Valedictory, 1819 – 1834

Kitty Scott Forbes c.1860. © A. Henderson Esq.

24

Bombay, 1832 – Aberdeen, 1893

Frederick had always taken a brotherly interest in Kitty and Aleck. Despite the differences in their early upbringing they kept in touch, and the clever and accomplished young doctor worried about the poor prospects of his less talented half-brother. According to him, Aleck's handwriting was 'execrable' and he despaired of his ever getting any decent employment. But on the 20th June 1831, in a neat and legible hand, Aleck had written a polite letter to Sir Charles Forbes. He tells Sir Charles that he is 'bound an apprentice for three years with Mr Black of Willowbank, general agent in this town'.

'As one of the trustees on the estate of my late Father Theodore Forbes and wishing also to follow the mercantile profession,' he asks if Sir Charles 'would have the kindness to interest himself,' at the termination of his apprenticeship, in 'procuring a situation' for him 'in any respectable House.' Sir Charles was, at the time, still involved in the lengthy business of unravelling Theodore's estate, dealing with Eliza's desperate pleas, and accounting for James's part in the whole sorry muddle, all with Alexander on his case. He must have longed to see the end of the whole wearisome episode of the Forbes brothers' involvement in his company. But it would be surprising if his well-known genial nature did not lead him to overlook Aleck's unfortunate connections and offer him a position in Forbes & Co. or recommend him to another 'respectable house'.

Aleck's descendants believe that he returned to India when still a child because he was homesick and that he later came back to Scotland and worked as an insurance agent in Arbroath, where he married aged fifty, and had two children. Family correspondence reveals that he stayed in Scotland at least until he came of age in 1836. Perhaps he returned to India then because he knew that it was his father's dying wish that he should remain there; or because he wanted to follow his half-brother Frederick to India; or because he wanted to help his mother financially; or perhaps it was because, when he finished his apprenticeship with Mr Black of Aberdeen, Sir Charles did give him an introduction to someone else's 'respectable house' in Bombay.

Frederick had arrived in Bombay in June 1832, almost three years after James's mysterious death. The passenger list of his voyage out to Bombay records that he was accompanied by a female servant. It was not uncommon for a servant being returned to India to be sent at a reduced rate in the service of one of the paying passengers. But is it possible that Fazagool had stayed with Kitty, for all those years? When Frederick left Scotland, Kitty had just turned nineteen, and Aleck was bound apprentice to Mr Black of Willowbank. Was Fazagool, perhaps, the female servant who accompanied Frederick? At this time correspondence from Forbes & Co. concerns the amount by which Eliza was to have her allowance cut, but no mention is made of Fazagool's annuity; was this because she had been in Scotland all the time since Theodore's death?

Frederick was attached to the Indian Navy as a ship's surgeon. In 1833 his ship, the brig *Tigris*, was sent to the Red Sea, and he found himself in his father's old sphere of influence. His ship twice put in to Mocha, but it is unlikely that he knew that he was treading the very ground where his father and step-mother started their married life together and where his younger half-sister and brother were both born. Many of the concerns that occupied Theodore during his three and a half years in office were still the same when Frederick visited Mocha: piracy; the ambitions of Mehmet Ali Pasha; the decline of Ottoman influence; and the ever-present threat from the Wahabees in Yemen. Fortunately, peace with France had long been concluded and now the French and British were allies in support of Greek independence within the declining Ottoman Empire.

About the same time as Frederick was on his tour of duty in the Red Sea area, a letter from the Bombay office of Forbes & Co., Bombay, arrived in London addressed to Sir Charles Forbes and John Stewart. It was a statement of James's account with the House. It also gave details of payments to Eliza from Theodore's estate. It transpires that she had so far received not only the full one hundred rupees per month that Theodore had left her, but:

'We likewise enclose a statement of the account on our books – "James Forbes Esq. For E.K." Commencing 14th November 1823, and exhibiting under date July last (1832), a principal balance of Rupees 11,057. 97 in our favor... the last mentioned account being unconnected with the estate of Mr. Theodore Forbes, remains for settlement hereafter on adjusting the affairs of the estate of Mr James Forbes.' In other words James's estate would be in debit to Forbes & Co. not only for his EK account, but also for the advance that Sir Charles had made to him to take Theodore's place as a partner.

Even assuming that James may have paid Aleck's fees for Eliza during the brief time he was at school in Bombay, and perhaps the fare of around a thousand rupees for his passage aboard the *James Sibbald*, it is difficult to understand why he should feel the need to charge such a large amount 'For E.K' to his own account with Forbes & Co. It throws up a barrage of questions: Was his desire for his brother's widow the cause of his falling into debt – had they become lovers? Was this the reason he disregarded Theodore's wish that Aleck should remain in Surat with his mother? Had he hoped to win her over with generosity to match his older brother's? Was his fatal fall really an accident or was it perhaps suicide? They must have met quite frequently; Forbes & Co. held records of regular sums of money advanced to E.K. by James over a period of six years. Whatever the answers to these questions might be, the outcome is the same: James was dead. Eliza remained in Surat, a young widow, within a dwindling Armenian community, in a city which, like her, had lost its former wealth and status. Both her children were on the other side of the world, and year on year were becoming strangers to her and their past. Her young brother-in-law had run himself into debt for her and, now that he was dead, the execution of Theodore's will and James's had reverted to the senior partners of Forbes & Co. They had no personal interest in either estate or knowledge of the beneficiaries. Along with a statement of James's indebtedness to the house, Forbes & Co., London, sent up to Scotland a copy of a letter they had sent to Eliza, still in Surat:

'We beg to acquaint you that as the assets of the estate are insufficient to pay the legacies in full, with interest, and as you have hitherto enjoyed the full amount of your bequest, independent of a considerable sum advanced to you by the late Mr James Forbes, and as a refund will be necessary from some of them, to place the whole of the legatees in the like situation, we think it right, until we receive instructions from the executors, to limit your allowance to Rupees fifty, and we have instructed

Dinshaw Eduljee accordingly.'

This was a terrible shock to poor Eliza. Her income would now be less than a quarter of what it had been before Theodore died, and she no longer had James to support her. She replied to Forbes & Co. by return. Her account of the situation does not agree with James's record on Forbes & Co.'s books: 'I beg to inform you,' she retorts, 'that I have received this intimation with surprise and much grief, for Mr Forbes engaged that I should receive 200 Rupees monthly – and that sum on his lamented death was reduced to 100 Rupees. At that period I was considerably involved in debt and owing to such reduction, I have never been able to extricate myself from difficulty. I am now reduced to circumstances of real distress, having no possible means of paying off any part of the sums due to different persons, and fearing that my creditors will seize on my goods, now that I can no longer pay the usual instalments. I beg also to mention in allusion to that part of your communication which states that Mr James Forbes advanced me a considerable sum, that I never received any sum, large or small from Mr James Forbes, and indeed the full amount of my lottery prize of Rupees 5,000 which during Mr Forbes lifetime remained in his hands, has never been paid me.'

This letter is composed in much better English than her earlier ones, there is no hint of her accent – it sounds more like someone whose first language is English – but in the absence of the original, it is impossible to say whether it was written by a scribe. Three months later Eliza wrote directly to Sir Charles Forbes in London. She appeals to him to 'order Messrs Forbes & Co. to alter their determination regarding my monthly allowance', and begs him to consider what Theodore would have said about the matter. 'Could it ever have his imagination that the poor mother of his children would be reduced to beggary and wretchedness?' she asks.

In April 1834, the final statement for Theodore's estate came into Alexander's hand from Sir Charles Forbes and John Stewart. It outlined the settlement the House had arrived at with regard to Eliza's legacy. Aleck was not yet twenty, but Kitty had reached her majority the previous December. In the letter the two trustees tell him that Eliza's monthly allowance is the only matter still in dispute:

'We did entertain some doubt regarding the monthly allowance to Eliza Kewark, and although there can be none as to the intention of the testator to secure to her the full annuity, we deemed it advisable to take the opinion of Sergeant Spankie, and then of Sir Edward Sugden and Mr Lewis, on the point in question. – They not being by any means conclusive, but rather contradictory, – we obtained the opinion of Mr Wigram, an eminent Chancery barrister on the case, who thinks that the claim of Eliza Kewark, to be paid her annuity in full, cannot be supported... You will no doubt agree with us that it is much to be regretted that the obvious intention of the testator cannot be carried into effect... It will be for the consideration of the children of Eliza Kewark by your late brother, to make up or contribute towards the full allowance which their father intended she should enjoy.'

With the statement came 'a letter for Miss Katherine Scott Forbes from her mother Eliza Kewark'. Eliza's letter to Kitty has not so far been found among the Ogilvie-Forbes archive nor among the Crombie papers, some of which passed into the possession of Cambridge University. Unfortunately it may have been among the papers of Rear-Admiral John Harvey Forbes Crombie, which are said to have been lost in the bombing of Portsmouth during the Second World War. This seems likely since many of the letters he deposited in Cambridge were addressed to Kitty, and would presumably have passed down from Kitty's children through the Crombie family not the Ogilvie-Forbes's.

Later in the year 1834, Captain Thomas Dickinson chanced to meet Frederick at the offices of Forbes & Co., Bombay, when he was chasing his son Sebastian's legacy and Frederick was there enquiring about the final settlement of his own inheritance. It was two years after Frederick's arrival from Scotland. Had he, during that time, been able to visit Surat and give Eliza any assistance? Surely Kitty would have asked him to take a letter from her out to India with him and deliver it to Eliza? If the female servant who accompanied him was Fazagool, she may have taken letters and presents from Kitty and Aleck back to Surat. 'It is said that Eliza died a wealthy woman.' This is the one family tradition that has yet to be proved; all the others: 'they were married after the manner of the country where they lived'; they had three children, 'one of whom died young'; 'he was not allowed to keep Eliza in Bombay with him'; have turned out to be true. Perhaps it is not too much to hope that, sometime in the future, letters or other documents might turn up and shed some light on the matter.

Frederick Forbes MD. Theodore's illegitimate son, by Anne MacDonnell.
'Barbarously murdered by Ibrahim Khan, Beloochee' in Afghanistan, on the
banks of the Hari Rud, in September 1841.

Photo © Susan Harvard. Photographed by kind permission of the
Brose family of Boyndlie.

Photo © Susan Harvard

The memorial to Peter Morison, Frederick's Dominie at Inverkeithny

Photo ©Susan Harvard

A humble grave in in Invekeithny kirkyard; is this Frederick's mother's grave?
The headstone is inscribed to A,McDonald with the N back to front.

Macdonnell is a variant of Mac Donald or McDonald.
Frederick left his mother an annuity but no lump sum.
She may not have saved enough to pay a professional mason

Photo ©Susan Harvard

In 1837, after five years' service in India, Frederick returned overland to Scotland on leave, with the aim of having a minor operation and enrolling at Edinburgh University to improve his medical knowledge and qualify for his MD. In October he wrote to Kitty from Balmeer: 'It is now a long time since I received your most welcome letter informing me of your approaching marriage with Mr Crombie.' He sends her his best wishes for her future happiness which, he adds, she 'so well' deserves. In fact, by the time he sent his letter, Kitty had already been married for six months. The marriage of Miss Katherine Scott Forbes to James Crombie Esq. of Cothal Mills had taken place in the cathedral church of St. Nicholas, Aberdeen on 30th March 1837. Dr Ogilvie gave his niece away, and by the time her half-brother's letter of congratulations arrived the couple were already expecting their first baby.

In a letter to Kitty, written in July 1838, Frederick describes how he has just arrived in Baghdad from staying with Col. Robert Taylor's son in Bussora, now Basra in present day Iraq. When he reached Baghdad, he tells her, he was received 'very kindly' by Col. Taylor the British Resident, whose 'family consists of his wife, an Armenian by birth but educated in England, and two daughters just come out, he... has three sons, one in India, another in England and a third in Bussora.' This was the very same Rosa Taylor whose kidnap and ransom by pirates, along with her baby son, had caused such a stir in Bombay in 1809 and may perhaps have inspired Theodore to feel he could marry Eliza and take her with him to Mocha without damaging his career prospects within the Secret and Political Department.

Frederick stayed with the Taylors for about a week, and then he continued his journey, taking time to visit any interesting or little-known places along the way, including the Sinjar Hills and, helped by letters of introduction from Colonel Taylor, was able to travel safely through the region and study the little-known Yezidi people and their faith. His observations were set down in a paper he presented to the Royal Geographical Society entitled *A Visit to the Sinjár Hills in 1838, with Some Account of the Sect of Yezídís, and of Various Places in the*

Mesopotamian Desert, between the Rivers Tigris and Khábúr. The account was published by the RGS in 1839.

When Frederick arrived back in Scotland, he was delighted to find Kitty and James happily settled in New Machar. The couple already had a baby daughter, Helen Forbes Crombie, baptised at New Machar on 26th March 1838. Another baby was swiftly on its way and Kitty's firstborn son John was baptised just twelve months and nine days later. Like Aleck, he was dark complexioned and later, at the Grandholm Mills, became known as 'black Jock'. Frederick used his furlough constructively; as well as writing up his paper on the Yezidis he also presented a paper before a meeting of the Royal Geographical Society entitled *Some Account of the Western Portion of Marwar, Commonly Called Mullani*, and he received his MD from Edinburgh University.

In 1841, on his return journey from Scotland to Bombay overland, he wrote frequently to Katherine and James Crombie during the early part of his journey. The first Afghan War was in its early stages when he had to pass through Afghanistan on his route from Persia to India. He had reached the borders of the province of Helmand and lingered there to explore the ancient ruins around Lake Seistan. Pledged safe conduct and provided with an armed escort of Baluchis with Ibrahim Khan at their head, he continued on his way towards Kandahar. When they reached the Hari Rud [river] his escort, who had charged their *jezails* earlier under the pretext of looking for game, first fired on him as he was crossing by raft, and then, as he turned back in mid-stream and attempted to wade back and reason with him, Khan cut down the doctor with his *tulwar*. His Persian attendant escaped and made a deposition before the British Political Resident, in Kandahar, the young Henry Rawlinson, later to become an eminent orientalist, famous as the decipherer of ancient Mesopotamian cuneiform script. It later transpired that this savage murder of a defenceless man was supposedly in retribution for the British Army's storming of Khelat in November 1840. Rawlinson recognised in Frederick's papers the observations and writings of a fellow academic and commented when he sent them to Bombay, that they were worthy of publication.

A small article appeared in the Scottish press relating how Dr Forbes had been 'barbarously murdered by Ibrahim Khan Beloochee'. The news spread quickly and Alexander's fears, expressed several months earlier, for his nephew's safety, were shockingly confirmed. The Rev. James Milne, vicar of Inverkeithny, on his way to hand over her allowance to her, met Frederick's mother hurrying on foot to ask if the rumours were true. Only weeks before his violent death, Frederick was in Teheran. He must have been made aware of the dangers of travelling through Afghanistan, because he drew up and deposited a will there. Though British politicians insisted that the country was subdued, the Army had made no attempt 'to win hearts and minds'. General Nott, the commander of the garrison at Kandahar had only recently declared that the conduct of the British had 'bared the throat of every European in this country to the sword and knife of the revengeful Afghan and bloody Belooch'. How right he was.

In his will Frederick left an annuity to his mother and a legacy to Aleck, whose story ends happily; though it is not known how long he stayed in India, records show that in June 1865, at the age of fifty, he was married to a twenty-nine-year-old lass from Dundee. The registration of his marriage to Elizabeth Cobb gives his age as forty nine but his fiftieth birthday had passed six months earlier. Elizabeth was the daughter of a weaver from Dundee. They had two children, named after his siblings; a boy named Frederick, and a girl, Catherine. He and Kitty had kept in touch and in her will she left the same sum of money to her niece as she did to her granddaughters, who were about the same age. The entry confirms that Alexander's father was 'Theodore Forbes, merchant in Bombay, deceased', and that his mother is given as 'Eliza Forbes' whose maiden surname is 'Quark'. Eliza is not described as deceased.

The entry of Kitty Scott Forbes into the Crombie family had brought James Crombie the acceptance of the old landed families of Aberdeenshire and Banff. James was an astute businessman, and had already made enough money to uphold the position in society which his bride's family enjoyed. And so, from this union between a mill owner and a girl of good family but indeterminate background, the Crombie family moved steadily up through the middle and professional classes into the ranks of the nobility. Kitty's sons were prosperous businessmen, and her daughters married into the professions. Soon there were connections with royalty; her grandson Adrian Crombie was elected to the Queen's Bodyguard for Scotland – the Royal Company of Archers; her great-granddaughter Ruth married into the peerage and became Lady Fermoy, woman-of-the-bedchamber, friend and confidante of HRH Queen Elizabeth, the Queen Mother. In the relentless upward march of Eliza's descendants Ruth's daughter, Frances, married an Earl, and her granddaughter, the Lady Diana Spencer, famously, married the Prince of Wales.

The disputed union of Theodore and Eliza was founded on physical love and mutual respect; their separation was caused by the 'vaulting ambition' of one party and the prejudice of society against the other. Their marriage, solemnised when each placed a crown on the other's head in the Armenian Church, can now be recognised as, literally, the crowning moment of an imperfectly remembered royal lineage, threaded back through two centuries of social change. It was to find a parallel in their descendants, Prince William, Duke of Cambridge and his brother Prince Harry, marrying, 'not for love of jewels money, riches etc.' but only for 'heartly love', as Eliza said of her own marriage. But Prince William and his brother Harry have inherited from Eliza something more substantive; their descent from her, in the direct female line, is integral to their physical being, for their unique mitochondrial DNA, passed to a child only from its mother, is therefore Diana's, Frances's, the two Ruth's, Jane Crombie's, Kitty's, Eliza's, Eliza's half-Armenian mother's and her Indian grandmother's. Chance has consolidated a series of tenuous links into an unbroken chain that stretches far back into the turbulent history of India; it is rooted in the great movements of peoples across the subcontinent from Armenia in Central Asia, through Persia to the north of India; in a serendipitous connection from the mountain regions of Kashmir and the plains of Rajputana, to the sacred city of the Mughals, Surat; and ultimately carried halfway across the world to Scotland in the person of a little girl born on the Red Sea coast of Arabia. It seems fitting that Eliza's fortitude and her faithfulness to the symbolism of the crown that Theodore placed on her head so lovingly in Surat should ultimately lead to the very real crown of Great Britain.

When Eliza gave up Kitty, she did so for love; for love of Theodore as well as for love of their little girl. She truly believed that her sacrifice was in Kitty's best interest, but at the same time she hoped to win Theodore back and reunite their family. She remained confident that her physical attraction and the memory of the close and loving relationship they had shared in Mocha would bring him back to her. She had always believed that if only she could make him look her in the face 'eyes to eyes' he could not find it in his heart to tell her they must part. She trusted too in the spiritual bond that held them together; the holy estate of matrimony solemnised in her church, and her faith never wavered. Her obedience to Theodore's wishes with regard to Kitty had always been part of a wider plan to reinstate their marriage 'with full affection'. Circumstantial evidence supports the assumption that her plan had succeeded. But Theodore's two years of dissipation in Bombay meant that his failing health had robbed her of the successful outcome of her dreams; that he would return to her, as loving and generous as before, as one of the élite of the Honourable East India Company and take up a 'fine station' with her at his side – perhaps as Governor of Surat.

Kitty appears in the census of 1891 as the head of her household in Bon Accord Square, Aberdeen. She has been elevated to the wealth and position her mother had wished for her; little Kitty Scott Forbes had become Katherine Crombie, a wealthy Scottish widow, matriarch of a large, prosperous and upwardly mobile family. Over the last seventy years she had become accustomed to the harshness of the Scottish climate, the adamantine granite of its buildings, the sombre dress of its people. Everything she had known up to the age of six had been so different to the life she had grown into. But vague as the memories of her colourful early childhood might have been after such a long time, flickering impressions of Mocha and Surat may still have burned through the cool fabric of her life in Scotland, like the last smouldering embers radiating heat from the ashes of a dying fire.

In this, the last of the six censuses taken during her lifetime, in April 1891, she had written the word 'Arabia' in response to the question 'where born' and it was the first time that the true answer, though vague, had been given. It seems that, only at the very end of her life, had she discovered the beginning. As she wrote the word Arabia, did some faint remembrance of her childhood come to the fore? Perhaps she could still recall another self – a lively child, beckoning her from across a wide expanse of time and tide. When two years later she lay on her deathbed, with her own children at her side, she may, perhaps, have felt the warmth of the early years of her parents' marriage and the love that surrounded her in Mocha. Perhaps it brought her peace in her final hours.

Bon Accord Square has changed very little over the years since the 1820s when it was built – it is still much as it was in 1893 when Katherine Scott Crombie died in her home at Number Sixteen. Archibald Simpson's graceful development is now surrounded by the bustling commercial streets and noisy traffic of the great city of Aberdeen. But peace and harmony are implicit in the name, and the square today resounds with echoes of its former gentility. It is not really a square but a long rectangle, with entries to it only along East and West Craibstone Street at either short end. The south and north terraces on the long sides face each other across a little park in the middle. A gentle movement of the trees in the central oasis of green seems to soften the resolute integrity of the opposing ranks of houses, and to validate the choice of name.

In Kitty Scott Crombie's day the square rang with the jingle of horses' harness and the echo of hooves on granite. Top-hatted professional gentlemen; ladies in rustling silk; nannies with wicker perambulators; and children bowling their hoops along the pavement, are but ghosts of the imagination. Today it is cluttered with parked cars and bicycles; scurrying office workers and casual visitors who linger at the sculpted monument to its architect. Passers-by hurry on, ignorant of its history. The solid cast-iron gas lanterns, so familiar to Kitty and her family, stand guard still at regular intervals along the kerbside, and the same stout iron railings form a serried line to defend the basement areas of the houses against rude incursions from the common pavement. Number Sixteen is still there with its secrets, locked into the north-west corner.

The End

TAIL PIECES

Forbes/Crombie Genealogy

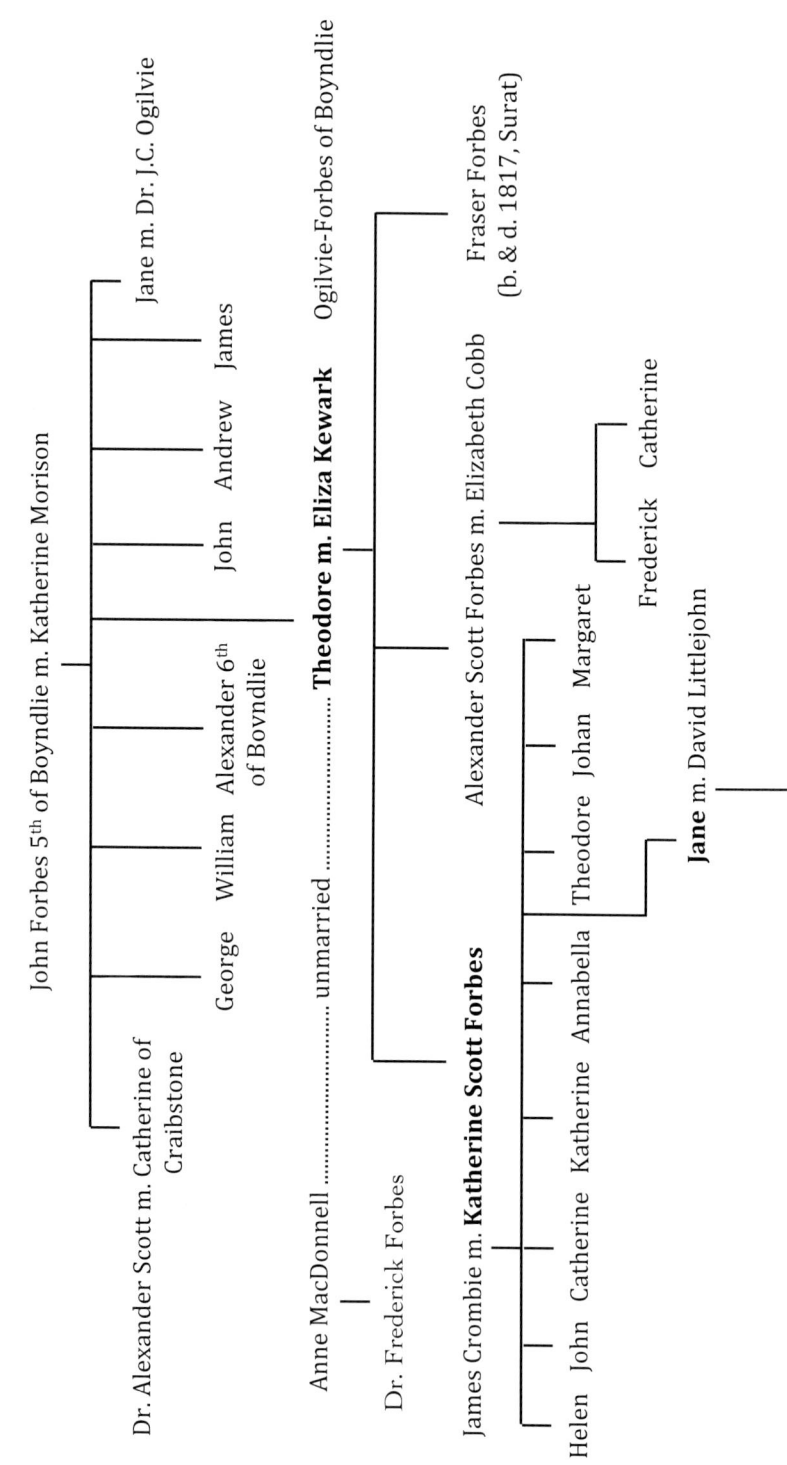

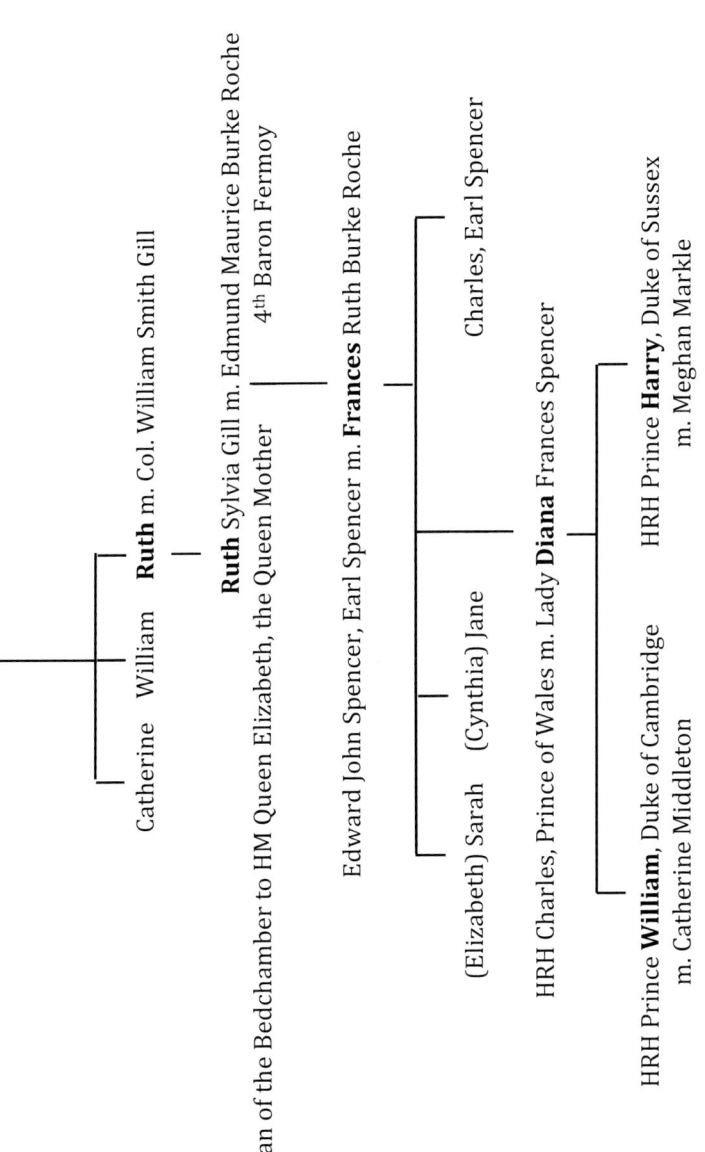

Eliza's Indo/Armenian Ethnicity and Genealogy

Jim Wilson, Professor of Human Genetics at the Usher Institute, Edinburgh University analysed DNA from several of Eliza's descendants, both male and female, and made the following comment:

'The issue of how Indian Eliza is, is not one that is straightforward to answer using the descendants alive today. We have two copies of our DNA: one from mum and one from dad. Although we get exactly half of our DNA from mum and half from our dad, we do not get exactly 25% from each of our grandparents. For any given part of the genome, mum and dad pass on one of the two copies they have, that is the DNA from only one grandparent in each case. It is random which one. It is exactly like a deck of cards or rolling a die: governed by the laws of chance. It is not uncommon to have say 20% total from one grandparent and 30% total from the other (plus 50% from the other parent's parents). Repeat this process going forward and you can appreciate that the DNA percentage becomes only a rough guide to the number of generations back. So, you get an approximate idea, but cannot rule out one generation forward or back.'

Professor Wilson further stressed that the information above is nothing to do with mtDNA (which is only passed down by the female, in the egg) but relates to the rest of the genome.

The proposition derived from the DNA analysis is that Eliza was either half or one quarter Indian. Any further assumptions had to be based on the limited knowledge of her immediate family gleaned from their correspondence. A further complication within the letters from Armenian correspondents is the fact that they are all written in English by a Parsee scribe. They are therefore transliterated at a time when spelling was not standardised anyway. Thus 'Guyane' can be written 'Khayanee' and 'Kevork' can be 'Kework'/'Kewark' reflecting the soft 'v' often used in the spoken word, and the frequency of pronouncing 'w' in a similar way. In the same way, the scribe writes the name 'Goodwin' as 'Goodveen'.

Theodore's habit of noting, on the reverse of every letter, the sender's name; date and method of dispatch; the date when he received it; if and how it was answered, means that most of Eliza's family were recorded with their honorific family titles. In 1817 Theodore refers to Eliza's aunt Mariam Khatchatoor, as 'Mukhanee Khalah'.

Professor Wilson has ascertained that Armenian language distinguishes between a maternal Aunt (Khalah) and a paternal Aunt (Chachi). Ageenah is 'Khalah' and is therefore Eliza's mother's sister. This might point to Eliza's maternal grandmother being Indian as she has given one of her daughters the name Ageenah, which looks most likely to be a Hindi name; we do not know Eliza's mother's name, it may or may not be Indian. Eliza and her sister, Guyane, both have Armenian forenames, and would have taken their surname Kevork from their father whose Christian name would have been Kevork (George).

Considering how few Armenians were left in Surat by 1820 Eliza's Aunt Mariam is almost certainly the same Mariam Vardanian, named by Mesroub Jacob Seth, in *Armenians in India From the Earliest Times*, as being one of the 'seven souls' who were Armenian heads of household living in Surat at that time. It would be reasonable to assume that she is the same 'Lady Mariam' whose tombstone inscription in the Armenian cemetery of Surat, recently translated by Professor Sebouh Aslanian and published by Liz Chater, relates that she was the 'wife of Paron [Baron/ Lord/Sir] Vartan' and that she died aged 90 in 1826. Considering that she was born in 1736, Mariam must have been of the same generation as Eliza's grandparents. It is unlikely that Paron Vartan would have married her had she been half Indian. An aunt on her mother's paternal side would also be known as Khalah. It is quite possible therefore that Mariam was Eliza's maternal grandfather's sister and that therefore he was also a Khatchatoor, and that his wife was Indian.

Partial Armenian Genealogy deduced from correspondence in *Ms. 2740.*

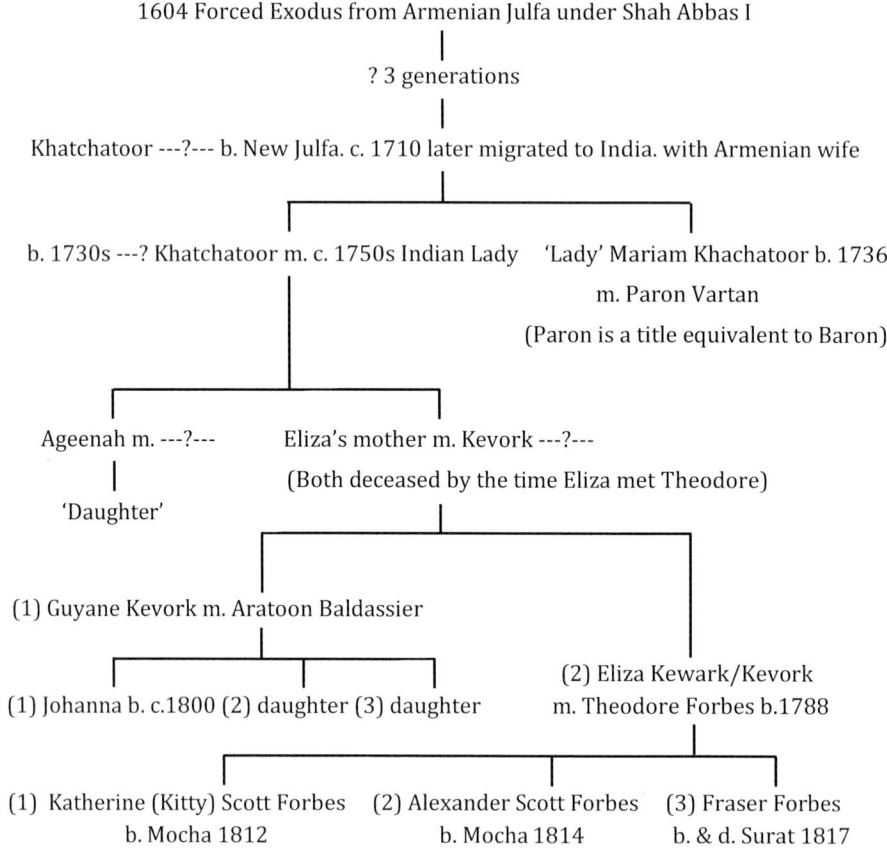

1604 Forced Exodus from Armenian Julfa under Shah Abbas I

? 3 generations

Khatchatoor ---?--- b. New Julfa. c. 1710 later migrated to India. with Armenian wife

b. 1730s ---? Khatchatoor m. c. 1750s Indian Lady   'Lady' Mariam Khachatoor b. 1736

m. Paron Vartan

(Paron is a title equivalent to Baron)

Ageenah m. ---?---   Eliza's mother m. Kevork ---?---

(Both deceased by the time Eliza met Theodore)

'Daughter'

(1) Guyane Kevork m. Aratoon Baldassier

(1) Johanna b. c.1800 (2) daughter (3) daughter

(2) Eliza Kewark/Kevork
m. Theodore Forbes b.1788

(1) Katherine (Kitty) Scott Forbes   (2) Alexander Scott Forbes   (3) Fraser Forbes
b. Mocha 1812   b. Mocha 1814   b. & d. Surat 1817

Maps

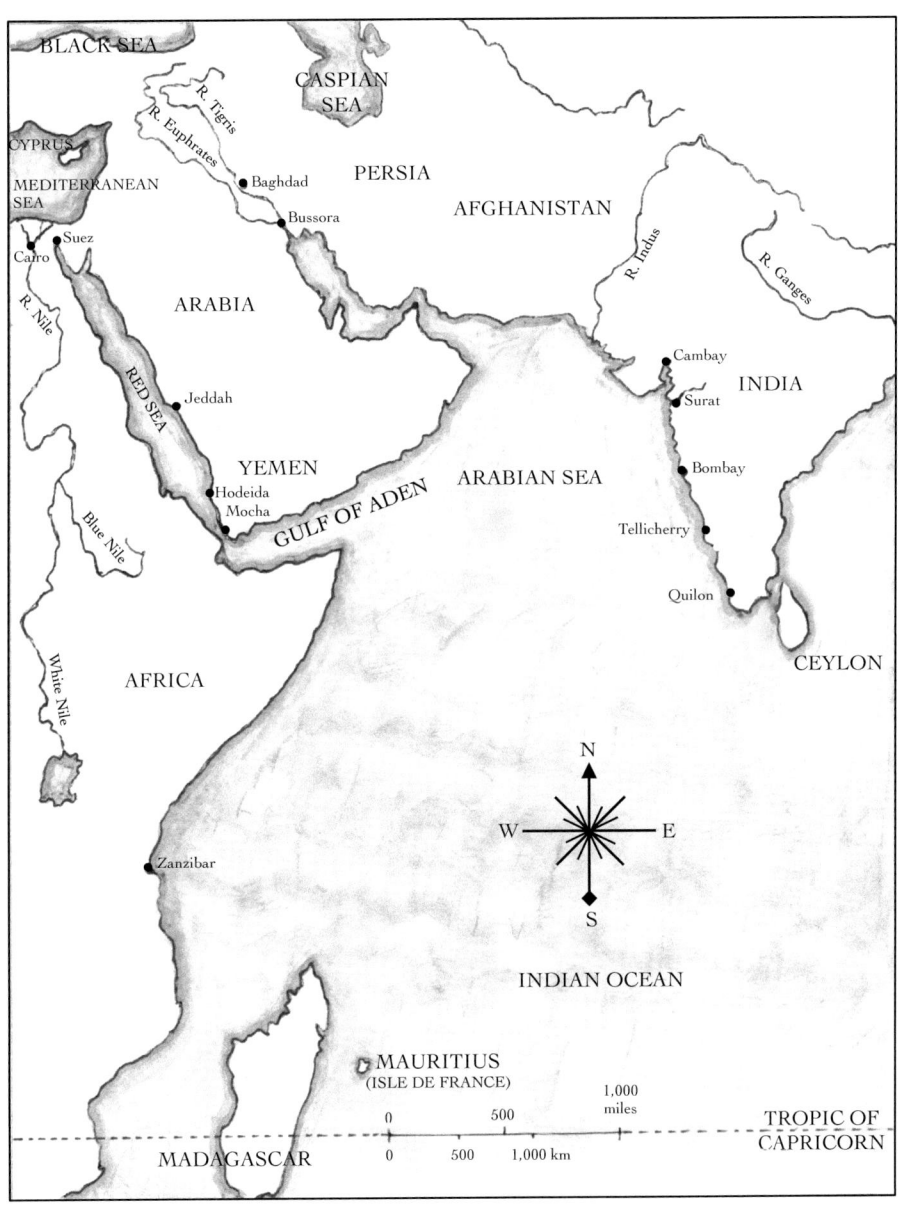

Indian Ocean – old Anglicised names.

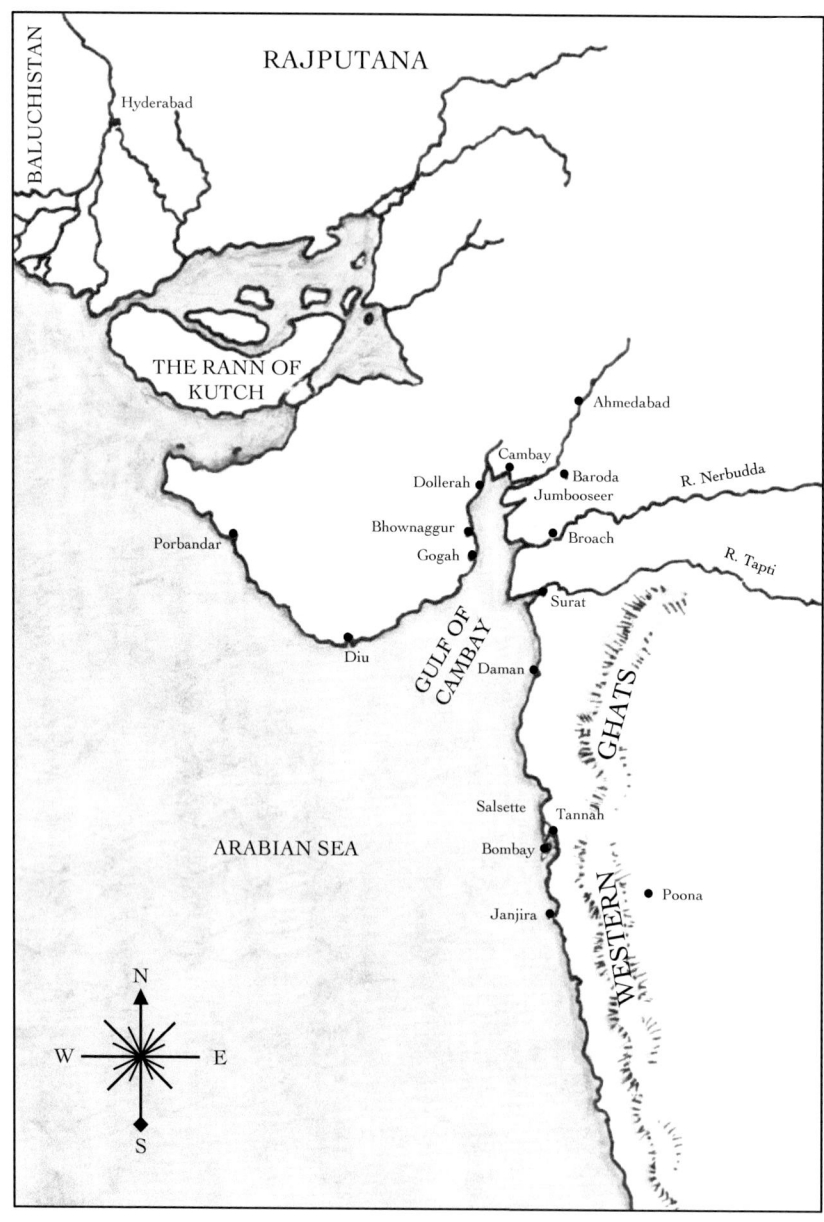

Bombay Presidency – 1820 names.

Sources

Most of the details of the couple's relationship are taken directly from primary sources: principally the correspondence in the special collections of Aberdeen University *Ms. 2740* (Ogilvie-Forbes archive), and Cambridge (Crombie papers). Quotations or references from contemporary published sources are attributed within the text,

My aim was to give the reader an uninterrupted chronological, semi-narrative representation of the couple's troubled marriage, without the need for constant reference to footnotes. The story is set within its historical, political and social context.

Though I have read widely on the relevant subjects, no specific works have informed my descriptions of people, places or incidents. Any that can be called a source are quoted and referenced within the text. The book is aimed at the general reader. Theodore's political career in Yemen during the years 1812-15 seems to have been largely overlooked by historians.

Names and Nouns

I have retained the spelling of all the old versions of place names as they appear in the correspondence and have also retained them in the text, for the sake of consistency, e.g. Bombay and Broach; Mocha and Jumbooseer.

Many of the letters contain idiosyncratic spellings and wayward grammar. Spelling had not yet been standardised c. 1810-20 and so I have chosen not to pepper the passages I have quoted with (sic), preferring rather to rely on the intelligence of the reader to follow the meaning, and not to demean the writer by inferring his/her ignorance.

In the few instances when the meaning of a phrase or passage may not be obvious, I have added my understanding of it within square brackets.

Select Bibliography

Adkins, Lesley, *Empires of the Plain, Henry Rawlinson and the Lost Languages of Babylon.*

Barber, William J., *British Economic Thought and India 1600-1858.*

Bradley, Chris, *Discovery Guide to Yemen.*

Bridges, Roy, *People and Places in New Machar Past and Present.*

Brogden, W. A., *Aberdeen: An Illustrated Architectural Guide.*

Buckingham, James Silk, *Autobiography.*

Bulley, Anne, *Free Mariner, John Adolphus Pope in the East Indies.*

Bulley, Anne, *The Bombay Country Ships.*

Chaudhuri, K. N., *Trade and Civilisation in the Indian Ocean, an Economic History from the Rise of Islam to 1750.*

Comrie, Bernard (Ed.), *The Major Languages of South Asia, the Middle East and Africa.*

Craven, Roy C., *Indian Art.*

Davies, Charles E., *The Blood-Red Arab Flag, An Investigation into Qasimi Piracy 1797-1820.*

Dossal, Mariam, *Mumbai, Theatre of Conflict, City of Hope, 1660 to Present Times.*

Downing, Charles, *Armenian Folk Tales and Fables Retold.*

Douglas, James, *Glimpses of Old Bombay and Western India, with other papers.*

Drewitt, Frederic Dawtrey, *Bombay in the Days of George IV, Memoirs of Sir Edward West.*

Gardner, Brian, *The East India Company.*

Greig, Alexander M., *Fate of The Blenden Hall, East Indiaman: With An Account Of Her Wreck.*

Gupta, Ashin Das and M. N. Pearson (Ed.), *India and the Indian Ocean 1500-1800.*

McIntyre, Ben, *Josiah the Great.*

Mackintosh, Robert James, *Memoirs of the Right Honourable Sir James Mackintosh.*

Macro, Eric, *Yemen and the Western World since 1571.*

Manley, Deborah, and Ree, Peta, *Henry Salt Artist, Traveller, Diplomat, Egyptologist.*

Mansel, Philip, *Levant.*

Moorehead, Alan, *The White Nile.*

Moorehead, Alan, *The Blue Nile.*

Nightingale, Pamela, *Trade and Empire in Western India 1784-1806.*

Pramar, V. S., *Wood Carvings of Gujarat.*

Pratapaditya Pal & Vidia Dehejia, *From Merchants to Emperors, British Artists and India 1757-1930.*

Al Qassimi, H. H. Sheikh Sultan Mohammed, *The White Shaik.*

Sebouh, David Aslanian, *From the Indian Ocean to the Mediterranean, The Global Trade Networks of Armenian Merchants from New Julfa.*

Starkey, Paul & Janet (Ed.), *Travellers in Egypt.*

Smith, Robert, *One Foot in the Sea.*

Tillotson, Sarah *Indian Mansions a Social History of the Haveli.*

Tindall, Gillian, *City of Gold, The Biography of Bombay.*

Um, Nancy, *The Merchant Houses of Mocha.*

Usick, Patricia, *Adventures in Egypt and Nubia, the Travels of William John Bankes (1786-1855).*

Waterfield, Gordon, *Sultans of Aden.*

Wilkinson, Theon, *Two Monsoons, The Life and Death of Europeans in India.*

Yule, Henry & Burnell, A. C., *Hobson Jobson, Concise Edition.*

PRINTED AND BOUND BY:

Copytech (UK) Limited trading as Printondemand-worldwide,
9 Culley Court, Bakewell Road, Orton Southgate.
Peterborough, PE2 6XD, United Kingdom.